PSYCHOLOGY OF EMOTIONS, MOTIVATIONS AND ACTIONS

UNDERSTANDING SUICIDAL IDEATION

PSYCHOLOGY OF EMOTIONS, MOTIVATIONS AND ACTIONS

Additional books and e-books in this series can be found on Nova's website under the Series tab.

PSYCHOLOGY OF EMOTIONS, MOTIVATIONS AND ACTIONS

UNDERSTANDING SUICIDAL IDEATION

DAVID LESTER
EDITOR

nova
science publishers
New York

Library of Congress Cataloging-in-Publication Data

Names: Lester, David, PhD, Stockton University, Galloway, NJ, USA, editor.
Title: Understanding Suicidal Ideation
Description: New York: Nova Science Publishers, [2019] | Series: Psychology of Emotions, Motivations and Actions | Includes bibliographical references and index.
Identifiers: LCCN 2019957084 (print) | ISBN 9781536169997 (hardcover) |
ISBN 9781536170009 (adobe pdf)

Published by Nova Science Publishers, Inc. † New York

CONTENTS

PREFACE

Suicide is difficult to study, of course, because those who die by suicide are unavailable for questioning. As a result, researchers have studied those who attempt suicide and those who have suicidal ideation in order to gain some understanding of suicidal behavior – the *method of substitute subjects* as Charles Neuringer called this methodology over 50 years ago. On the other hand, suicidal ideation and suicide attempts are important in their own right because the assessment and therapeutic treatment of these individuals requires time and money.

In addition to these considerations, one of the most powerful predictors of whether an individual will choose to die by suicide is the presence of suicidal ideation. It was an established "fact" for many years that those who talk about suicide do not die by suicide, but this was exposed as a myth many years ago.

For all of these reasons, understanding suicidal ideation, the topic of this book, is important. Not only might a better understanding of suicidal ideation increase our knowledge of suicide, since many of those with suicidal ideation (past or current) are at an increased risk of suicide, but improved understanding of suicidal ideation would help mental health professionals better help those patients. The present volume presents chapters by experts in this field, with reports of original research, reviews of the research on important issues, and case studies.

In: Understanding Suicidal Ideation
Editor: David Lester
ISBN: 978-1-53616-999-7

Chapter 1

RAPE AND SUICIDE AMONG MEN*

Steven Stack

ABSTRACT

Previous research on male suicidality has largely neglected rape as a predictor. The present study reviews and integrates the work on the psychological distress (e.g., PTSD and depression) reported by male rape victims. It then explores the degree to which rape victimization predicts suicide ideation among males. All data were taken from the Youth Risk Behavior Survey for 6,947 high school males. Suicide ideation (SI) referred to ever having seriously considered suicide. Bivariate analysis showed that male rape victims were 3.87 times more likely to report SI than non-victims. Controlling for measures of the other variables, including depression, male rape victims were now only 1.56 times more likely than non-victims to report SI. These results suggest that rape victimization be included in future work on male suicide, especially for at-risk young males.

---

* This is a revised version of a paper presented at the annual meetings of the American Association of Suicidology, Seattle, Washington, April 28-May 1, 2006.

Until recently, the idea that men rape men, indeed the possibility that men can be raped, was a notion that was not frequently acknowledged in mainstream society. Often male rape is thought to occur mainly in prisons, while research on rape in society has centered largely on female rape victims. For example, many criminological texts tend to give very little attention to male rape victims, and rape prevention efforts have tended to be focused on females (Daigle & Muftic, 2016; Karmen, 2016; Schmalleger, 2009; Thio, 2006). However, U.S. surveys document significant victimization of men by male predators. For example, in the Youth Risk Behavior Survey approximately 5% of male and 10% of female high school students report having been raped (Stack, 2006). In juvenile detention facilities, a national survey found that 9.7% of males vs. 6.9% of females reported sexual victimization (Beck, 2013). Male rape victims suffer many of the same psychological consequences of being raped as do female victims of rape. These include PTSD, depression, anger, and lower self-esteem (Davies, 2002; McLean, Baldwin, & White, 2005; Walker, Archer, & Davies, 2005).

Rape has been a neglected area in suicidology. For example, a search through major textbooks found no mention of rape in the indexes and little on related topics such as sexual abuse (Hawton & Vanheeringen, 2000; Lester, 2000; Maris, 2019; O'Connor & Pirkis, 2018). However, one book does mention rape as a cultural justification for suicide in ancient China (Wasserman & Wasserman, 2009). Rape is apparently typically omitted as a risk factor in models of suicidality.

RAPE AND PSYCHOLOGICAL DISTRESS

Data from a national co morbidity study found 65% of raped men develop PTSD vs. 46% of raped women (Kessler 1995; Sageman 2003). This is a higher prevalence of PTSD than that found among combat veterans. As with female victims, male rape victims have been found to have elevated levels of depression, anger, self-blame, sleep disorders, sexual dysfunction, and other problems that can elevate suicide risk (e.g.,

Daigle & Muftic, 2016; Goyer, & Eddleman, 1984; Karmen, 2016; Mezey & King, 1989; Isely & Shim, 1997; Rentoul & Appleboom, 1997; Walker, Archer, & Davies, 2005; Sageman, 2003; Tewksbury, 2009). For example, in a detailed study of 40 male rape victims, the long-term psychological effects affected a large majority. These included the following (with the percentage affected): depression 97%, revenge fantasies 95%, flashbacks 93%, anxiety 93%, anger 80%, low self-esteem 78%, alcohol abuse 63% and drug abuse 53% (Walker, Archer, & Davies, 2005). A much larger sample of 1,679 male rape victims yielded many negative consequences of rape including depression 92%, nightmares 59%, flashbacks 69%, sexual dysfunction 51%, and a fear being perceived as gay since most male rape victims are heterosexuals (Isely & Shim, 1997).

HELP SEEKING

The impact of rape on men may be greater than the effect on women since men are less apt than women to seek help after a rape event. A culture of homophobia can intensify this pattern. A relative lack of help seeking can make male rape victims more vulnerable to depression, suicide and other negative consequences of being raped (e.g., Walker, Archer, & Davies, 2005; WHO 2003). It is often found that men fear being blamed for their own victimization and not being taken seriously by the criminal justice system (Hodge & Cantor 1998; Mezey & King 1989; Walker Archer, & Davies 2005). Male rape victims who do report victimization, as in the case of women victims, tend not to report the event for over a year after the rape. In one study the mean time between the rape event and coming to a counseling center was 16 years (King & Woollette, 1997).

Given evidence of the substantial negative psychological impact of rape on male victims, the present chapter extends the analysis of rape to suicidal ideation (SI). To fully explore the association between rape and SI, we build a model that incorporates variables from a wide range of alternative predictors of suicide drawn from the literature (e.g., Lester, 2000; Maris, 2019). These constructs include violence involvement, school integration, and a range of socio-demographic constructs. The central hypotheses to be tested are:

Hypothesis 1: Males who have been raped will be more apt than their counterparts to have suicide ideation.

Hypothesis 2: The association between rape and SI will remain after controlling for a wide array of possible mediators taken from the literature.

The present study explores the association between male rape victimization and suicide ideation using a national representative sample of young males from the CDC National Youth Risk Behavior Survey. A key concern is with depression as a mediator, a factor which has a long history of support for predicting suicidality (e.g., Lester, 2000; Maris, 2019), while depression is also a consequence of rape (e.g., Walker, Archer, & Davies, 2005).

PREVIOUS RESEARCH

The previous investigations of the association between sexual assault and suicidality have been overwhelmingly based on female samples (see reviews in Daigle & Muftic, 2016; Thio, 2005; Ullman & Najdowski, 2009). This line of work has generally found support for a strong link between sexual assault and female suicide ideation and suicide attempts. In contrast to females, systematic research on the association between rape and suicidality specific to male rape victims, has been sparse. Even recent research that has included males, often lump males together with females. In these pooled samples of males and females, a possible gendered effect is not assessed in (e.g., Annor, Clayton, Gilbert, et al., 2018).

A search was undertaken for research on male rape. Studies were included if they met the following criteria: (1) a measure of suicidality, (2) included male rape victims, (3) included a comparison group of male non-rape victims, (4) reported quantitative findings on the presence or absence of an association between rape and male suicidality, and (5) were based on

American samples. Examples of investigations that were excluded were literature reviews, case studies, opinion papers with no new research findings and studies using SI, along with many other socio-demographic variables to predict rape victimization (e.g., Shrier, Pierce, Emmans, et al., 1998). A total of three papers met the inclusion criteria.

The works generally assessed the relationship between male rape and a wide variety of outcome variables. In these large epidemiological studies, it was not possible to provide an in-depth analysis of rape victimization and suicidality (Buzi, Tortolero, Roberts, et al, 2003; Howard, Yang, & Yan, 2007; Lowry, Crosby & Brenner, 2014). For example, Howard, Wang and Yan (2007) report findings on the links between male rape victimization and each of 14 other youth risk behaviors including fighting, drug use, and carrying a gun, but not suicide ideation. The findings of the three investigations are mixed. Two investigations (Buzi, Tortolero, Roberts, et al., 2003; Lowry, Crosby & Brenner, 2014) briefly report a significant association between rape and SI. One does not find a significant link (Howard, Wang, & Yan, 2007). No study performed a systematic review of the literature on the psychological consequences of being raped or perform a detailed analysis of the mediators accounting for any association between male rape victimization and SI. The present study fills this gap.

In order to address the association between rape and SI, controls for possible mediators are included from the literature (e.g., Annor, Clayton, Gilbert, et al., 2018, Buzi, Tortolero, Roberts, Ross, et al., 2003; Howard, Wang, & Yan, F., 2007; Lowry, Crosby, & Brenner, 2014; Shrier, Pierce, Emmans, & DuRant, 1998; Stack, 2014; Ullman & Najdowski, 2009). Measures of constructs were available in the YRBS. These are grouped into several major categories. Psychiatric controls include depression, eating disorders, and substance abuse; measures of violence involvement include fighting resulting in injuries, and dating violence. Violence involvement has been interpreted as a contributor to suicidality to the extent that it desensitizes the person to painful experiences which are thought to increase the capability for suicide (Joiner, 2005). Risky sexual behaviors, which may be associated with rape through such mechanisms as opportunity factors, include number of sex partners and causing pregnancy. Measures of school integration are based on grade point average and membership on sports teams. These have been widely used in the work on delinquency and deviant behavior from the standpoint of social bonds and control theory (Hirschi, 1969; Stack, Wasserman, & Kern, 2004). A set of demographic controls often included in previous work are employed and include ethnicity, age, region of the nation, and urban vs. rural residence.

METHODOLOGY

All data are taken from the 2001 Youth Risk Behavior Survey (YRBS). YRBS data are collected annually by the Centers for Disease Control, USA. Data were collected following a multistage cluster sampling strategy. This started with a sample of 52 of the nation's 3,000 counties, then 189 schools within counties, and ending with 2 randomly selected classes within each of the selected schools. The student response rate was 89%. The year 2001 was selected at the time of data analysis since it was a year for which data were available in the YRBS on key constructs. Unlike some years, the 2001 survey has some advantages for model specification. It contains a measure of major depression, an important psychiatric control. Complete data were available for 6,947 males. For further details on the YRBS, see Centers for Disease Control (2003).

Suicide Ideation

The dependent variable is suicide ideation. The specific item employed is: "During the past 12 months, did you ever seriously consider attempting suicide?" This variable is coded as a binary variable where 1 = yes and 0 = no. Given the dichotomous nature of the dependent variable, logistic regression techniques are appropriate (Menard, 2002).

Rape victimization is measured by the available item in the YRBS: "Have you ever been physically forced to have sexual intercourse when you did not want to?" This is coded as a dichotomous variable where 1 = yes and 0 = no. A total of 353 males, or 5.3%, reported yes.

Psychiatric Controls

A battery of four available psychiatric control variables was incorporated.

Depression

This is measured using the available item in the YRBS which is an apparent crude measure of major depression since it requires 2 weeks of ongoing anguish: "During the past 12 months did you ever feel so sad or hopeless almost every day for two weeks or more in a row that you stopped doing some usual activities?" The responses were coded as binary variable where 1 = yes, others = 0.

Several measures of substance abuse are incorporated. *Binge Drinking* is measured using the following available YRBS item: "During the past 30 days, on how many days did you have five or more drinks of alcohol in a row, that is, within a couple of hours"

The responses were coded as: 3 or more days = 1, all others = 0. *Marijuana Use* was measured by the item: "During the past thirty days how many times did you use marijuana?" The following codes were employed: 10 or more times = 1, all others = 0. It is noted that 10.8% reported 10 or more times. *Cocaine Use* was measured using the item: "During the past 30 days how many times did you use any form of cocaine including powder, crack, or freebase?" For this, 3 or more times = 1, all others = 0. It is noted that 2.1% report 3 or more. *Bulimia*. The presence of an eating disorder was referenced by the item on Bulimia: "During the past

30 days did you vomit or take laxatives to lose weight or to keep from gaining weight?" where yes = 1 and no = 0.

Violence

Following previous work on suicidology (e.g., Stack, 2014), controls are included for involvement in violence. Aggressive teens are at higher risk of suicide ideation. The first measure is: "During the past 12 months, how many times were you involved in a physical fight in which you were injured and had to be treated by a doctor or nurse?" For this, 1 or more times = 1, all others = 0. Involvement in dating violence is measured using the following YRBS item: "During the past 12 months did your boyfriend or girlfriend ever hurt, slap, or physically hurt you on purpose?" with Yes = 1 and No = 0.

Risky Sexual Behavior

Two items tap involvement in risky sexual behavior. The number of actual sex partners is measured as none through 6 or more in the last three months. Having got someone pregnant is measured by responses to the question: "How many times have you gotten someone pregnant? with "0 times" = 0, "1 time," or "two or more times" = 1.

School Integration

From a control theory of deviant behavior (e.g., Hirschi 1969) we used two available binary measures on bonds to school thought to predict deviant behavior including suicidality. These are low GPA (getting mostly D's & E's. (0,1) and participation in sports: is also a binary variable using "belongs to one or more sports teams" (0,1).

Demographic Controls

A set of demographic controls include: race: a series of binary variables: Asian (0,1), Black (0,1), Hispanic (0,1), Other (0,1,) with Whites as the benchmark category; age (in years); urbanism: series of binary variables: Urban (0,1); Suburban (0,1) with rural as the benchmark category; region of nation: a series of binary variables: Midwest (0,1), South (0,1), West (0,1), (northeast = benchmark category).

The analysis follows a forced stepwise multiple logistic regression analysis. First, only rape is entered in the prediction equation for SI. Second, psychiatric morbidity indicators, including depression, are added to assess the extent to which the bivariate relationship between rape and suicide is diminished or becomes insignificant. Third, the violence involvement and risky sexual behavior variables, are added. Fourth, school integration and demographic controls are added. The analysis will help to assess whether the link between rape and SI endures through controls for possible mediators of the association and which variables are most responsible for decreases in the strength of the original link.

RESULTS

Table 1.1 presents the forced stepwise logistic regression analyses. Equation 1 presents the bivariate analysis. It shows that rape is a significant predictor of SI. The logistic regression coefficient for rape is 1.35, and this is over 11 times its standard error. From the odds ratio, males who report being a rape victim are 3.87 times more likley than their counterparts to be suicide ideators.

In analyses not fully reported here, rape also predicted depression, a firmly established correlate of suicide (Lester, 2000; Maris, 2019). Rape victims are 3.25 times more apt than their counterparts to report depression.

Also, as anticipated, depression predicts SI. Males who report depression are fully 8.93 times more apt than males without depression to be marked by SI. Given that rape is associated with both SI and depression, and that depression predicts SI, it is plausible that some of the association between rape and SI is due to rape's association on depression.

Equation 2 shows that, after controlling for depression and the other psychiatric risk factors, rape is still associated with SI. However, the rape coefficient in equation 2 and its corresponding Wald chi-square statistic (not shown) are smaller than in equation 1. The logistic regression coefficient declines from 1.35 in equation 1, to 0.67 in equation 2. The odds ratio for rape decreases from 3.87 in equation 1, to 2.60 in equation 2. Men who have been raped are now just 1.98 times more likley than men who have not been raped to report suicide ideation. This suggests that some of predictive power of rape is mediated through its association with depression and/or the other psychiatric variables in equation 2.

Controlling for the other variables in equation 2, depression is associated with a higher risk of SI. The coefficient for depression is 26 times its standard error. From the odds ratio, depressed males are fully 8 times more likly than their counterparts to be suicide ideators. Three other psychiatric predictors are also significant predictors of suicide: bulimia (OR = 2.56), marijuana use (OR = 1.49), and binge drinking (OR = 1.24). The model explains 23.8% of the variance in SI according to the Nagelkerke r- squared statistic.

Equation 3 adds the variables of violence involvement and risky behaviors to the analysis. Controlling for these and for the other factors, the variable of being a rape victim remains a significant predictor of SI. However, its coefficient and odds ratios are reduced. Rape victims are now only 1.49 times more apt than other males to be marked by SI. Both measures of involvement in violence predict SI. For example, being involved in fighting increases the odds of SI by 1.64 times. Depression remains a significant predictor with an odds ratio (OR = 8.28) close to that of equation 2. The significant model chi-square statistic suggests that the equation provides a good fit to the data.

Table 1.1. Logistic regression results: Equation 1. Suicide ideation (SI) predicted by rape; Equation 2. SI predicted by rape with addition of psychiatric controls; Equation 3. Addition of violence involvement and risky sexual behavior; Equation 4 addition of social integration and demographic controls. Youth Risk Behavior Survey, N = 6,627 males

Constructs/Variables	Equation 1	Equation 2	Equation 3	Equation 4
		B, se, OR Odds Ratio	B, Se, OR	B,se,OR
Rape Victim	1.35* se = .118 OR = 3.87	.67* se = .14 OR = 1.98	.40* se = .16 OR = 1.49	.44* se = .17 OR = 1.56
Psychiatric Morbidity				
Depression		2.08* se = .08 OR = 8.03	2.11* se = .085 OR = 8.28	2.12* se = .086 OR = 8.37
Bulimia		.94* se = .17 OR = 2.56	.90* se = .21 OR = 2.46	.92* se = .21 OR = 2.52
Marijuana		.40* se = .11, OR = 1.49	.39* se = .12 OR = 1.49	.31* se = .12 OR = 1.37
Cocaine User		.05 se = .19 OR = 1.05	-.05 se = .22 OR = .94	-.10 se = .23 OR = .90
Binge Drinking		.21* se = .11 OR = 1.24	.21* se = .11 OR = 1.23	.10 se = .12 OR = 1.11
Violence & Risky Sex Behavior				
Fighting Victim			.54* se = .16 OR = 1.72	.49* se = .16 OR = 1.64
Dating Violence Victim			.50* se = .12 OR = 1.65	.47* se = .12 OR = 1.61
Number Sex Partners			-.05 se = .02 OR = .94	-.02 se = .03 OR = .98
Made someone pregnant			.35* se = .16 OR = 1.42	.46* se = .17 OR = 1.59
School Integration				
Low GPA				.34* se = .13 OR = 1.41
Sports Team member				-.21* se = .08 OR = .80
Demographics				
Race: Black				-.79* se = .14 OR = .45
Hispanic				-.49* se = .12 OR = .61

Table 1.1. (Continued)

Constructs/Variables	Equation 1	Equation 2	Equation 3	Equation 4
Asian				-.32 se = .25 OR = .71
Ref: white 1.00				1.00
Age				-.03 se = .03 OR = .97
Region: South				.27 se = .17 OR = 1.32
West				.11 se = .18 OR = 1.12
Midwest				.31 se = .20 OR = 1.37
Ref: N.E. 1.00				1.00
Urban				.36* se = .16 OR = 1.43
Suburban				.23 se = .15 OR = 1.26
Ref: Rural 1.00				1.00
Constant	-1.99* se = .03	-2.87* se = .06	2.87* se = .08	-2.56* se = .16
Nagelkerke R-squared	.031	.238	.254	.271
Model chi-square	112.4*	915.4*	897.9*	962.0*
Cases correctly classified	86.8%	87.2%	87.%	87.9%

Key: * = $p < .05$; B = logistic regression coefficient; se = standard error; OR = odds ratio.

Finally, equation 4 adds the range of school integration and demographic controls. Controlling for all the other predictor variables, rape victimization continues to be a significant predictor of SI. Its logistic regression coefficient is 2.6 times its standard error. Male rape victims are found to be 1.56 times (OR = 1.56) more apt than other males to be suicide ideators.

As anticipated, both school integration measures predict SI. African American and Hispanic males are less likely than whites to be suicide ideators. From the odds ratios, blacks are 55% (1-0.45) less likely, and Hispanics are 39% less likely than whites to be suicide ideators. Region of residence (South, West, Midwest) is not related to SI. However, urban residents are 1.43 times more likely than rural residents to be suicide ideators. From the Nagelkerke r squared and model chi-square, equation 4 provides a reasonable fit to the data.

Conclusion

Previous work on male suicidality in the U.S. has generally neglected rape as a predictor (e.g., for reviews see Lester, 2000; Maris, 2019; Wasserman & Wasserman, 2009). There are many works on the negative psychological effects of being raped (e.g., Daigle & Muftic, 2016; Goyer, & Eddleman, 1984; Karmen, 2016; Mezey & King, 1989; Isely & Shim, 1997; Rentoul & Appleboom, 1997; Walker, Archer, & Davies, 2005; Sageman, 2003; Tewksbury, 2009), but these do not systematically extend the analysis to SI. The few papers that assess the association between rape and SI are descriptive. Furthermore, most are not focused on male rape and SI, but on other concerns such as the trend in youth suicidality over two decades (Lowry, Crosby, & Brener, 2014), and rape's association with a broad range of outcomes including substance abuse, fighting, and risky sexual behavior (Buzi, Tortelero, Roberts, et al., 2003; Crosby, & Brener, 2014; Howard, Wang, & Yan, 2007). For example, rape is a dependent variable, not an independent variable in one study (Buzi, Tortelero, Roberts, et al., 2003). These studies do not focus on male rape and SI. Little attention is paid to integrating the work on the effects of rape on its victims, such as depression and PTSD, with the work on to suicide risk.

The present chapter reviews and then applies the work on the consequences of rape for male victims to the problem of subsequent SI. It finds that the association between rape and male SI remains after controlling for a wide range of theoretically relevant factors including psychiatric constructs, involvement in violence, risky sexual behavior, school integration, and a range of demographic factors.

The findings of the present study are consistent with two previous descriptive studies (Buzi, Tortolero, Roberts, et al., 2003; Lowry, Crosby & Brenner, 2014). They are not consistent with another investigation, however. One study where rape victimization does not predict SI needs qualification. Howard, Wang, and Yan (2007) included suicide attempts as a control in the equation predicting SI. Since SI and suicide attempts are highly correlated, it is not surprising that male rape did not predict SI at the multivariate level when suicide attempts were also included in the same equation.

Theoretically, the findings are consistent with Joiner's (2005) interpersonal theory of suicide as it pertains to the capability for suicide. Controlling for all the other constructs, experience with violence predicted SI. Both fighting involving an injury requiring medical attention and dating violence enhanced the odds of SI in the adjusted model. In addition, being a victim of rape is also a measure of involvement in violence. The present results add to the literature on how violence involvement indicators are a viable measure of capability for suicide (e.g., Stack, 2014). Such experiences are argued to desensitize the subject to the pain and violence involved in the act of suicide.

Caution needs to be exercised in the interpretation of the findings of the present research. Importantly, it is based on cross-sectional evidence. This makes it difficult to establish causality. It is not clear if the SI occurred before, after, or simultaneously with rape. However, in a related area of research, the findings based on cross sectional research are essentially the same as in longitudinal research. In a meta-analysis of 47 studies of the effect of early childhood sexual abuse on suicidality (Ng, Yong, Ho, et al., 2018), the pooled odds ratio found in cross sectional research was 1.98 (CI: 1.7 to 2.15, $p < .001$) compared to an odds ratio of 1.64 (CI: 1.37 to 1.93, $p < .001$) in longitudinal studies. The level of risk of child abuse on suicidality was about the same in both cross sectional and longitudinal designed studies. Nevertheless, future work is needed to assess the association between male rape victimization and suicidality in the context of longitudinal research designs.

Future work is needed to assess the association between male rape and SI for adult populations. The findings based on a teenage student sample may differ from those of the general population in their 20's and older age groups. Rape generally becomes less common for older age groups vs. younger age groups. In addition, research is needed on other forms of suicidality such as suicide attempts, suicide plans, and suicide deaths.

Finally, there may be a contextual effect based on variation in the cultural approval of homosexuality. There are sizable differences in homophobia among nations (Adamczyk, 2017). It is anticipated that regions of the U.S. would also vary in the cultural support of homophobia, a social context where public opinion is very negative toward homosexuals. Where this is high, male rape victims may be especially reluctant to report their victimization and seek help. As such, the potential for suicide at the individual level would be expected to be relatively high. Data on attitudes measuring homophobia are available by region in the American General Social Survey and could be used to address this problem.

REFERENCES

Adamczyk, A. (2017). *Cross national public opinion about homosexuality*. Berkeley: University of California Press.

Annor, F., Clayton, H., Gilbert, L. K., et al., (2018). Sexual orientation discordance and non-fatal suicidal behaviors in U.S. high school students. *American Journal of Preventive Medicine, 54,* 530-538.

Beck, A. J. (2013). *Sexual victimization in juvenile facilities reported by youth 2012*. Washington, DC: Bureau of Justice Statistics.

Buzi, R. S., Tortolero, S. R., Roberts, R. E., Ross, M. et al., (2003). Gender differences in the consequences of coercive sexual experience among adolescents attending alternative schools. *Journal of School Health, 73,* 191-196.

Centers for Disease Control. (2003). *2001 National school-based youth risk behavior survey: Public use data documentation*. Atlanta, GA: Author.

Daigle, L. E., & Muftic, L. R. (2016). *Victimology*. Los Angeles, Sage.

Davies, M. (2002). Male sexual assault victims. *Aggression & Violent Behavior*, 7, 203-214.

Goyer, P. F., & Eddleman, H. C. (1984). Same sex rape of nonincarcerated men. *American Journal of Psychiatry, 141,* 576-579.

Hawton, K., & van Heeringen, K. (Eds.) (2000). *International handbook of suicide and attempted suicide*. New York: John Wiley & Sons.

Hirschi, T. (1969). *The causes of delinquency*. Berkeley, Ca.: University of California Press.

Hodge, S., & Cantor, D. (1998). Victims & perpetrators of male sexual assault, *Journal of Interpersonal Violence*, *13,* 222-239.

Howard, D., Wang, M. Q., & Yan, F. (2007). Prevalence and psychological correlates of forced sexual intercourse among U.S. high school adolescents. *Suicide & Life-Threatening Behavior, 42,* 629-643.

Isely, P., & Shim, D. G. 1997. Sexual assault of men in the community, *Journal of Community Psychology, 25,* 159-166.

Joiner, T. (2005). *Why people die by suicide*. Cambridge, MA.: Harvard University Press.

Kessler, R. (1995). Post-traumatic stress disorder in the national comorbidity survey. *Archives of General Psychiatry*, 52, 1048-1060.

Karmen, A. (2016). *Crime victims*. Boston, MA: Cengage Learning.

King, M., & Woollette, E. (1997). Sexually assaulted males: 115 men consulting a counseling service. *Archives of Sexual Behavior*, *26,* 579-588.

Lester, D. (2000). *Why people kill themselves*. Springfield, IL: Charles Thomas.

Lowry, R., Crosby, A. E., & Brenner, N. D. (2014). Suicidal thoughts and attempts among high school students: Trends and associated health risk behaviors, 1991-2011. *Journal of Adolescent Health, 54*, 100-108.

McLean, I. A., Balding, V., & White, C. (2005). Further analysis of male on male rape and sexual assault in greater Manchester. *Medicine, Science & the Law*, *45*, 223-232.

Maris, R. (2019). *Suicidology: A comprehensive biopsychological perspective*. New York: Guilford.

Menard, S. (2002). *Applied logistic regression analysis*. Thousand Oaks, CA: Sage.

Mezey, G. & King, M. (1989). The effects of sexual assault on men: A survey of 22 victims. *Psychological Medicine*, *19,* 205-209.

Ng, Q. X., Yong, B. Z. J., Ho, C. Y. X. et al., (2018). Early life sexual abuse is associated with increased suicide attempts. *Journal of Psychiatric Research, 99,* 129-141.

O'Connor, R. C. & Pirkis, J. (eds.) (2016). *The International Handbook of Suicide Prevention*. London, UK: John Wiley.

Rentoul, L., & Appleboom, N. (1997). Understanding the psychological impact of rape and serious sexual assault of men: A literature review. *Journal of Psychiatric & Mental Health Nursing, 4,* 267-274.

Sageman, S. (2003). The rape of boys and impact of sexually predatory environments. *Journal of the American Academy of Psychoanalysis & Dynamic Psychiatry, 31,* 563-580.

Schmalleger, F. (2009). *Criminology Today*. 5th edition. Columbus, Ohio: Prentice Hall.

Shrier, L., Pierce, J. D., Emmans, J., & DuRant, R. H. (1998). Gender differences in risk behaviors associated with forced or pressured sex. *Archives of Pediatric & Adolescent Medicine. 152,* 57-63

Stack, S. (2006). Male rape victims and suicide: A hidden crisis. *Paper read at the annual meetings of the American Association of Suicidology*, Seattle, Washington, April.

Stack, S. (2014). Differentiating suicide ideators from attempters: Violence. *Suicide & Life-Threatening Behavior, 44,* 46-57.

Stack, S., Wasserman, I., & Kern, R. (2004). Adult social bonds and use of internet pornography. *Social Science Quarterly, 85, 75-88.*

Tewksbury, R. (2009). Male rape. In J. Wilson (Ed.), *The Praeger handbook of victimology* (pp. 161-163). Santa Barbara, CA: Praeger.

Thio, A. (2006) *Deviant Behavior*. 8th edition. Boston, MA: Allyn and Bacon.

Ullman, S. E., & Najdowski, C. (2009). Correlates of serious suicide ideation and attempts in female adult sexual assault survivors. *Suicide & Life-Threatening Behavior* 39, 47-57.

Walker, J., Archer, J., & Davies, M. (2005). Effects of rape on men. *Archives of Sexual Behavior, 34*, 69-80.

Wasserman, D., & Wasserman, C. (2009). *Oxford textbook of suicidology and suicide prevention*. New York: Oxford University Press.

WHO. (2003). *Guidelines for medico-legal care for victims of sexual violence*, Geneva, Switzerland: WHO.

In: Understanding Suicidal Ideation
Editor: David Lester
ISBN: 978-1-53616-999-7

Chapter 2

Religiosity and Suicidal Ideation

Karolina Krysinska and David Lester

Abstract

This chapter reviews research on whether religiosity is a protective factor for suicidal ideation. The results of the research are mixed, with the evidence suggesting a protective effect from religiosity, except for psychotic patients. The results differ by age and sex, and the protective impact of religiosity is more apparent for attempted and completed suicide than for suicidal ideation.

Suicidal ideation and behavior result from complex interactions among a wide range of risk and protective factors encompassing the entire life span of an individual (Lester, 2000). Although there are differences between age, gender and race/ethnic groups, factors related to an elevated risk for suicide include individual characteristics, such as mental health problems and psychiatric hospitalization, current suicidal ideation and previous suicidal behavior, physical illness, negative life events and low coping potential, as well as neurobiological and psychological factors, especially hopelessness. A family history of psychopathology and suicidal behavior and a lack of social support may also affect the level of suicide risk. In addition, socioeconomic and cultural factors, such as a permissive attitude towards suicide and easy access to lethal means, can increase the risk.

Sufficiently strong protective factors can outweigh the impact of risk factors. Several factors which can reduce the risk of suicide have been identified, including good physical health, hopefulness, strong reasons for living, effective problem-solving and coping skills, cognitive flexibility, having plans for the future, constructive use of leisure time, and the propensity to seek help. Availability of family and nonfamily social support, significant and stable relationships, children under the age of 18 living at home, employment, and restricted access to lethal means of suicide can reduce the risk of suicide. Sociocultural factors, such as negative attitudes towards suicide and cultural continuity among the First Nations and other Indigenous peoples, have also been found to protect against suicidal ideation and behavior.

Religion and Suicidality

Religion *per se* impacts suicidal ideation and behavior. For example, Eskin, et al. (2019), in a study of 5,572 students from 12 countries, found that Muslim students were less likely to report suicidal ideation than students with other religious affiliations.

Research and clinical evidence indicate that religion can be linked to a lower risk of both suicidal ideation and behavior, that is, suicide attempts and suicide (Gearing & Alonzo, 2018; Moreira- Almeida et al., 2006). A meta-analysis of international studies, including case-control and retrospective cohorts, found an overall protective effect of religion against suicide (Wu, et al., 2015). About three quarters of the studies published to-date, including studies in Western (predominantly Christian) and in Middle Eastern (predominantly Muslim) countries, have reported a significant inverse relationship between at least one aspect of religion and at least one dimension of suicidality (Koenig, et al., 2012; Stack & Kposowa, 2011). Attendance at religious services was found to be protective against suicide in two U.S.-based general population studies (Kleinman & Liu, 2014; Nisbet, et al., 2000). In a longitudinal follow-up study, Kleinman and Liu (2014) found that attending religious services 24 times each year or more was a long-term protective factor against suicide. Similarly, Nisbet, et al., (2000) found that, in older age groups (ages 50 and older), participation in religious activities reduced the odds of suicide versus natural death, even after controlling for the frequency of social support. An inverse association between suicide and religious commitment was also found in young (aged 15–34 years) male members of the Church of Jesus Christ of Latter-Day Saints (Hilton, et al., 2002). In 162 regions within 22 European nations, Stack and Laubepin (2019) found that religiousness was associated with lower suicide rates, even after controlling for measures of economic strain, level of economic development, and education.

In contrast, some studies have found no evidence for the protective effect of religion or they report both positive and negative effects, implying a conditional, moderated or mediated protective effect from a range of variables (Lawrence, Oquendo & Stanley, 2015; Stack & Kposowa, 2011). For instance, a longitudinal population study in Northern Ireland found the same suicide risk in those with and without self-reported religious affiliation (O'Reilly & Rosato, 2015). Interestingly, the only group with a lower relative risk (at least up to the age of 55) was the more conservative Christian group. The lack of the relationship between religion and suicide found in Northern Ireland may be related to the rise in individualized approaches to religious beliefs and practices. This phenomenon may ameliorate differences in religiosity between those who are affiliated with a major religion and the non-affiliated who "believe without belonging" (Davie, 2007), especially among younger adults; a group with the highest suicide rates (O'Reilly & Rosato, 2015). Also, Wu, et al., (2015) found significant protective effects of religiosity in studies conducted in Western cultures, in areas with high religious homogeneity, and among older populations. This effect has not been found in Eastern countries, in areas with low religious homogeneity, and among younger populations.

Another example of the complexity of the suicide-religion relationship, and the role of the changing broad socio-cultural context, is a study comparing suicide rates among people aged 64 years and over in predominantly religious versus non-religious countries (Pritchard & Baldwin, 2000). Contrary to the expectations based on the assumed protective effect of religious affiliations and extended family traditions, elderly suicide rates, especially among men, were higher in Catholic and Orthodox societies than in non-Catholic or non-orthodox countries. One of the suggested explanations for the observed paradox refers to a relative scarcity of services available for the elderly in societies, which traditionally depended upon extended family systems and traditional values (which are currently eroding). Sisask, et al., (2010) also reported cross-cultural differences in the protective effects of three dimensions of religiosity (religious denomination, subjective religiosity and organizational religiosity) for attempted suicide. The strongest protective effect across the different study sites, including Brazil, Estonia, the Islamic Republic of Iran and Sri Lanka, was found for subjective religiosity, that is, considering oneself to be a religious person, while the results for the more objective indicators of religiosity were mixed.

Gender may moderate the relationship between religion and suicide. Neeleman, et al., (1997) reported that the protective effect of religious belief against tolerance of suicide in 19 Western countries was different in men and women. In men, it depended upon their own religious beliefs, as well as upon the salience of religion in their social environment. In women, the associations between religiousness and suicide tolerance were attributable to their own beliefs, irrespective of their level of exposure to a religious environment.

Religion can have an impact on suicidal behavior through sanctioning particular means of suicide. Social acceptability, influenced by culture, tradition and religion, can influence the choice of a particular suicide method (Ajdacic-Gross, et al., 2008). For instance, epidemiological studies show that self-immolation is one of the frequently used female suicide methods in India, a phenomenon which can probably be linked to the easy access to kerosene and the cultural and religious meaning of the method

(Wu, et al., 2012). Cultural factors give meanings to suicide methods, and "suicide by self-immolation in many Asian countries reflects the cultural connotation of fire, and the use of fire symbolizes protest against injustices in life. Carrying the symbolic meaning of God and the purifier in Hinduism, fire is important in Hindu rituals and in prevalent ancient practices of *sati* (burning of the Hindu widow) and *jauhar* (women's honorary self- immolation before their men go to battlefield)" (Wu, et al., 2012, p. 1149). Of note, a relatively high incidence of suicide by burning has also been reported in women of Indian origin in England and Wales. Between 1988 and 1992, one in four female victims of suicide by burning in the UK was an Asian woman (Raleigh, 1996).

Religious sanctions may negatively affect the process of the collection and quality of national mortality data. A study on suicide in 49 countries worldwide, based on the World Health Organization (WHO) data, found lower suicide rates in countries with religious sanctions against suicide than in countries without such sanctions (Kelleher, et al., 1998). A stronger protective impact of moral/religious objections against suicide in women than in men was found in this study and in a study of hospitalized depressed patients (Lizardi, et al., 2007). Although religious sanctions as such may protect against suicide, an alternative explanation must be considered. Kelleher, et al. observed that countries with religious sanctions were less likely to provide suicide mortality data to the WHO than other countries. Furthermore, religious sanctions may decrease the reliability of suicide data through their detrimental impact on the recording and reporting procedures, as the relatives of the deceased and professionals may try to conceal the stigmatized or socially unacceptable cause of death (Khan & Hyder, 2006; Mishara & Weisstub, 2015).

Suicidal Behavior and Religiosity: Clinical Population Studies

Religiosity can have a protective effect on suicidality in populations with a high risk of suicide, such as people with a history of suicidal ideation or a suicide attempt, people with diagnosed mental health problems, and individuals in a psychological crisis. In general, studies show lower levels of religiosity in people who have made a suicide attempt. Caribé, et al., (2012) reported significantly lower levels of intrinsic religiosity and organizational and non-organizational religious activities in people hospitalized after a suicide attempt than in a control group. This difference remained significant even after controlling for mental illness, impulsivity and sociodemographic variables. In a group of women who had recently attempted suicide, having no current religious affiliation was one of the predictors of suicide five years later (Wandrei, 1985). Spirituality and religion were also found to play a significant role in mental health help-seeking in young people aged 14-18 who made a suicide attempt (Bullock, et al., 2012). In this group, religious communities can act as a bridge or a provider of mental health services, and a religious or spiritual discourse can be embedded in the process of counselling. Many young people reported changes in their level of interest in spirituality and religion before the suicide attempt. In the words of one of the interviewed participants: "It's not more so that the religion affected it, it was more the mental health affected the religion aspect of my life; it's that I just wanted to avoid everything and push it out of my life and so it's pretty much just the opposite way" (Bullock, et al., 2012, p. 190).

Contact with psychiatric services, confiding in family and friends, self-help, and religion are among the resources used, and perceived as helpful, by patients with severe psychiatric illness who are in crisis (Eagles, et al., 2003). In a study of the frequency and helpfulness of contact when patients felt at their most despairing (Eagles, et al., 2003), almost half (49%) of the participants reported that they thought about their religious beliefs when in crisis, and one in three (37%) prayed to cope with the difficult situation. One in four (25%) said that their religious beliefs actually prevented them from engaging in suicidal behavior, and prayers and talking to a member of the clergy was "a great deal" or at least "a bit" helpful in a suicidal crisis.

A series of studies conducted with patients diagnosed with depression and bipolar disorder indicate the preventive potential of religiosity, operationalized within the reasons for living framework (Linehan, et al.,

1983). Reasons for living are the individual's beliefs which may help to inhibit suicidal behavior or "beliefs potentially important as reasons for not committing suicide" (Linehan, et al., 1983, p. 276). These include survival and coping beliefs, responsibility to family, child-related concerns, fear of social disapproval, fear of suicide, and moral objections to suicide, such as "I believe only God has the right to end a life," "My religious beliefs forbid it" and "I am afraid of going to hell." Studies found that depressed patients with a lifetime history of suicide attempts endorsed a significantly smaller range of reasons for living, including moral objections to suicide (Dervic, et al., 2004; Malone, et al., 2000). In addition, patients without religious affiliation had significantly more lifetime suicide attempts and more first-degree relatives who had committed suicide than religiously affiliated patients (Dervic, et al., 2004). Religious affiliation *per se* did not differentiate patients with and without a history of a suicide attempt, leading to a conclusion that reasons for living may be a more sensitive indicator of the protective effect of religious beliefs than objectively measured religious persuasion (Malone, et al., 2000).

Reasons for living, including moral/religious objections against suicide, can also have a predictive utility regarding future suicidal behavior. In a two-year follow up study, hospitalized patients with a major depressive episode and a higher score on the reasons for living scale made significantly fewer suicide attempts than their counterparts with lower scores (Lizardi, et al., 2007). This protective effect was observed only in female, and not in male, patients. In addition, in this study, hospitalized patients with depression who had a history of a suicide attempt more often reported no religious affiliation than hospitalized patients, who were non-attempters. The protective effect of the higher score on the moral or religious objections to suicide was also found in depressed bipolar patients (Dervic, et al., 2011). Besides reasons for living, intrinsic religiosity and non-organizational religious activities, can have a protective effect against suicidal behavior in patients with a depressive episode (Mosqueiro, et al., 2015) and bipolar type-1 outpatients, even after controlling for variables, such as gender, impulsivity, and psychiatric comorbidity (Caribé, et al., 2015).

Notwithstanding its preventive potential, in some cases religiosity can play an incentive role in suicidal behavior in clinical populations. A study exploring the role of religion in the decisions about suicide in both in psychotic (schizophrenia or schizoaffective disorders) and non- psychotic patients, found that religion may play a protective or an incentive role (or may be unrelated to suicidality) (Huguelet, et al., 2007). The majority of patients (64%) reported no relationship between religion and their suicide attempts. For one fourth of the patients (25%) religion appeared to be a protective factor through religious coping, religious condemnation of suicide, and finding the meaning of life through religion. The remaining patients (11%) reported an incentive role of religion in their suicidal behavior related to their wish to die in order to be with God, to experience death or to live another life after death. Also, religious delusions and hallucinations, anger with God, loss of faith, and breaking with their religious community contributed to suicide attempts for some patients (Huguelet, et al., 2007). It has also been observed that patients with symptoms of psychosis may misinterpret biblical verses from the Gospel of Matthew associated with self-mutilation as giving instructions to engage in self-injury involving eyes, hands, feet or genitalia (Schwerkoske, et al., 2012). Moreover, in depressive patients in the bipolar spectrum, high religious involvement may increase the risk of suicidal behavior through aggravation of the guilt feelings or the perceived sinful character of hypomanic experiences (Azorin, et al., 2013).

Maltsberger (1997) introduced the phenomenon of "ecstatic suicide" into the literature, referring to suicidal behavior where "[the] aim in dying is self-transformation, to escape from an insupportable present into a better future beyond death" (p. 290). Such acts do not stem from melancholia and sadness. Instead, they are linked to elated mood and grandiose beliefs about death and suicide, which are perceived as a "passage to glory" (p. 293) and have been observed in patients with borderline, narcissistic, and bipolar features.

Complex Interactions between Religiosity, Suicidal Ideation and Suicidal Behavior

Lawrence, Oquendo & Stanley (2015) conducted a systematic review which focused on three specific dimensions of religion (affiliation, service attendance, and doctrine) and three specific aspects of suicidality (ideation, suicide attempt, and suicide). Their aim was to test a hypothesis that religious affiliation and service attendance protect against suicidal behavior, but not suicidal ideation ("I think about suicide but would never do it because of my religion"). Although, in general, religious affiliation was protective against suicide attempts and dying by suicide, it did not necessarily protect against suicidal ideation. Service attendance, after adjusting for social support, was also found to have a protective affect against suicidal attempts, and possibly also suicide, but not suicidal ideation. Religion may thus prevent a person with suicidal thoughts from engaging in self-harming behavior by offering access to community support, providing a source of hope and ways to interpret suffering, as well as shaping their beliefs about suicide. Also, for some people, prayer can be helpful in coping with suicidal thoughts (Osafo et al., 2013). Nonetheless, although religious affiliation can offer community connection, affiliation with a religious minority group may lead to social isolation, and the protective effect can also be lower in socio-cultural contexts opposing religion in general or specific religions. Moreover, negative religious coping, such as experiencing spiritual tension or doubt, internal religious conflict and struggle with God, as well as perceiving God as the source of difficulties or the only agent of control (Pargament et al., 1998) may increase suicide risk, including suicidal ideation (Lawrence et al., 2015).

Religiosity and Suicidal Ideation

The next section focuses on *religiosity* rather than religion and reviews research on this topic, focusing on suicidal ideation and on questionnaire measures of religiosity.

University Students

Krysinska, et al. (2015) studied 165 American undergraduates and found that a history of lifetime suicidal ideation was negatively associated with religiosity (using a scale devised by Francis [1992]), whereas current suicidal ideation was not associated with religiosity. In a factor analysis of the variables measured in the study, religiosity clustered with gratitude, reasons for living, and social support. In a multiple regression, only depression, stress and social support predicted lifetime suicidal ideation. Lester and Francis (1993) studied 103 American undergraduates and found that both past and current suicidal were negatively associated with religiosity (as measured by Francis's scale). These associations held up after controls for depression and controls for locus of control but not after controls for a measure of neuroticism.

Walker and Bishop (2005) studied 459 undergraduates and found that intrinsic religiosity, but not extrinsic religiosity, was negatively associated with suicidal ideation as measured by the Beck Scale for Suicidal Ideation, along with depression, and this was found for both European Americans and African Americans.[1] Lester and Walker (2017) studied 419 American undergraduates and found that, in general, intrinsic religiosity, but not extrinsic religiosity, predicted suicidal ideation (using the suicidal ideation scale of Reynolds [1991]). Intrinsic religiosity was a protective factor for women, but not for men, and for European Americans but not for African Americans.

Hills and Francis (2005) studied 501 students in Wales and found that, in a multiple regression analysis, neither intrinsic nor extrinsic religiosity predicted past suicidal ideation, but *quest orientation* was positively associated with past suicidal ideation, that is those seeking a meaning in existence through religion.

---

[1] Intrinsic religiosity refers to people who are religious because of the beliefs and practices of their religion, whereas extrinsic religiosity refers to the side benefits of being religious such as the social networks it provides.

(A typical item on this subscale was: I am constantly questioning my religious beliefs). In a study of 149 American undergraduates, Lester (2012) found that past suicidal ideation was *positively* associated with extrinsic religiosity but not associated with intrinsic religiosity.

Lytle, et al. (2018) studied past year suicidal ideation in 21,247 university students and their rating of the importance of religion for their personal identity. Religiosity was a protective factor for male and female heterosexual students, but a risk factor for female lesbian and questioning students. Religiosity was not associated with past-year suicidal ideation for bisexual students of either sex.

Zhang and Jin (1996) studied 320 Chinese and 352 American undergraduates using their own specially constructed measure of 5 items to measure religiosity. Suicidal ideation in the past year was negatively associated with religiosity in the American sample, but positively associated with suicidal ideation in the Chinese sample. In a study of 375 undergraduates from Ghana and the United States, Eshun (2003), found that suicidal ideation in the past year was not associated with Zhang and Jin's measure of religiosity in either the Ghanaian or the American students. Clearly, culture plays a major role in the association between suicidal ideation and religiosity.

The results of these studies are quite inconsistent. Two studies reported a protective effect of religiosity (Krysinska, et al., 2015; Lester & Francis, 1993); two studies reported a protective effect but only for intrinsic religiosity (Lester & Walker, 2017; Walker & Bishop, 2005); and two studies found no effect of religiosity (Hill & Francis, 2005; Eshun, 2003). One study reported that religiosity was a risk factor for suicidal ideation (Lester, 2012).

The other research found a qualified protective effect of religiosity: for heterosexual but not for LBGTQ students (Lytle, et al., 2018), for women but not for men, for European Americans but not for African Americans (Lester & Walker, 2017), and for American but not Chinese students (Zhang & Jin, 1996).

Adolescents

Nkansah-Amankra (2013) studied 9,421 American adolescents who were followed up on three subsequent occasions, until young adulthood (1995-2008). They were asked to rate the importance of their religious faith in 1995 and suicidal ideation in the past year at each of the four interviews.

He found that the importance of religion was negatively associated with suicidal ideation in the past year when they were adolescents, but not when they were young adults. Social support and self-esteem eliminated the statistical significance of religiosity.

Boyas, et al. (2019) studied past suicidal ideation and intrinsic religiosity in 3,116 Hispanic American adolescents and found a weak, but significant, correlation.

In a study of 702 Mexican high school students, Hoffman and Marsiglia (2014) found that recent suicidal ideation (in the past week) was not associated with responses to a question "How important is religion to you?" (labelled internal religiosity) but was negatively associated (at a marginal level of statistical significance: $p < 0.10$) with "How often do you attend religious services at your church, mosque, synagogues or temple?" (labelled external religiosity).

Muallem and Israelashvilli (2015) studied 209 Christian and Muslim Arab adolescents in Israel using Reynolds's (1991) suicidal ideation questionnaire and a religiosity scale adapted for adolescents of both religions. They found that religiosity was associated with less suicidal ideation, but only for the Christian adolescents.

Thus, three of these studies found qualified support for a protective effect of religiosity on suicidal ideation: for adolescents but not young adults, for extrinsic religiosity but not intrinsic religiosity, and for Christians but not Muslims. The fourth study contradicted one of the preceding three by finding that intrinsic religiosity was a protective factor.

Adults

Walker, et al. (2014) recruited 236 African American adults from the community in a city in the United States. They found that suicidal ideation as measured using the scale from Reynolds was associated negatively with intrinsic religiosity but not with extrinsic religiosity, but not when other variables (such as depression) were controlled for.

Burshtein, et al. (2016) studied 5,200 Israeli Jewish young adults and asked them how religious they were (classified as secular, partially observant and religious) and found that the incidence of lifetime suicidal ideation was higher in the secular subjects (9.4%) than in the partially observant (6.7%) and religious (6.2%), but not significantly so.

In contrast, Wingate, et al. (2005) studied 299 adult American men aged 15-54. The intent of the study was to study the impact of living in the South, and so their results for religiosity are not clear, but lifetime suicidal ideation appeared to be unrelated to religiosity.

Of these three studies, two found a protective effect from religiosity (but, in one study, only for intrinsic religiosity), while one study found no impact from religiosity.

Psychiatric Patients

Nad, et al. (2008) studied 45 Croatian war veterans with PTSD. They found that intrinsic religiosity scores were associated negatively with suicidality as assessed with a suicide assessment scale.[2]

[2] The scale they used has 3 questions on suicidal ideation, but also 17 other questions.

Practical Guidelines for the Assessment of Religiosity and Suicide Risk

General population and clinical studies show that religious beliefs, behaviors and networks can play a significant protective role against suicide risk. Despite this accumulating evidence, standard clinical assessments often overlook religiosity and relevant guidelines have not been established. Addressing this gap, Gearing and Lizardi (2009; Gearing & Alonzo, 2018) proposed a set of general practice guidelines which may help clinicians to assess the impact of their clients' religiosity on suicide risk.

1. Assessing the importance of religion to the client, client's identity, support networks and significant others, for example:
   - What is the client's degree of religious affiliation and activity?
   - Does he/she socialize with members of religious community?
   - How strongly does he/she identify with the tenets of the religion?
   - Has there been a recent change in his/her religious commitment?
2. Assessing the role of religiosity during times of stress and past difficulties, for example:
   - Has the client's religiosity served as a source of comfort or a coping mechanism in the past?
   - Has his/her religiosity neither positively nor negatively influenced the level of distress?
   - If religion has been used, how?
   - If religion has not been used, why?
3. Assessing how suicide is conceptualized in the client's religion, for example:
   - Are there religious sanctions against suicide?
   - Is suicide acceptable under some circumstances?

- Is there conflict between clients' personal beliefs about suicide and the religious viewpoint?
- If so, how is this conflict resolved and does it have an impact on the client's faith?

4. Assessing the value of strengthening client's religiosity and religious participation during the treatment process, for example:
   - Which elements of the client's religiosity provide protection against suicide?
   - How can the religious support be maximized?
   - Which elements of the client's religiosity have attenuated his/her distress?
   - How can these harmful effects be minimized?

CONCLUSION

As in many psychological research studies, the measures used tend to over-simplify the constructs being measured. The beliefs of religious people can vary tremendously. Some devout people may view death as leading to an afterlife that is pleasant. They believe that will be reunited with their loved ones and live happily ever after. Others may believe in a Day of Judgment and fear that they will be judged harshly. Some religions allow for confession and forgiveness while others do not. Beshai and Lester (2013) developed a scale to measure the belief in a Day of Judgment and found that scores on the scale were moderately associated with scores on Francis's measure of religiosity (Pearson r = 0.79), but were not associated with the fears of death and dying for oneself or for others.

This review of research on the association of religiosity and suicidal ideation found mixed results. The majority of the studies found that religiosity was a protective factor, but perhaps only for intrinsic religiosity. Other research found qualified support, with religiosity being a protective factor for some subgroups of the sample, a risk factor for other subgroups and irrelevant for other subgroups. Clearly, more research is needed on this topic.

References

Beshai, J. A. & Lester, D. (2013). Belief in a day of judgment and death anxiety. *Psychological Reports*, *112*, 100-105.

Bouas, J. F., Kim, Y. J., Villarreal-Otálora, T. & Sink, J. K. (2019). Suicide ideation among Latinx adolescents. *Children & Youth Services Review*, *102*, 177-185.

Burshstein, S., Dohrenwend, B. P., Levav, I., Werbeloff, N., Davidson, M. & Weiser, M. (2016). Religiosity as a protective factor against suicidal behavior. *Acta Psychiatrica Scandinavica*, *133*, 481-488.

Eshun, S. (2003). Sociocultural determinants of suicidal ideation. *Suicide & Life-Threatening Behavior*, *33*, 165-171.

Eskin, M., Poyrazli, S., Janghorbani, M., Bakhshi, S., Carta, M. G.,…….& Taifour, S. (2019). The role of religion in suicidal behavior, attitudes and psychological distress among university students: *Transcultural Psychiatry*, in press.

Francis, L. J. (1992). Reliability and validity and the Francis scale of attitude towards Christianity. *Panorama*, *4*(1), 17-19.

Gearing, R. E. & Alonzo, D. (2018). Religion and suicide: new findings. *Journal of Religion and Health*, *57*(6), 2478-2499.

Hills, P. R. & Francis, L. J. (2005). The relationships of religiosity and personality with suicidal ideation. *Mortality*, *10*, 286-293.

Hoffman, S. & Marsiglia, F. F. (2014). The impact of religiosity on suicidal ideation among youth in central Mexico. *Journal of Religion & Health*, *53*, 255-266.

Krysinska, K., Lester, D., Lyke, J. & Corveleyn, J. (2015). Trait gratitude and suicidal ideation and behavior. *Crisis*, *36*, 291-296.

Lester, D. (2000). *Why people kill themselves*. 4th Edition. Springfield, IL: Charles Thomas. Lester, D. (2012). Spirituality and religiosity as predictors of depression and suicidal ideation. *Psychological Reports*, *110*, 247-250.

Lester, D. & Francis, L. J. (1993). Is religiosity related to suicidal ideation after personality and mood are taken into account? *Personality & Individual Differences*, *15*, 591-592.

Lester, D. & Walker, R. L. (2017). Religiosity is a protective factor for suicidal ideation in European American students but not in African American students. *Omega*, *74*, 295-303.

Lytle, M. C., Blosnich, L. R., De Luca, S. M. & Brownson, C. (2018). Association of religiosity with sexual minority suicide ideation and attempt. *American Journal of Preventive Medicine*, *54*, 644-651.

Muallem, H. K. & Israelashvilli, M. (2015). Religiosity as a buffer against suicidal ideation. *Mental Health, Religion & Culture*, *18*, 838-849.

Nađ, S., Marčinko, D., Vuksan-Aeusa, B., Jakovljevič, M. & Jakovljevic, G. (2008). Spirituality well-being, intrinsic religiosity, and suicidal behavior in predominantly Catholic Croatian war veterans with chronic posttraumatic stress disorder. *Journal of Nervous & Mental Disease*, *196*, 79-83.

Nkansah-Amankra, S. (2013). Adolescent suicidal trajectories through young adulthood. *Suicide & Life-Threatening Behavior*, *43*, 439-459.

Reynolds, W. M. (1991). Psychometric characteristics of the adult suicidal ideation questionnaire in college students. *Journal of Personality Assessment*, *56*, 289-307.

Stack, S. & Laubepin, F. (2019). Religiousness as a predictor of suicide: An analysis of 162 European regions. *Suicide and Life-Threatening Behavior*, *49*(2), 371-381.

Walker, R. H. & Bishop, S. (2005). Examining a model of the relation between religiosity and suicidal ideation in a sample of African American and white college students. *Suicide & Life-Threatening Behavior*, 35, 630-639.

Walker, R. H., Salami, T. K., Carter, S. F. & Flowers, K. (2014). Perceived racism and suicide ideation. *Suicide & Life-Threatening Behavior*, *44*, 548-559.

Wingate, L. R., Bobadilla, L., Burns, A. B. & Joiner, T. E. (2005). Suicidality in African American men. *Suicide & Life-Threatening Behavior*, *35*, 615-629.

Zhang, J. & Jin, S. (1996). Determinants of suicide ideation. *Adolescence*, *31*, 451-467.

In: Understanding Suicidal Ideation
Editor: David Lester
ISBN: 978-1-53616-999-7

Chapter 3

"BUT WORDS CAN NEVER HURT ME:" EXAMINING THE ROLE OF PEER VICTIMIZATION IN THE DEVELOPMENT OF SUICIDAL THOUGHTS

John F. Gunn III

ABSTRACT

A significant number of adolescents and young adults experience peer victimization throughout their lives. Research has supported a number of detrimental effects linked to exposure to peer victimization. Those who experience peer victimization, as either victims, perpetrators, or both, have elevated rates of suicidal thoughts and behaviors. The present chapter will review the evidence for this increased risk as well as how exposure to peer victimization fits into three modern theoretical frameworks of suicide.

"'You're so ugly, stupid, lame, pathetic, useless, idiotic, just go away, no one even likes you, you're a waste of space, just go kill yourself already; you're better off dead." Comments like those are why I'm

> depressed, why I cut myself, why I believe I'm not important, why I can't accept compliments or even believe I'm beautiful".

The quote that opens this chapter comes directly from a 19-year-old girl who died by suicide. Before her death, she posted a video online in which she used flashcards to explain her story. This quote highlights the impact that experiences of peer victimization can have on the development of suicidal thoughts and, subsequently, death by suicide. While bullying and suicide are not causally linked, bullying is sometimes a contributing factor in the development of suicidal thoughts and is most salient at specific developmental periods (Gunn & Goldstein, 2016). The present chapter will review the prevalence of bullying, the evidence for a suicide-bullying link, and explore modern theories of suicide that may account for the relationship between bullying and suicidal thoughts.

However, before progressing to these considerations, it is important to outline just what is meant by the term "peer victimization." In this chapter, peer victimization is used as an umbrella term to refer to any of a number of different forms of aggression faced by individuals. These forms of aggression are: (1) physical aggression, (2) relational aggression, (3) verbal aggression, and (4) cyber aggression/cyberbullying. There is substantial variation in who experience and engage in these various forms of peer victimization, but all forms have been linked to suicidal thoughts and behaviors by previous researchers (Gunn & Goldstein, 2018).

PREVALENCE OF PEER VICTIMIZATION

According to reports from the U.S. Department of Education for the year 2015, 20% of students aged 12-18 reported being exposed to some form of bullying (U.S. Department of Education, 2016). The two most commonly reported forms of peer victimization reported were being made fun of, insulted, or called names (13.3%) and having rumors spread about them (12.2%).

A meta-analysis by Modecki and colleagues (2014) found that the mean prevalence rate across 80 studies was 35% for traditional forms of bullying and 15% for cyber victimization.

These percentages relate to populations as a whole, but there is also a need to consider risk among subpopulations. Looking at a large sample of American youth, Berlan et al., (2010) found an increased risk for peer victimization among gay males, bisexual females and lesbians compared to heterosexual males and females. Drawing on the Youth Risk Behavior Survey (YRBS), Kahle (2017) found that LGBQ youth experience all types of bullying victimization at greater rates than do heterosexual youth. DeSmet and colleagues (2018) also found elevated experiences of traditional victimization among LGBQ youth compared to their heterosexual counterparts.

LGBTQ+ youth are not the only group to experience greater exposure to peer victimization. Work by Rose, Simpson, and Moss (2015) points to increased experiences of relational victimization, cyber victimization, and physical victimization among students with disabilities. Even after controlling for a number of other bullying risk factors, Chatzitheochari, Parsons and Platt (2016) found that youth in the United Kingdom who had disabilities were more likely to experience peer victimization than non-disabled youth. Beckman, Hellstrom, and von Kobyletzki (2019) found a tendency for children and young adults with neurodiversity to be involved in cyber bullying (as a victim, perpetrator and victim-perpetrator) at a higher frequency than non-neurodiverse controls.

PEER VICTIMIZATION AND SUICIDE

Both those who experience peer victimization as a victim and who engage in it as a perpetrator experience suicidal thoughts and behaviors at an elevated rate. Cleary (2000) found that, among those participating in the Youth Risk Behavior Survey, experiences of peer victimization were associated with increased suicidal behavior as well as outwardly-directed violent behavior.

This was particularly relevant to males, who experience increased suicidal behavior and violent behavior after exposure to peer victimization. Work by van der Wal and colleagues (2003) found that, for both boys and girls, experiences of peer victimization increased the incidence of suicidal thoughts, and this association was particularly strong for exposure to indirect (i.e., relational) victimization. Heikkila and colleagues (2013) reported that those who engage in victimization as perpetrators and experience victimization as victims were at the greatest risk for developing suicidal thoughts. Additionally, those who were only victims more often reported suicidal thoughts than those who were only perpetrators.

Kim and colleagues (2009) also found a greater risk of suicidal thoughts among those who were victims and perpetrators of peer victimization. Their findings indicated that peer victimization was a significant risk factor for suicidal thoughts even when anxiety and depression, aggressive behavior, and conduct problems were controlled for.

Reviewing a number of cross-sectional and longitudinal studies on the peer victimization and suicide link, Klomek and colleagues (2010) found that the research supported both a peer victimization and suicide link as well as previous findings that those who experience both peer victimization and engage in perpetration are at the greatest risk for suicidal thoughts and behaviors.

Litwiller and Brausch (2013), exploring both the role of in-school victimization and cyber victimization, found that both forms of victimization were associated with suicidal thoughts and behaviors. Finally, a recent meta-analysis of the literature concluded that cyber victimization may be even more impactful on suicidal thoughts than traditional forms of victimization (i.e., physical aggression and relational aggression (van Geel et al., 2014). It is worth noting that cyber victimization does not occur in a vacuum, and those who are typically exposed to one form of victimization often face other forms as well (Hase et al., 2015).

How Peer Victimization Fits into Modern Theories of Suicide?

While research has established that an association between exposure to peer victimization and suicidal thoughts and behaviors exists, little work has explored the mechanism by which bullying may contribute to suicidal thoughts. The present section will discuss three theoretical frameworks for suicide and outline how the victimization-suicide link might be explained by them. The three theoretical frameworks that will be discussed in relation to the victimization-suicide link are: (1) Interpersonal-Psychological Theory of Suicide (IPTS), (2) Three-Step Theory of Suicide (3ST), and (3) Social Pain Model (SPM).

Interpersonal-Psychological Theory of Suicide (IPTS)

The IPTS was first proposed by Joiner (2005) and then expanded upon by Van Orden and colleagues (2010). According to the IPTS, suicide is the result of three risk factors for suicide: (1) perceived burdensomeness, (2) thwarted belongingness, and (3) the acquired capability for suicide. This is illustrated in Figure 3.1.

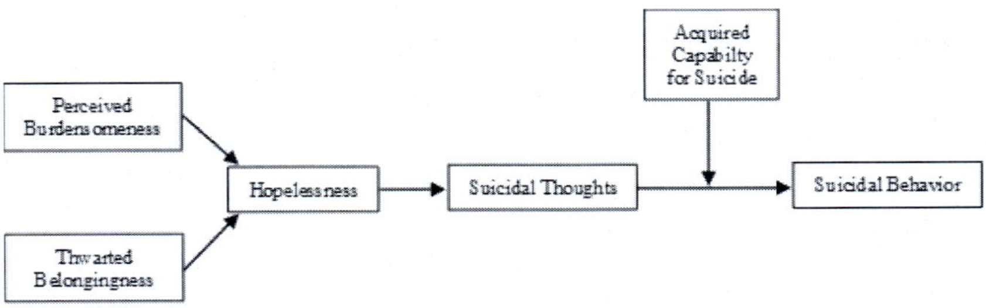

Figure 3.1. Interpersonal-Psychological Theory of Suicide (IPTS), Figure based on Van Orden, et al., 2010.

Perceived burdensomeness is the belief that you are a liability or a burden on those around you. Statements such as “Others would be better off if I were gone” and “I’m such a burden on my family” would be characteristic of someone experiencing perceptions of burdensomeness. Thwarted belongingness is the belief that you have weak social ties and that you lack support. Statements such as “Nobody cares about me” and “I am so alone” would be characteristic of someone experiencing a heightened sense of thwarted belongingness.

When both perceived burdensomeness and thwarted belongingness are present in the minds of an individual, people are said to have the motivation for suicide, the desire to die by suicide and therefore those factors can be viewed as motivational factors. However, according to the IPTS, in order to transition from the motivation to death by suicide, one must also have the acquired capability for suicide. The acquired capability for suicide is a lowered fear of death and increased pain tolerance and is often associated with repeated self-injury, exposure to violence, and other experiences often present in the lives of those who die by suicide.

Three-Step Theory of Suicide (3ST)

Recently, Klonsky and May (2015) presented a Three-Step Theory (3ST) focused on explaining the transition from suicidal thoughts to suicidal behaviors (an ‘ideation-to-action’ framework). As the name implies, the 3ST explains suicide through three steps that confer increased risk. Figure 3.2 highlights these steps. As can be seen in this figure, step 1 focuses on whether or not an individual is experiencing both pain and hopelessness. If both are present, suicidal thoughts will be experienced. At step 2 the question is whether or not the pain is greater than their sense of connectedness. If an individual is experiencing pain, but they have strong social connections, then only moderate suicidal thoughts will be experienced, but if it is not, stronger suicidal thoughts will develop. Finally, step 3 askes whether or not the individual is capable of suicide, drawing on the acquired capability discussed by the IPTS but expanding it.

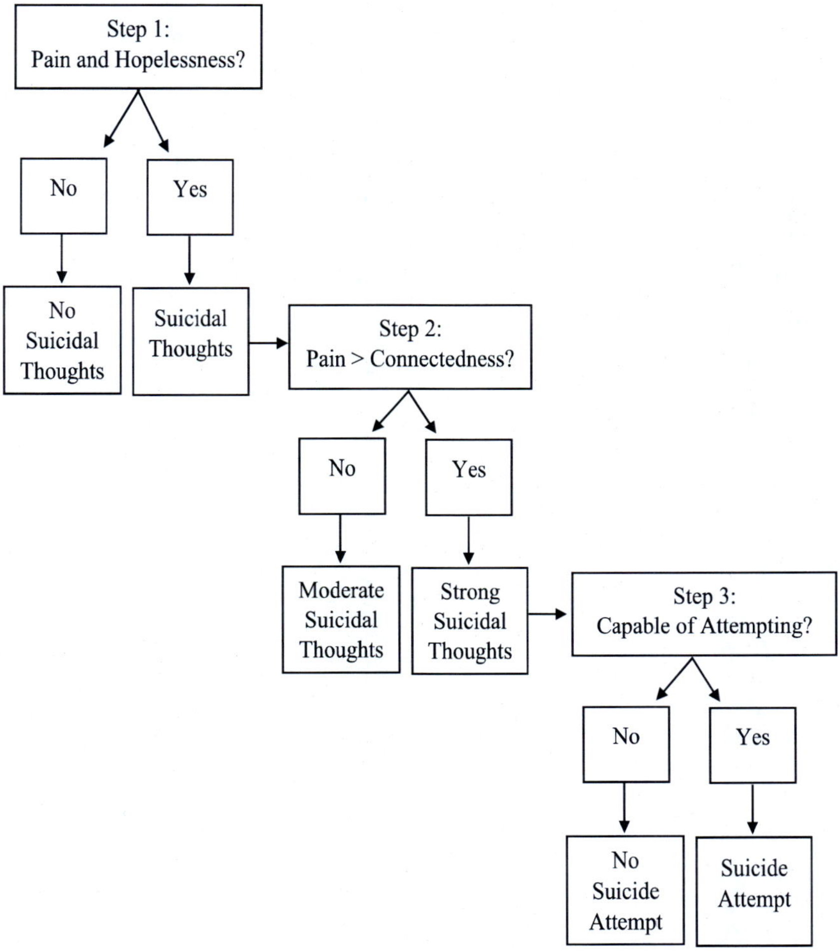

Figure 3.2 Step Theory. Figure based on Klonsky & May, 2015.

Capability, according to Klonsky and May (2015), has *dispositional* qualities, *acquired* qualities, and *practical* qualities. Dispositional qualities are factors that are largely out of the control of an individual, such as genetic predispositions (e.g., to pain sensitivity). Acquired qualities are a direct reference to the acquired capability discussed in the IPTS. Finally, practical qualities refer to factors that make suicide attempts easier, such as access to means.

Social Pain Model of Suicide (SPM)

Building from the IPTS, 3-ST, and recent theoretical explanations of suicide from an evolutionary perspective (Soper, 2018), Gunn (2017) proposed the Social Pain Model (SPM) as an explanation for suicidal behavior that considers suicide within the context of evolutionary psychology and social neuroscience. Figure 3.3 shows an updated model from that proposed by Gunn (2017).

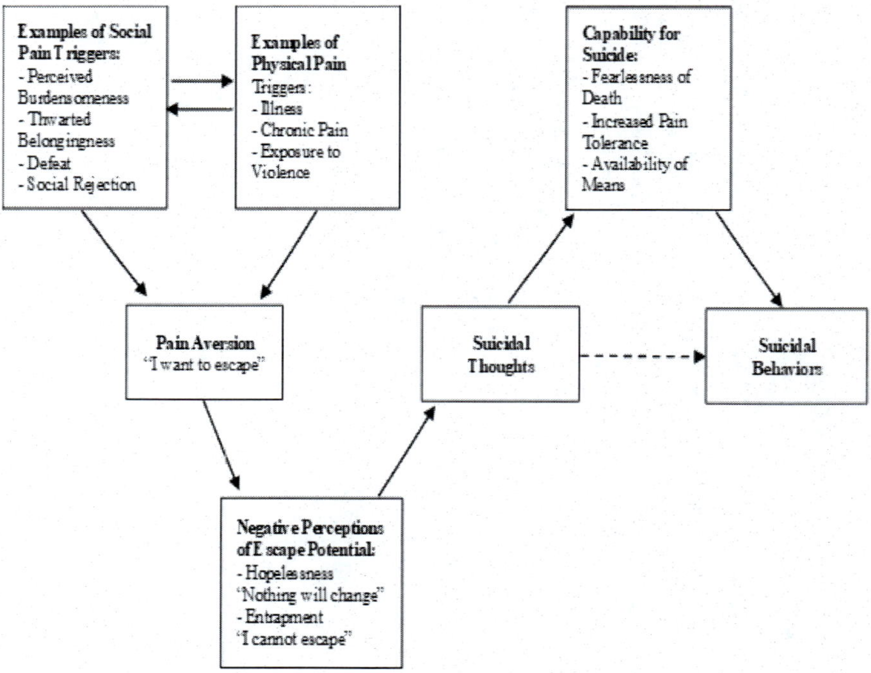

Figure 3.3 Social Pain Model of Suicide (SPM; Figure based on Gunn, 2017).

According to the SPM, the motivational force driving suicidal behavior is the evolutionary adaptation of pain aversion. Suicidal individuals experience a desire to escape pain, typically associated with social pain (such as that experienced when social rejection or ostracism occurs). This desire to escape pain develops into suicidal thoughts when there are perceptions of negative escape potential, which is characterized by hopelessness ("Nothing will change") and a sense of entrapment ("I cannot escape").

APPLICATION OF THEORY TO PEER VICTIMIZATION

Examining the theories outlined above, it can be seen how each can be applied to understanding the association between exposure to peer victimization and subsequent suicidal behavior. (However, it is important to note that these theories deal with the psychology of suicide and not the influence of social forces). Drawing from the IPTS, those who are experiencing peer victimization will likely experience thwarted belongingness, feeling as if they do not belong or are alone. Additionally, feelings of burdensomeness may be increased by a devaluation of the self in light of the victimization that an individual is facing. Being ostracized or victimized by their peers may drive many who experience the various forms of bullying to view the self in a negative light. The 3ST, drawing from the IPTS, would apply to bullying in a similar way as the IPTS, with increased burdensomeness and decreased belongingness. In addition to this, those exposed to peer victimization may also develop greater feelings of hopelessness that contribute to their suicidal behaviors. Finally, the SPM would view peer victimization as contributing to suicidal thoughts and behaviors through the experience of pain. Those exposed to peer victimization may experience both social pain (e.g., from ostracism) and/or physical pain (e.g., from physical victimization) that motivate the individual to escape the pain.

Research has attempted to apply these theories to peer victimization. Opperman, et al., (2015) explored the role of perceived burdensomeness and various forms of connectedness (e.g., peer and family) among adolescents who had experienced peer victimization as well as those perpetrating bullying. Adolescents who were experiencing low family connectedness combined with high perceived burdensomeness were more lily to report suicidal ideation. Mitchell, et al., (2018) found that perceived burdensomeness, but not thwarted belongingness, mediated the association between experiences of cyber victimization and suicidal thoughts. Moberg and Anestis (2015) explored the role of negative online interactions on the development of thwarted belongingness in an undergraduate population. The findings found that negative social interactions increased a sense of thwarted belongingness among participants. Recently, Brailovskaia, et al., (2019) found that thwarted belongingness and perceived burdensomeness fully mediated the relationship between peer victimization and suicidal thoughts.

Conclusion

The present chapter set out to explore the problem of peer victimization and the impact it has on the development of suicidal thoughts and behaviors. Specifically, the association between peer victimization and suicide was explored through the lens of three theoretical frameworks for suicide: the IPTS, 3ST, and SPM theories. Each of these models emphasize the social nature of suicidal behavior, highlighting the potential role of social connectedness, or the lack thereof, thereby indicating how peer victimization can result in experiences of suicidal thoughts and behaviors. Often peer victimization is talked about as a risk factor for suicide, but the mechanisms by which peer victimization leads to suicidal behavior is less often discussed. By viewing peer victimization through these three theoretical frameworks, it becomes more apparent how suicidal behavior can result from exposure to peer victimization.

References

Beckman, L., Hellstrom, L., & von Kobyletzki, L. (2019). Cyber bullying among children with neurodevelopmental disorders: A systematic review. *Scandinavian Journal of Psychology,* online first.

Berlan, E. D., Corliss, H. L., Field, A. E., Goodman, E., & Austin, S. B. (2010). Sexual orientation and bullying among adolescents in the growing up today study. *Journal of Adolescent Health, 46,* 366-371.

Brailovskaia, J., Ujma, M., Friedrich, S., & Teismann, T. (2019). Thwarted belongingness and perceived burdensomeness mediate the association between bullying and suicide ideation. *Crisis,* online first.

Chatzitheochari, S., Parsons, S., & Platt, L. (2016). Doubly disadvantaged? Bullying experiences among disabled children and young people in England. *Sociology, 50,* 695-713.

Cleary, S. D. (2000). Adolescent victimization and associated suicidal and violent behaviors. *Adolescence, 25(140),* 671-682.

DeSmet, A., Rodelli, M., Walrave, M., Soenens, B., Cardon, G., & De Bourdeaudhuij, I. (2018). Cyberbullying and traditional bullying involvement among heterosexual and non-heterosexual adolescents, and their associations with age and gender. *Computers in Human Behavior, 83,* 254-261.

Fite, P. J., Stauffacher, K., Ostrov, J. M., & Colder, C. R. (2008). Replication and extension of Little et al.'s (2003) forms and functions of aggression. *International Journal of Behavioral Development, 32,* 238-242.

Gunn, J. F. III, & Goldstein, S. E. (2016). Bullying and suicidal behavior during adolescence: A developmental perspective. *Adolescent Research Review, 2,* 77-97.

Hase, C. N., Goldberg, S. B., Smith, D., Stuck, A., & Campain, J. (2015). Impacts of traditional bullying and cyberbullying on the mental health of middle school and high school students. *Psychology in the Schools, 52(6),* 607-617.

Heikkila, H., Vaananen, J., Helminen, M., Frojd, S., Marttunen, M., & Kaltiala-Heino, R. (2013). Involvement in bullying and suicidal ideation in middle adolescence: A 2-year follow-up study. *European Journal of Child & Adolescent Psychiatry, 22,* 95-102.

Kahle, L. (2017). Are sexual minorities more at risk? Bullying victimization among lesbian, gay, bisexual, and questioning youth. *Journal of Interpersonal Violence,* online first.

Kim, Y. S., Leventhal, B., Koh, Y., & Boyce, T. (2009). Bullying increased suicide risk: prospective study of Korean adolescents. *Archives of Suicide Research, 13,* 15-30.

Klomek, A. B., Sourander, A., & Gould, M. (2010). The association of suicide and bullying in childhood to young adulthood: A review of cross-sectional and longitudinal research findings. *Canadian Journal of Psychiatry, 55,* 282-288.

Klonsky, E. D. & May, A. M. (2015). The three-step theory (3ST): A new theory of suicide rooted in the "ideation-to-action" framework. *International Journal of Cognitive Therapy, 8,* 114-129.

Little, T. D., Jones, S. M., Henrich, C. C., & Hawley, P. H. (2003). Disentangling the 'whys' from the 'whats' of aggressive behavior. *International Journal of Behavioral Development, 27,* 122-133.

Mitchell, S. M., Seegan, P. L., Roush, J. F., Brown, S. L., Sustaita, M. A., & Cukrowicz, K. C. (2018). Retrospective cyberbullying and suicide ideation: The mediating roles of depressive symptoms, perceived burdensomeness, and thwarted belongingness. *Journal of Interpersonal Violence, 33,* 2602-2620.

Moberg, F. B., & Anestis, M. D. (2015). A preliminary examination of the relationship between social networking interactions, internet use, and thwarted belongingness. *Crisis, 36,* 187-193.

Opperman, K., Czyz, E. K., Gipson, P. Y., & King, C. A. (2015). Connectedness and perceived burdensomeness among adolescents at elevated suicide risk: An examination of the Interpersonal Theory of Suicidal Behavior. *Archives of Suicide Research, 19,* 385-400.

Rose, C. A., Simpson, C. G., & Moss, A. (2015). The bullying dynamic: Prevalence of involvement among a large-scale sample of middle and high school youth with and without disabilities. *Psychology in the Schools, 52,* 515-531.

U.S. Department of Education (2016). Student reports of bullying: Results from the 2015 school crime supplement to the National Crime Victimization Survey. Retrieved from https://nces.ed.gov/pubsearch/pubsinfo.asp?pubid=2017015.

Van der Wal, M. F., de Wit, C. A. M., & Hirasing, R. A. (2003). Psychosocial health among young victims and offenders of direct and indirect bullying. *Pediatrics, 111,* 1312-1317.

Van Geel, M., Vedder, P., & Tanilon, J. (2014). Relationship between peer victimization, cyberbullying, and suicide in children and adolescents: A meta-analysis. *JAMA Pediatrics, 168,* 435-442.

In: Understanding Suicidal Ideation
Editor: David Lester
ISBN: 978-1-53616-999-7

Chapter 4

MATTERING AND SUICIDAL IDEATION

Mahboubeh Dadfar

ABSTRACT

Mattering is a construct related to the sense of belonging to and with others, thereby reducing the sense of isolation and reducing the lack of communication within the social context. The present chapter reviews relationship between mattering, suicidal ideation and psychological concepts and reports a study to explore whether mattering and loneliness are associated with previous and current suicidal behavior. In a sample of psychiatric outpatients in Iran, both mattering and loneliness were associated with past suicide ideation and attempts and current suicidal ideation and suicide risk. No differences by sex were identified. The results indicate that mattering may be a useful construct, both theoretically and clinically, for understanding suicidal ideation and suicidal behavior in psychiatric patients and supports the development and practice of mattering-focused therapy in the treatment of suicidal psychiatric outpatients.

The mattering construct, as described by Rosenberg and McCullough (1981), is a feeling that others depend on us, are interested in us, are concerned with our fate, or experience us as an ego-extension. Mattering is a social-psychological concept and an important self-concept that is a personal motivator. Mattering has three elements: awareness (I am the object of other's attention), importance (I am the object of other's concern), and reliance (Others rely on me) (Elliott, Kao and Grant 2004, Elliott 2009). Mattering to others, actual or perceived, is an emotional and cognitive concept related to the sense of belonging to and with others, thereby reducing the sense of isolation and reducing the lack of communication within the social context (Baumeister and Leary 1995; Marcus and Rosenberg 1987; Marcus 1991; Schieman and Taylor 2001; France 2011). Mattering is a key issue in building community (Schlossberg 1989).

Marshall and Lambert (2006) found that mattering is not a stable trait, but dependent on the way in which individuals understand their interactions with others. A lack of mattering may lead to a greater sense of general existential meaningless for some people, while those who perceive a sense of social purpose and meaning in their life are more likely have a strong sense of mattering (Marshall 1998, 2001; Marshall, and Tilton-Weaver 2019). Marshall (2004) pointed out that "mattering facilitates a unique feeling or we-ness" that helps people socialize and lessens their feeling of isolation. Having meaningful interactions with others, based on the individual's evaluation of these interactions and also the number of their interactions, is a learned social behavior that has different implications in different cultures.

Drabenstott (2019) noted that mattering can be integrated into Joiner's (2005) Interpersonal Psychological Theory of Suicide (IPTS). Mattering is related to perceived burdensomeness for, if an individual's sense of mattering is strong, that person will not think that he or she is a burden to others. Mattering is also related to thwarted belongingness.

Rashid, et al. (2016, 2017) reported that there was a significant negative relationship between mattering and suicidal behavior in Iranian college students although, after for controlling interpersonal needs, this relationship disappeared. Kiani Chalmari, Jamshidian, and Rashid (2018) found that mattering correlated with interpersonal needs and also with suicidal behavior (mediated by interpersonal needs) in Iranian college students, and they suggested that mattering has a role in the prevention of suicide.

The present chapter reports a study of mattering and suicidal ideation in Iranian psychiatric outpatients, the first such study. The aims of the present study were: (1) to explore the association of mattering with suicidal behavior, and (2) to explore sex differences.

PARTICIPANTS

A convenience sample of 102 Iranian volunteer psychiatric outpatients was recruited from the psychiatric and psychological clinics at the School of Behavioral Sciences and Mental Health-Tehran Institute of Psychiatry affiliated with Iran University of Medical Sciences.

PROCEDURE

The purpose of the study was explained to the patients. The confidentiality of the patients' information was maintained. The patients were invited to participate voluntarily in the study and provided written informed consent after they completed an interview with a psychiatrist. The study protocol was approved by the Institutional Review Board at Iran University of Medical Sciences. The patients were administered the scales individually. All patients completed the scales fully.

MEASURES

The Interpersonal Mattering Scale (IMS)

The Interpersonal Mattering Scale (IMS) was developed by Elliott, Kao, and Grant (2004) based on Rosenberg and McCullough's conceptualization of mattering. The IMS is a 24-item self-report inventory, answered using a 5-point Likert-type format from strongly disagree to strongly agree. The IMS measures the sense of mattering or the individual's perceptions of the degree to which they matter to others (all people who are in contact with them). The IMS has three subscales: awareness, importance, and reliance. Previous studies indicated high reliability and validity in different samples and various settings (e.g., Elliott et al. 2004, Bernardon 2012).

Previous Preference for Death

Previous Preference for Death was evaluated with a question written by the present author: In the previous month, have you felt that you would rather be dead? This item comes from the EURO-D, a face-to-face administered measure of depression (Ayalon and Shiovitz-Ezra 2011). Response options are yes versus no.

Previous Suicidal Thoughts

Previous suicidal thoughts were evaluated with the question: "Have you ever had suicidal thoughts?" Response options were yes versus no.

Previous Suicidal Attempts

Previous suicidal attempts were evaluated with a question: Have you ever made a suicidal attempt?" Response options were yes versus no.

The Suicidal Behavior Questionnaire-Revised (SBQ-R)

The Suicidal Behavior Questionnaire-Revised (SBQ-R, Osman, Bagge, Gutierrez, Konick, Kopper et al. 2001) has 4 items for evaluating previous and future suicidal thoughts and behaviors: the presence and frequency of previous of suicidal ideation and attempts, communication of suicidal thoughts to others, and how likely is a future suicidal attempt. The SBQ-R has high internal consistency and high test-retest reliability) (Osman et al. 2001).

Loneliness

Loneliness was evaluated with the question, "How frequently have you felt lonely over the previous week?" This item comes from the Center for Epidemiological Studies of Depression questionnaire (CES-D) (Radloff 1977; Shiovitz-Ezra and Ayalon 2010). Response options are: not at all (1), part of the time (2), most of the time (3), and almost all the time (4), with a higher score indicating greater loneliness.

RESULTS

The mean age of the patients was 31.1 years (SD = 9.6); the mean duration of their mental disorder was 6.5 years (SD = 5.4); 28.4% had a BA degree; 82.4% were female; 49.0% were single; 43.0% were married and 7.0% divorced; 56.7% had a depressive disorder; 31.7% an anxiety disorder; 8.3% a mixed depressive anxiety disorder; 1.7% a personality disorder, and 41.2% had missing data; 44.1% had a previous preference for death; 39.2% had lifetime suicidal thoughts; and 20.6% had lifetime suicidal attempts.

The internal reliability of the total score and subscale scores for the IMS were moderate, ranging from 0.43 to 0.68. A factor analysis of the 24 items of the IMS identified 7 factors indicating a large degree of heterogeneity in the scale items. Men and women did not differ in IMS scores (mean 67.0, SD = 9.9 for men and 70.4, SD = 8.6 for women, t = 1.09, df = 100).

The correlations between the IMS score and the variables of interest were: previous preference for death $r = 0.28$ ($p < .01$), previous suicidal thoughts $r = 0.35$ ($p < .01$), previous suicidal attempts $r = 0.35$ ($p < .01$), the SBQ-R *total score* $r = 0.48$ ($p < .01$), and loneliness $r = 0.35$ ($p < .01$), all in the expected direction.

Discussion

The research presented in this chapter sought to identify psychological variables that are associated with the suicidal ideation. Using an Iranian clinical sample, mattering was found to have significant positive correlations with a previous preference for death, previous suicidal thoughts, previous suicidal attempts, and current suicidal ideation.

Previous empirical studies have identified associations between mattering and suicidal ideation (Elliot, Colangelo and Gelles 2005; Holden et al. 2018; Olcon, Kim and Gulbas 2017; Van Orden et al. 2008). Elliot et al. (2005) also studied the association of loneliness with suicidal ideation and concluded that, while loneliness is correlated with a higher risk of suicidal behavior, mattering acts as a protective factor. Elliott (2009) suggested that a lack of mattering (often a result of rejection by others) can lead to feelings of worthlessness and shame. Flett, Khan and Su (2019) found that lack of mattering feeling was uniquely involved in depression and suicidality among college and university students. Loneliness can be considered to be a lack of belongingness (de Jong Gierveld et al. 2006), while mattering is associated with belongingness (Chang 2012), and so both variables are relevant to Joiner's (2005) Interpersonal Theory of Suicide which proposed that perceived burdensomeness and thwarted belongingness increased the risk of suicide.

The Farsi version of the mattering scale was reasonably reliable, although somewhat lower than in previous research (e.g., Elliott et al. 2004; Racque-Bogdan et al. 2011). The present study found no sex differences in mattering scores, whereas Dixon Rayle (2005) found that female adolescents reported higher levels of perceived mattering to their family than did male adolescents, and Dixon Rayle and Chung (2007) found that female college students reported higher levels of mattering to friends and their college environment. However, the present study was on psychiatric outpatients rather than normal adolescents, and this may account for the different results.

The present study extends the evidence base regarding the role of mattering in suicidal ideation and suicidal behavior to Iranian psychiatric outpatients. The results indicate that mattering may be a significant construct, both theoretically and clinically, in understanding suicidal ideation and suicidal behavior in such patients. Future research should explore whether the results would differ by psychiatric diagnosis, and a long-term follow-up study that examines subsequent suicidal behavior would be useful.

CONCLUSION

The results of this study support the relevance of mattering in the development of psychotherapeutic strategies for the treatment of Iranian psychiatric outpatients. A focus on the improvement of interpersonal relationship for the patients might facilitate reducing their risk of suicidal behavior. Furthermore, because the association between IMS and SBQ-R scores was only 0.48, using the IMS and SBQ-R together when assessing patients might provide a better predictor of future suicidal behavior than either used alone.

ACKNOWLEDGMENTS

I would like to thank all the psychiatric outpatients for their participation in the study and my research assistants for helping in the collection of data.

REFERENCES

Ayalon, L. and Shiovitz-Ezra, S. (2011). The relationship between loneliness and passive death wishes in the second half of life. *International Psychogeriatrics*, 23, 1677-1685.

Baumeister, R. F. and Leary, M. R. (1995). The need to belong desire for interpersonal attachments as a fundamental human motivation. *Psychological Bulletin,* 117, 497-529.

Bernardon, S. J. M. (2012). *An examination of relationship experiences in relation to loneliness and depressive symptomatology in emerging adulthood.* Ph.D. dissertation submitted to the Graduate School of Wayne State University, Detroit, Michigan. Wayne State University Dissertations. Paper 564.

Chang, S. (2012). *Loneliness and mattering: Investigating distinctions among university students*. A thesis submitted in partial fulfillment of the requirements for the degree of Master of Social Work. The Faculty of Graduate Studies (Social Work), University of British Columbia (Canada).

de Jong Gierveld, J., van Tilburg, T. and Dykstra, P. A. (2006). Loneliness and social isolation. In L.A. Peplau and D. Perlman (Eds.), *Loneliness: A sourcebook of current theory, research and therapy* (pp. 485-499). New York: John Wiley.

Dixon Rayle, A. and Chung, K. (2007). Revisiting first-year college students' mattering: Social support, academic stress, and the mattering experience. *Journal of College Student Retention,* 9, 21-37.

Dixson Rayle, A. (2005). Adolescent gender differences in mattering and wellness. *Journal of Adolescence*, 28, 753-763.

Drabenstott, M. (2019). A matter of life and death: Integrating mattering into the Interpersonal-Psychological Theory of Suicide. *Suicide & Life-Threatening Behavior,* in press.

Elliott, G. C. (2009). *Family matters: The importance of mattering to family in adolescence.* London, UK: Wiley-Blackwell.

Elliott, G., Colangelo, M. F. R. and Gelles, R. (2005). Mattering and suicide ideation: Establishing and elaborating a relationship. *Social Psychology Quarterly,* 68, 223-238.

Elliott, G., Kao, S. and Grant, A.-M. (2004). Mattering: Empirical validation of a social-psychological concept. *Self & Identity,* 3, 339-354.

Flett, G., Khan, A. and Su, C. (2019). Mattering and psychological well-being in college and university students: Review and recommendation campus-based initiatives. *International Journal of Mental Health & Addiction*, online first.

France, M. K. (2011). *Introducing the unified measure of university mattering: Instrument development and evidence of the structural integrity of scores for transfer and native students*. Ph.D. dissertation submitted to the Graduate Faculty of James Madison University.

Holden, R. R., Lambert, C. E., Bianchini, G., Wong, R. E., Towheed, S., Yeung, C. and Fekken, G. C. (2018). Response surface modeling of how love mitigates the associates between a need to belong and suicidality. *Personality & Individual Differences*, 134, 210-213.

Kiani Chalmari, A., Jamshidian, Y. and Rashid, S. (2018). Analyzing the mediating role of the Interpersonal Model of Suicide (perceived burdensomeness and thwarted belongingness) in relation between mattering and suicide. *Journal of Thought & Behavior in Clinical Psychology*, 12(7), 57-66.

Marcus, F. M. (1991, August). *Mattering: Its measurement and theoretical significance for social psychology.* Paper presented at the annual meeting of the Eastern Sociological Association, Cincinnati, OH.

Marcus, F. M. and Rosenberg, M. (1987). *Mattering: Its measurement and significance in everyday life*. Paper presented at the 57th annual Eastern Sociological Society Meeting, Boston, MA.

Marshall, S. K. (1998). Mattering attitudes: Validating the construct. *Dissertation Abstracts International,* 59, 3121B.

Marshall, S. K. (2001). Do I matter? Construct validation of adolescents' perceived mattering to parents and friends. *Journal of Adolescence*, 24, 473-490.

Marshall, S. K. (2004). Relative contributions of perceived mattering to parents and friends in predicting adolescents' psychological well-being. *Perceptual and Motor Skills*, 99, 591-601.

Marshall, S. K. and Lambert, J. D. (2006). Parental mattering: A qualitative inquiry into the tendency to evaluate the self as significant to one's children. *Journal of Family Issues*, 27, 1561-1582.

Marshall, S. K. and Tilton-Weaver, L. (2019). Adolescents' perceived mattering to parents and friends: Testing cross-lagged associations with psychosocial well-being. *International Journal of Behavioral Development*. In press.

Olcon, K., Kim, Y. and Gulbas, L. E. (2017). Sense of belonging and youth suicidal behaviors: What do communities and schools have to do with it? *Social Work in Public Health*, 32, 432-442.

Osman, A., Bagge, C. L., Gutierrez, P. M., Konick, L. C., Kopper, B. A., and Barrios, F. X. (2001). The Suicidal Behaviors Questionnaire-Revised (SBQ-R): Validation with clinical and nonclinical sample. *Assessment*, 8, 443-454.

Radloff, L. S. (1977). The CES-D scale: a self-report depression scale for research in the general population. *Applied Psychological Measurement,* 1, 385-401.

Raque-Bogdan, T. L., Ericson, S. K., Jackson, J., Martin, H. M. and Bryan, N. A. (2011). Attachment and mental and physical health: Self-compassion and mattering as mediators. *Journal of Counseling Psychology,* 58, 272-278.

Rashid, S., Kiani Chalmari, A. R., Khorramdel, K, Gholami, F. and Sanobar, L. (2016). The relationship between Interpersonal Psychological Theory of Suicide constructs (loneliness, perceived social support, thwarted belongingness and burdensomeness) and suicidal behavior among Iranian students. *Health Education & Health Promotion*, 4(2), 35-48.

Rashid, S., Kiani Chalmari, A. R., Yeganeh, N. and Zeinaddini, S. (2017). The relationship between death anxiety, mattering, perceived burdensomeness and thwarted belongingness with suicidal behavior in college students (The Interpersonal-Psychological Theory for suicide). *Iranian Journal of Emergency Care*, 1(1), 32-42.

Rosenberg, M. and McCullough, B. C. (1981). Mattering: Inferred significance and mental health among adolescents. *Research in Community & Mental Health*, 2, 163-182.

Schieman, S. and Taylor, J. (2001). Statuses, roles, and the sense of mattering. *Sociological Perspective*s, 44, 469-484.

Schlossberg, N. K. (1989). Marginality and mattering: Key issues in building community. *New Directions for Student Services,* 48, 5-15.

Shiovitz-Ezra, S. and Ayalon, L. (2010). Situational versus chronic loneliness as risk factors for all-cause mortality. *International Psychogeriatrics*, 22, 455-462.

Van Orden, K. A., Witte, T. K., James, L. M., Castro, Y., Gordon, K. H., Braithwaite, S. R., Hollar, D. L. and Joiner, T. E., Jr. (2008). Suicidal ideation in college students varies across semesters: The mediating role of belongingness. *Suicide & Life-threatening Behavior,* 38, 427-435.

In: Understanding Suicidal Ideation
Editor: David Lester ISBN: 978-1-53616-999-7

Chapter 5

UNDERSTANDING SUICIDAL IDEATION IN CHINESE UNDERGRADUATE STUDENTS

Jenny Huen, Bob Lew and David Lester

ABSTRACT

The present study of 2,074 undergraduates at two Chinese universities was designed to identify risk and protective factors for suicidal ideation. Suicidal ideation in the past year was reported by 22.3% of the students, a higher percentage than found in previous studies of Chinese and Western university students. Students reporting suicidal ideation also reported higher levels of depression, anxiety and stress, greater hopelessness, less of an orientation to finding a meaning in life through pleasure, and engagement in passive rather than active coping strategies. Some of the differences would seem to provide ideas for strategies for counselors when trying to help suicidal students.

INTRODUCTION

Undergraduate students are known to have relatively high intelligence, achievements and aspirations, but they are also known to have an increased incidence of suicide ideation compared with the general population. In a meta-analysis of 41 studies involving 160,339 Chinese undergraduate students, Li, et al. (2014) found that the prevalence of suicidal ideation among Chinese undergraduate students was relatively high (ranging from 1.2% to 26.0% with the overall pooled prevalence rate being 10.7%), although their suicide rate was lower than that of the general population. Suicidal ideation is frequently a precursor of subsequent suicidal behaviors. To prevent suicide among Chinese undergraduate students, it is, therefore, important to understand suicidal ideation in this population and to identify risk and protective factors for suicidal ideation. Risk factors for suicidal ideation are factors that make it more likely for individuals to develop suicidal ideation, whereas protective factors for suicidal ideation refer to factors that make it less likely for individuals to develop suicidal ideation. Both risk and protective factors may encompass biological, psychological and social factors in the individual, family, and environment.

The present authors and fellow researchers, therefore, joined together to conduct a mental health survey to estimate the prevalence of suicidal ideation among Chinese undergraduate students and to explore a variety of socio-demographic and psychological factors as potential risk and protective factors. The findings could inform suicide prevention strategies by identifying the key risk and protective factors that are associated with suicidal ideation in Chinese undergraduate students.

THE MENTAL HEALTH SURVEY

The mental health survey, approved by the Institutional Review Boards and Ethics Committee of the Shandong University School of Public Health, was administered in November 2016 to undergraduate students at the Shandong University and Shandong University of Traditional Chinese Medicine in Jinan, the capital of Shandong province in China. Shandong province lies on the coast of Eastern China and has the second largest population (about 100 million) at the provincial level. In each university, three to four classes in each year of studies (i.e., from Year 1 to Year 4) in two faculty colleges were randomly sampled, using the stratified-clustered-random sampling method. All students in the sampled classes who were present on the day of the survey were invited to participate in the survey. Participation was voluntary and anonymous in nature. It took participants approximately 15 minutes to complete the questionnaire which contained a battery of measures (see below). A high response rate of 94.40% was obtained (2,074 responses out of the 2,197 questionnaires distributed). The respondents (706 males and 1,368 females) had a mean age of 19.8 (SD = 1.4) and were in the following year of studies: Year 1 (27.7%), Year 2 (25.127%), Year 3 (29.9%), and Year 4 (17.4%).

MEASURES

In addition to questions relating to socio-demographic variables, the following psychological inventories were administered.

Suicidal ideation. Suicidal ideation was measured by one question of the Suicidal Behaviors Questionnaire-Revised (SBQ-R; Osman et al., 2001): How often have you thought about killing yourself in the past year? Among the five response options to this question ("Never"; "Rarely (1 time)"; "Sometimes (2 times)"; "Often (3 to 4 times)"; "Very Often (5 or more times)"), those who responded "Never" were categorized as the non-suicidal ideation group whereas those who responded any of the other four options were categorized as the suicidal ideation group for the analysis in this study.

Depression, anxiety, and stress. Three different negative emotional states (depression, anxiety and stress) were measured by 21 items of the Depression Anxiety Stress Scales (DASS-21; Lovibond & Lovibond, 1995). DASS-21 has seven items for each of the three subscales (depression, anxiety and stress) and has been widely used as the assessment of symptoms of the corresponding negative emotional states. Three sample items, one item each for depression, anxiety, and stress are "I was unable to become enthusiastic about anything," "I felt scared without any good reason," and "I found it difficult to relax" respectively. Respondents were asked to rate from 0 (*did not apply to me at all*) to 3 (*applied to me very much, or most of the time*) the extent to which they experienced each of the symptoms over the past week. A higher subscale score (e.g., depression score) indicates higher levels of severity of corresponding symptoms (e.g., depressive symptoms) experienced over the past week.

Hopelessness. Hopelessness was measured by 20 items of the Beck Hopelessness Scale (BHS; Beck, Weissman, Lester, & Trexler, 1974). One sample item is "My future seems dark to me." Responses to the BHS on a 5-point Likert scale ranging from 1 (*completely opposite*) to 5 (*in full agreement with*). A higher hopelessness score indicates more negative attitudes about the future.

Future orientation. Future orientation, in terms of positive focus, negative focus and suicide orientation, was measured by 24 items of the Future Dispositional Inventory (FDI-24; Osman, et al., 2010). The FDI-24 has 8 items for each of the subscales (positive focus, negative focus, and suicide orientation). Three sample items, one item each for positive focus, negative focus and suicide orientation are "I expect things to turn out better," "All I see ahead of me are hardships," and "I think that by ending my life, all problems will go away" respectively. Responses to the FDI-24 items range from 1 (*not at all true of me*) to 5 (*extremely true of me*). A higher subscale score (e.g., suicide orientation) indicates higher levels of corresponding future related thoughts and feelings (e.g., future related thoughts and feelings that are associated with suicide-related risk behaviors).

Coping strategies. Coping strategies, are measured by the 14 subscales (two items for each subscale) of the Brief COPE Scale (BCS; Carver, 1997). One sample item for each of 14 coping strategies are: "I've been taking action to try to make the situation better (active coping)," "I've been thinking hard about what steps to take (planning)," "I've been trying to see it in a different light, to make it seem more positive (positive reframing)," "I've been making jokes about it (humor)," "I have been accepting the reality of the fact that it has happened (acceptance)," "I've been trying to find comfort in my religion or spiritual beliefs (religion)," "I've been getting emotional support from others (using emotional support)," "I've been getting help and advice from other people (using instrumental support)," "I've been turning to work or other activities to take my mind off things (self-distraction)," "I've been refusing to believe that it has happened (denial)," "I've been saying things to let my unpleasant feelings escape (venting)," "I've been using alcohol or other drugs to help me get through it (substance use)," "I've been giving up trying to deal with it (behavioral disengagement)," and "I've been blaming myself for things that happened (self-blame)." Responses to the BCS items range from 1 (*I haven't been doing this at all*) to 3 (*I've been doing this a lot*). A higher subscale score indicates higher degree to which one would take the corresponding strategy under stress.

Orientation to happiness. Two different orientations to happiness, life of meaning and life of pleasure, were measured by 6 items each from the Orientation to Happiness Questionnaire (OTH; Peterson, Park & Seligman, 2005). One sample item for life of meaning is "I have a responsibility to make the world a better place," and one sample item for life of pleasure is "Life is too short to postpone the pleasures it can provide." Respondents were asked to indicate the degree to which the OTH items applied to them on a 5-point scale from 1 (*very much unlike me*) to 5 (*very much like me*). A higher subscale score indicates a stronger endorsement of the respective way to be happy, that is, through meaning or through pleasure in life.

Meaning in life. Meaning in life, in terms of presence of and search for meaning of life, was measured by the 5 items each from the Meaning in Life Questionnaire (MLQ; Steger, Frazier, Oishi, & Kaler, 2006). One sample item for the presence of meaning in life is "I understand my life's meaning," and a search for meaning in life is "I am seeking for a purpose or mission for my life." Respondents were asked to rate the MLQ items on a 7-point scale from 1 (*absolutely untrue*) to 7 (*absolutely true*). A higher subscale score indicates one has a stronger presence of, or search for, meaning in life.

The Chinese version of these instruments were adapted from previous studies and, if not available, developed after translation and back-translation by local researchers.

Results and Discussion

Prevalence of Suicidal Ideation in Chinese Undergraduate Students

The 1-year prevalence of suicidal ideation among the students was 22.3%, relatively high compared to the results of a study by Wang, et al. (2019) of 9.2% and the meta-analysis of Li, et al. (2014) whose estimates ranged from 1.2% to 26.0%.

Socio-Demographic Variables

The frequencies and ORs of non-suicidal ideation group and suicidal ideation group for the statistically significant socio-demographic variables are presented in Table 5.1. The variables that differed significantly between the non-suicidal ideation and suicidal ideation groups were physical health, mental health, sleep quality, academic performance, internet and online gaming entertainment, father's physical health, mother's physical health, mother's education, and parents' marital relationship. Compared with the non-suicidal ideation group, the suicide ideation group was significantly more likely to have poor physical health, mental health, sleep quality, and academic performance. Chinese undergraduate students who spent more than 3 hours per day on internet and online gaming entertainment had a significantly higher risk of suicidal ideation. Having parents in a conflicting marital relationship and being separated/divorced/widowed significantly increased the risk of suicidal ideation. It was also found that having fathers and mothers with poor physical health significantly decreased the likelihood of suicidal ideation. Having mothers with high school education also decreased the likelihood of suicidal ideation compared with having mothers with less education.

There were no significant differences by suicidal ideation for sex, ethnicity (Han Chinese versus not), age, year of studies, urban/rural residence, being an only child, socio-economic status, political membership, participation in student clubs, smoking, drinking, exercise, religion, father's education, father's occupation and mother's occupation.

For some of the significant differences, it is impossible to know from this correlational study which variable is the cause and which is the effect. Suicidal ideation may lead to poor sleep quality or, alternatively, poor sleep quality may increase the risk of suicidal ideation. Similarly, it is generally understood that physical health, mental health, academic performance, and parents' marital relationship are associated with suicidal ideation among students, although a cause-and-effect relationship cannot be drawn. It is interesting that the mother's education, but not the father's education, was associated with suicidal ideation, and this difference merits further investigation. One speculation is that mothers usually play the roles of caregiver and counselor in the family, and thus mother's education can increase their understanding of ways to protect their children from suicidal ideation.

Internet and online gaming entertainment has become widespread and seems to threaten the physical and mental health of players. The Chinese government has introduced policies to prevent adolescents from spending too much time in front of computers, one of which was imposing restrictions or limitations to players after three hours of playing. In the present study, internet and online gaming entertainment for more than 3 hours per day was a risk factor.

The findings that Chinese undergraduate students with parents of poor physical health were less likely to have suicidal ideation may reflect the duty of filial piety in Chinese culture, that sons and daughters should be responsible for the health and care of their parents.

Table 5.1. Non-suicidal ideation group versus suicidal ideation group by significant socio-demographic variables

	Non-suicidal ideation group ($N = 1611$)		Suicidal ideation group ($N = 463$)		OR
Socio-demographic variable	*N*	%	*n*	%	
Physical health					
Poor	48	2.98	38	8.21	2.03**
Average	436	27.06	170	36.72	1.00
Good	1127	69.96	255	55.08	0.58***
Mental health					
Poor	33	2.05	53	11.45	2.70***
Average	282	17.50	168	36.29	1.00
Good	1296	80.45	242	52.27	0.31***
Sleep quality					
Poor	129	8.01	71	15.33	1.32
Average	402	24.95	168	36.29	1.00
Good	1,080	67.04	224	48.38	0.50***
Academic performance					
Poor	181	11.24	81	17.49	1.58**
Average	1,150	71.38	326	70.41	1.00
Good	280	17.38	56	12.10	0.71*
Internet and online gaming entertainment					
<3 hours per day	1076	66.79	270	58.32	1.00
>3 hours per day	535	33.21	193	41.68	1.44***
Father's physical health					
Poor	1103	69.28	287	63.22	0.74*
Average	392	24.62	138	30.40	1.00
Good	97	6.09	29	6.39	0.85
Mother's physical health					
Poor	963	60.30	239	52.18	0.77*
Average	458	28.68	148	32.31	1.00
Good	176	11.02	71	15.50	1.25
Mother's education					
Primary school	257	15.95	84	18.14	1.00
Middle school	542	33.64	157	33.91	0.89
High school	322	19.99	66	14.25	0.63*
Junior college	228	14.15	69	14.90	0.93
Undergraduate	232	14.40	78	16.85	1.03
Postgraduate	30	1.86	9	1.94	0.92
Parents' marital relationship					
Good	1177	73.06	279	60.26	1.00
Conflicting	338	20.98	146	31.53	1.82***
Separated/Divorced/Widowed	96	5.96	38	8.21	1.67*

Note: OR = odds ratio. $^{*}p < 0.05$. $^{**}p < 0.01$. $^{***}p < 0.001$.

Table 5.2. Non-suicidal ideation group versus suicidal ideation group by significant psychological factors

	Non-suicidal ideation group ($N = 1611$)		Suicidal ideation group ($N = 463$)		OR
Psychological factor (Measures)	*M*	*SD*	*M*	*SD*	
Depression, anxiety, and stress (DASS-21)					
Depression	2.58	3.13	5.21	4.17	1.21***
Anxiety	4.17	3.48	6.76	4.03	1.19***
Stress	4.72	3.82	7.57	4.17	1.18***
Hopelessness (BHS)	40.35	11.70	46.72	11.56	1.05***
Future Orientation (FDI-24)					
Positive focus	31.44	7.19	29.29	7.24	0.96***
Negative focus	15.63	6.01	19.46	6.41	1.10***
Suicide orientation	11.33	6.53	15.06	7.76	1.07***
Coping strategies (BCS)					
Active coping	6.65	1.35	6.24	1.36	0.81***
Planning	6.40	1.33	6.07	1.29	0.83***
Positive reframing	6.20	1.44	5.81	1.46	0.83***
Acceptance	6.27	1.33	6.06	1.29	0.89**
Humor	4.07	1.50	4.41	1.49	1.16***
Religion	3.49	1.40	3.84	1.52	1.18***
Using emotional support	5.57	1.52	5.60	1.55	1.02
Using instrumental support	5.97	1.47	5.80	1.49	0.93*
Self-distraction	5.75	1.45	5.88	1.42	1.06
Denial	3.58	1.34	4.01	1.43	1.24***
Venting	5.28	1.52	5.40	1.39	1.05
Substance use	2.68	1.27	3.19	1.64	1.27***
Behavioral disengagement	3.52	1.36	4.07	1.40	1.31***
Self-blame	4.93	1.40	5.45	1.44	1.29***
Orientation to happiness (OTH)					
Life of meaning	20.98	4.42	19.91	4.19	0.95**
Life of pleasure	20.22	4.49	19.83	4.35	0.98
Meaning in life (MLQ)					
Presence of meaning in life	26.72	5.49	24.36	5.43	0.93***
Search of meaning in life	27.35	5.77	26.17	5.77	0.97***

Note: *M* = mean; *SD* = standard deviation; OR = odds ratio; DASS-21 = Depression Anxiety Stress Scales; BHS = Beck Hopelessness Scale; FDI-24 = Future Disposition Inventory; BCS = Brief COPE Scale; OTH = Orientation to Happiness Questionnaire; MLQ = Meaning in Life Questionnaire.

$^{*}p < 0.05$. $^{**}p < 0.01$. $^{***}p < 0.001$.

Thus, it could be reasoned that by upholding the responsibility to take care of the health of their parents, Chinese undergraduates with parents of poor health less often think of suicide since their parents would be left uncared for.

Psychological Factors

The descriptive statistics and ORs for psychological factors are presented in Table 5.2. There were significant differences between the non-suicidal ideation group and suicidal ideation group in all the psychological factors examined: depression, anxiety, stress, hopelessness, future orientation, coping strategies, orientation to happiness and meaning in life.

The increased levels of depression, anxiety and stress replicate the results found for Western students (e.g., Farabaugh, et al., 2012; Garlow, et al., 2008; Hill, Castaellanos, & Petti, 2011; Lester, 2014). Adapting to the transition from adolescence to early adulthood as well as to the new environment in universities can be stressful because students are dealing with challenging homework, group projects and internships, and managing the tight schedule between academic study, extracurricular activities, favorite pastimes, and rest.

Hopelessness is another well-documented risk factor for suicidal ideation among undergraduate students (e.g., Chang, 2017; Lester, 2013). Consistent with the higher level of hopelessness in the suicidal students, a positive focus for future orientation was a protective factor whereas a negative focus was a risk factor.

Orientation to happiness through a life of pleasure was found to be significant protective factor whereas orientation to happiness through a life of meaning was not a significant protective factor. Yang, Li, and Kou (2017) found that Chinese adolescents with both orientations to happiness (i.e., pleasure and meaning) had the greatest subjective well-being, but this was not true for suicidal ideation in the present study. The present study also found that presence of and search for meaning in life were protective factors for suicidal ideation, which was consistent with previous research among Chinese undergraduate students (e.g., Xie, & Zou, 2012).

Coping strategies found to be protective factors were active coping, planning, positive reframing, acceptance, and using instrumental support, while the passive coping strategies of humor, religion, denial, substance use, behavioral disengagement, and self-blame were risk factors, consistent with the results reported by Zhang, et al. (2012). This finding provides ideas for counselors working with suicidal students who could, therefore, train the students to move from passive coping strategies to active coping strategies.

CONCLUSION

The present study of 2,074 undergraduates at two Chinese universities indicated that suicidal ideation was associated with socio-demographic variables and several measures of psychological disturbance and well-being. In particular, students with a history of suicidal ideation had worse coping strategies, and this may suggest ideas for strategies for counselors when trying to help suicidal students.

ACKNOWLEDGMENTS

The authors would like to thank Professor Cun-xian Jia of Shandong University Centre for Suicide Prevention Research for his involvement in planning the survey, finalizing questionnaires and instruments, and coordinating the data collation. The authors are grateful for the guidance and useful comments on research design and methodology from Professor Paul Yip, Professor Thambu Maniam, Professor Augustine Osman, Professor Kairy Kolves, and Ksenia Chistopolskaya. Special thanks also go to the students at Shandong University and Shandong University of Traditional Chinese Medicine who responded to this survey. This research was funded by Bob Lew and dedicated to all people interested in understanding suicide.

References

Beck, A. T, Weissman, A., Lester, D., & Trexler, L. (1974). The measurement of pessimism: The Hopelessness Scale. *Journal of Consulting & Clinical Psychology*, 42, 861-865.

Carver, C. S. (1997). You want to measure coping but your protocol's too long: Consider the brief COPE. *International Journal of Behavioral Medicine*, 4, 92-100.

Chang, E. C. (2017). Hope and hopelessness as predictors of suicide ideation in Hungarian college students. *Death Studies*, 41, 455-460.

Farabaugh, A., Bitran, S., Nyer, M., Holt, D., Pedrelli, P., Shyu, I., Fava, M. (2012). Depression and suicidal ideation in college students. *Psychopathology*, 45(4), 228-234.

Garlow, S. J., Rosenberg, J., Moore, J. D., Haas, A. P., Koestner, B., Hendin, H., & Nemeroff, C. B. (2008). Depression, desperation, and suicidal ideation in college students. *Depression and Anxiety*, 25, 482-488.

Hill, Castellanos, & Pettit (2011). Suicide-related behaviors and anxiety in children and adolescents: A review. *Clinical Psychology Review*, 31, 1133-1144.

Lester, D. (2013). Hopelessness in undergraduate students around the world: A review. *Journal of Affective Disorders*, 150, 1204-1208.

Lester, D. (2014). College student stressors, depression, and suicidal ideation. *Psychological Reports*, 114, 293-296.

Li, Z. Z., Li, Y. M., Lei, X. Y., Zhang, D., Liu, L., Tang, S. Y., & Chen, L. (2014). Prevalence of suicidal ideation in Chinese college students: A meta-analysis. *PLoS ONE*, 9, e104368.

Lovibond, P. F., & Lovibond, S. H. (1995). The structure of negative emotional states: Comparison of the Depression Anxiety Stress Scales

(DASS) with the Beck Depression and Anxiety Inventories. *Behaviour Research & Therapy*, 33, 335-343.

Osman, A., Gutierrez, P. M., Barrios, F, Wong, J. L., Freedenthal, S., Lozano, G. (2010). Development and initial psychometric properties of the University of Texas at San Antonio Future Disposition Inventory. *Journal of Clinical Psychology*, 66, 410-429.

Peterson, C., Park, N., & Seligman, M. E. P. (2005). Orientations to happiness and life satisfaction: The full life versus the empty life. *Journal of Happiness Stud*ies, 6: 25-41.

Wang, M., Kou, C., Bai, W., Song, Y., Liu, X., Yu, W., Li, W. (2019). Prevalence and correlates of suicidal ideation among college students: A mental health survey in Jilin Province, China. *Journal of Affective Disorders*, 246, 166-173.

Xie, X., Zou, B., & Huang, Z. (2012). Relationships between suicide attitudes and perception of life purpose and meaning of life in college students. Nan Fang Yi Ke Da Xue Xue Bao. *Journal of Southern Medical University*, 32, 1482-1485.

Yang, Y., Li, P., & Kou, Y. (2017). Orientations to happiness and subjective well-being in Chinese adolescents. *Child Indicators Research*, 10, 881-897.

Zhang, X., Wang, H., Xia, Y., Liu, X., & Jung, E. (2012). Stress, coping and suicide ideation in Chinese College Students. *Journal of Adolescence*, 35, 683-690.

In: Understanding Suicidal Ideation
Editor: David Lester
ISBN: 978-1-53616-999-7

Chapter 6

UNDERSTANDING SUICIDAL IDEATION IN PEOPLE WITH CHRONIC INVISIBLE ILLNESS

Cathy L. Pederson

ABSTRACT

Recent studies have demonstrated increased suicidal ideation and suicide attempts in the chronic illness community compared with the general population. Suicidal ideation is common in people who have been diagnosed with a variety of chronic invisible illnesses like chronic fatigue syndrome/myalgic encephalomyelitis (CFS/ME), Ehlers-Danlos syndrome, fibromyalgia, chronic Lyme disease, and postural orthostatic tachycardia syndrome (POTS). Numerous physical and psychosocial factors can contribute to suicidal ideation in this population. Physical factors, like sleep disturbance and pain, are common in chronic illness. Psychosocial issues, such as perceived burdensomeness (feeling like a burden to others), thwarted belongingness (lack of connection to a social group), hopelessness, and depression, may also contribute to an increased suicide risk in people with chronic invisible illness. More research is needed to better understand the underlying risk factors for suicidal ideation in this population. Putting suicide prevention programs in place that will target this under-represented group of physically ill patients is also necessary.

There are a variety of chronic invisible illnesses that significantly decrease quality of life and can ultimately increase the risk of suicide. These include chronic fatigue syndrome/myalgic encephalomyelitis (CFS/ME), Ehlers-Danlos syndrome, fibromyalgia, chronic Lyme disease, and postural orthostatic tachycardia syndrome (POTS). People with these conditions often have a myriad of significant physical problems, including bodily pain, poor general health, sleep, and physical and social functioning (Pederson & Brook, 2017a; Schmaling & Betterton, 2016).

Despite healthy outward appearances, the level of impairment for many with chronic invisible illnesses significantly decreases their quality of life. Tasks that involve concentration and memory, such as conversing, reading and watching television, are negatively affected by chronic illness, thereby affecting relationships, employability and leisure (Horton et al., 2010). In addition, functional disability is also a concern as most patients report activity limitations due to symptoms, and a significant minority require assistance with the activities of daily living (Pederson & Brook, 2017a). As a result, these chronically ill patients may be stigmatized in the workplace and at home, pressured to downplay their symptoms, and become afraid of triggering a symptom flare from subsequent over-activity (Horton et al., 2010).

Little is known about the etiology of these disorders, leaving many practitioners and loved ones to disregard complaints of fatigue, pain, dizziness, cognitive impairments, headaches and sensitivities to light, sound or smell as being "all in your head." These symptoms are typically difficult to quantify. Further exacerbating the problem, the vast majority of people with chronic invisible illnesses are women (Arout, Sofuoglu, Bastian, & Rosenheck, 2018; Boris & Bernadzikowski, 2018), who have historically been labeled as hysterical when presenting with psychogenic-type symptoms (Gould, Miller, Goldberg, & Benson, 1986).

Research into the etiology of these disorders is in its infancy. Many chronic invisible illnesses appear to develop following infection (Fedorowski, 2019), human papilloma virus vaccination (Blitshteyn, Brinth, Hendrickson, & Martinez-Lavin, 2018) or concussion (Miranda, Boris, Kouvel, & Stiles, 2018). There is growing evidence that a significant subset of people with CFS/ME (Loebel et al., 2016), fibromyalgia (Jeong, Kim, Park, Park, & Kim, 2019), chronic Lyme disease (Arvikar, Crowley, Sulka, & Steere, 2017), and POTS (Ruzieh, Batizy, Dasa, Oostra, & Grubb, 2017) may have autoimmune underpinnings that explain their illness. We must fund research on these chronic illnesses in order to understand their etiology and develop better treatment regimens for affected individuals.

Elevated Risk: Psychological Symptoms

Psychosocial factors can be significant predictors of suicidal ideation. In the general population, depression is an important risk factor for suicide. In the chronic illness community, however, other factors like perceived burdensomeness, hopelessness, and acquired capability for suicide appear to be more important in understanding suicidal ideation and attempts.

Depression

Chronically ill patients are often misdiagnosed with clinical depression and/or anxiety prior to receiving their correct physical diagnosis of CFS/ME, POTS, or another chronic invisible illness (Kavi et al., 2016). There is significant overlap between the physical symptoms of these chronic illnesses and the somatic complaints often attributed to depression and anxiety. Most psychological instruments include questions related to somatic complaints (appetite, sleep disturbance, fatigue, and ability to work) that can be explained by physical illness rather than depression in this population (Pederson, Gorman-Ezell, & Mayer, 2018). In addition, orthostatic symptoms like heart palpitations, lightheadedness, nausea and chest discomfort may be misinterpreted as anxiety (Raj, Opie, & Arnold, 2018). In fact, POTS patients do not have higher current or lifetime prevalence of clinical anxiety or major depressive disorder than the general population (Raj et al., 2018). Furthermore, a study of CFS/ME patients found that suicidal individuals were not typically depressed, but rather felt trapped by their illness and the lack of viable treatments (Devendorf, McManimen, & Jason, 2019).

That said, nearly half of individuals with chronic illness and/or chronic pain do suffer from depression (Alderson, Foy, & House, 2015; Nicholas, 2011), especially if they have autoimmune disorders or high levels of inflammation (Caneo, Marston, Bellón, & King, 2016). Depression and poor sleep are linked, with one study finding that 85% of patients who met the criteria for major depressive disorder also had clinically significant sleep disturbances (Zimmerman, Ellison, Young, Chelminski, & Dalrymple, 2015). When depression is correctly diagnosed in a chronically ill patient, it must be aggressively treated to improve their quality of life and decrease their risk of suicide.

Perceived Burdensomeness and Thwarted Belongingness

Many chronically ill people require more personal care and have less social interaction than their peers, which may increase suicidal ideation. Their illnesses drastically limit mobility and stamina to the point where teens and young adults require daily assistance for basic personal tasks like bathing and dressing. In addition, they may also require assistive devices (e.g., wheelchair, shower chair, and handicap placard). This can be humiliating and may also lead to a sense of perceived burdensomeness - feeling like a burden to family and friends (Khazem, 2018). Despite their need for assistance and the plethora of symptoms, they often have a healthy outward appearance and patients are often accused of being lazy, anxious or physically deconditioned (Stiles, Cinnamon, & Balan, 2018). Even within their support system, this misunderstanding about the level of illness and disability can lead to social isolation and thwarted belongingness, the feeling that one does not fit into a social group (You, Van Orden & Conner, 2011). When life experiences vary significantly from the norm, it can be hard to connect with other people in a meaningful way.

The interpersonal theory of suicide – that perceived burdensomeness and thwarted belongingness may increase suicidal ideation (Joiner, 2005) - may be relevant to the chronic illness community. Perceived burdensomeness is elevated in chronic pain populations (Kanzler, Bryan, McGeary, & Morrow, 2012) and can increase the risk of suicide (Wilson et al., 2017). In one study of POTS patients, 30% required assistance for basic personal care (Pederson & Brook, 2017a). This type of functional disability may lead to feelings of perceived burdensomeness and thwarted belongingness that can eventually lead to suicidal ideation. In those with chronic invisible illnesses, perceived burdensomeness is a stronger predictor of suicidal ideation than depression, thwarted belongingness, or loneliness (Pederson & Brookings, 2018).

Acquired Capability for Suicide

The acquired capability for suicide is perhaps one of the most important recent concepts in suicide research (Bauer, Martin, Allan, Fink-Miller, & Capron, 2018) and encompasses a person's diminished fear of pain, injury and death over time (Joiner, 2005). People can habituate to pain tolerance with practice. Therefore, those who self-harm may have a higher pain tolerance which may make transitioning from thinking about suicide to making an attempt more feasible (Koenig, Thayer, & Kaess, 2016). In essence, this theory proposes that the physical and psychological pain that accumulates over time can increase the likelihood of moving from suicidal thoughts to attempts (May & Victor, 2018).

Not all research supports this idea of acquired capability for suicide, however. One study found that neither age nor accumulating painful events have a significant effect on the acquired capability for suicide (Bauer, et al., 2018). Instead, some stages of development (teens and young adults) may be more vulnerable to quickly developing an acquired capability for suicide despite a relatively small number of painful events (Bauer, et al., 2019). Unfortunately, the acquired capability for suicide is not a strong predictor for differentiating between suicide attempters and non-attempters (Burke, Ammerman, Knorr, Alloy, & McCloskey, 2018).

Hopelessness

Hopelessness is a risk factor for suicidal ideation, attempt and death by suicide (Ribeiro, Huang, Fox, & Franklin, 2018). In the chronic illness community, many have lost hope that their symptom load will improve naturally or that new treatment options will soon be developed (Devendorf, et al., 2019). This hopelessness is often due to their specific circumstances (illness, financial ramifications, etc.), rather than depression (Devendorf, et al., 2019). The duration and intensity of the hopelessness is also important. Patients with longstanding hopelessness have increased suicidality compared with those who felt that their hopelessness was more temporary (Burr, Rahm-Knigge, & Conner, 2018). In young women, a small increase in hopelessness can lead to a significant increase in suicidal ideation (Wolfe, et al., 2019). A positive correlation between hopelessness and lethality of the suicide attempt has also been shown (Jaiswal, Faye, Gore, Shah, & Kamath, 2016).

Hopelessness may directly relate to other psychological factors that increase suicidality. Perhaps hopelessness is the link that can explain why some people with depression consider suicide while others do not (Jaiswal, et al., 2016). In addition, feeling hopeless about perceived burdensomeness and thwarted belongingness may be important in explaining suicidal ideation and suicide risk (Tucker, et al., 2018). Unfortunately, hopelessness is not particularly useful in separating suicide attempters from non-attempters (Qiu, Klonsky, & Klein, 2017).

ELEVATED SUIDICE RISK: POTENTIAL PHYSCIAL CAUSES

It is important to recognize that suicidal ideation in this population is not always related to psychological factors alone. There are well-documented physical challenges that may increase the risk of suicidal ideation or attempt in a chronically ill person. The illness itself, with a high symptom load and functional disability, can increase the risk of suicidal ideation. Chronic pain and sleep disturbances also increase risk. Recognition and aggressive treatment of these symptoms can help to improve quality of life and decrease suicide risk.

Chronic Illness

Suicide is prevalent in many chronic illness communities. Physical illness and functional disability are known risk factors for suicide (Cheung & Sundram, 2017; Pederson, 2018), and those with multiple physical illnesses are at significantly higher risk (Ahmedani, et al., 2017). In a large study of suicide attempters, 50% suffered from a physical illness. Of these, 42% reported that their physical illness played into their decision to attempt suicide (De Leo, et al., 1999). Suicide is the second leading cause of death for those with CFS/ME, with approximately 20% dying by suicide (Jason, Corradi, Gress, Williams, & Torres-Harding, 2006; Smith, Noonan, & Buchwald, 2006). Nearly half of POTS patients are at high risk for suicide, with 15% reporting a previous attempt (Pederson & Brook, 2017a). In those with fibromyalgia, 33% of patients experience suicidal ideation (Triñanes, González-Villar, Gómez-Perretta, & Carrillo-de-la-Peña, 2015), while 4% of people with hypermobile Ehlers-Danlos syndrome had attempted suicide (Cederlöf, et al., 2016). In the United States alone, approximately 1,200 patients with Lyme disease die by suicide each year (Bransfield, 2017). Clearly, suicide is a major concern for the chronic invisible illness community.

Among the physically ill, many who are considering suicide have no mental health diagnosis (Ahmedani, et al., 2017). While 40% of those with CFS/ME report suicidal ideation, nearly half of those did not meet the criteria for clinical depression (McManimen, McClellan, Stoothoff, & Jason, 2018). While suicidal thinking in the general population is often linked with depression, in the chronically ill population suicide can be a response to suffering from the chronic illness itself or a mechanism to permanently relieve physical and/or emotional distress (Alderson, Foy, Glidewell, McLintock, & House, 2012). Many patients who consider suicide do not want to die, but they do not want to continue living in their current state of illness (Newton-John, 2014).

Chronic Physical Pain

Chronic pain is common among those with chronic invisible illness. This pain can present in a variety of ways – migraine headaches or neuropathic, abdominal, muscular, and/or joint pain – and significantly decrease quality of life (Martín, et al., 2017; Pederson & Brook, 2017a; Schmaling & Betterton, 2016). Fibromyalgia is characterized by widespread pain lasting more than three months (Wolfe, et al., 1990). In CFS/ME patients, pain is pervasive and significantly associated with decreased overall functioning and quality of life (Strand, et al., 2019). People with chronic Lyme disease suffer with generalized musculoskeletal pain (Ranque-Garnier, Eldin, Sault, Raoult, & Donnet, 2019). One small study of people with hypermobile Ehlers-Danlos syndrome found that nearly all reported chronic pain, including joint and neuropathic pain (Bénistan & Martinez, 2019). In POTS, more than half report neuropathic pain, in addition to those with frequent headaches and abdominal pain (Deb, Morgenshtern, Culbertson, Wang, & DePold Hohler, 2015).

Chronic pain has been linked to both increased suicidal ideation and suicide attempts (Legarreta, Bueler, DiMuzio, McGlade, & Yurgelun-Todd, 2018). Pain can interfere with activities of daily living, eventually diminishing the feeling of control over their own lives (Pederson & Brook, 2017a). This can lead to increased perceived burdensomeness, thwarted belongingness, hopelessness, pain catastrophizing, and mental defeat often found in chronic pain patients (Racine, 2017).

People with chronic and/or frequent intermittent pain conditions (i.e., migraine headaches, abdominal pain) are at increased risk for suicide, with 25% of chronic pain patients reporting suicidal thoughts (Racine, 2017). In one study of people with a variety of chronic pain conditions, 19% reported current passive suicidal ideation, and another 13% reported active thoughts of suicide. Of these, 5% currently had a plan for suicide, and 5% had previously made an attempt (Smith, Edwards, Robinson, & Dworkin, 2004). In the CFS/ME community, 21% reported that their overwhelming physical pain increased their suicidal ideation (Devendorf, et al., 2019).

Sleep Disturbance

Sleep disturbances, including non-restorative sleep and insomnia, are typical for many people with chronic illness. Sleep disturbance is a common symptom in people with CFS/ME (Owen-Smith, et al., 2019), Ehlers-Danlos syndrome (Muriello, et al., 2018), fibromyalgia (Calandre, et al., 2015), chronic Lyme disease (Bransfield, 2018), and POTS (Pederson & Brook, 2017b). Nearly all of these patients report poor sleep and excessive fatigue that negatively impact their quality of life (Bagai, et al., 2016).

Sleep disturbance is one of the most important clinical risk factors for suicide prior to making an attempt (Ahmedani, et al., 2017). Sleep disturbance is related to increased suicidal ideation in patients with CFS/ME (Owen-Smith, et al., 2019), fibromyalgia (Calandre, et al., 2015), and POTS (Pederson & Brook, 2017b). Both insomnia and regular nightmares can independently increase suicide risk (Drapeau, et al., 2019). Loss of sleep may negatively impact neurocognitive performance and increase impulsivity the following day. These cognitive changes may result in an unplanned suicide attempt (Porras-Segovia, et al., 2019). Together, these highlight the need for better diagnosis and more aggressive treatment of sleep disturbances in an effort to improve quality of life and decrease suicide risk (Zullo, et al., 2017).

Quality of Life

Many with chronic invisible illnesses have a severely diminished quality of life as a result of chronic pain, sleep disturbances, fatigue and a myriad of other physical symptoms that impact all facets of their life (Mu, et al., 2019). Functional disability caused by chronic illness can increase isolation, perceived burdensomeness, and depression (Fässberg, et al., 2016). Many feel trapped by their illness and a lack of the personal and medical support that they need to thrive (Devendorf, et al., 2019).

Employment may be difficult for those who suffer from these invisible illnesses. Nearly 60% of fibromyalgia patients report work impairment, including both hours missed and decreased productivity when at work (Bateman, et al., 2016). Many CFS/ME patients and 25% of POTS patients develop such severe symptoms that they are unable to work or attend school and, in some cases, become housebound (Benrud-Larson, et al., 2002; Horton, et al., 2010).

In CFS/ME patients, the quality of life is worse than for people who have schizophrenia, depression, or cancer (Hvidberg, Brinth, Olesen, Petersen, & Ehlers, 2015), while POTS patients had a quality of life similar to those with rheumatoid arthritis, end-stage kidney disease (Bagai, et al., 2011), congestive heart failure, and chronic obstructive pulmonary disease (Benrud-Larson, et al., 2002).

Decreased quality of life is associated with both suicidal ideation and suicide attempt, even in those with well-understood illnesses like cardiovascular disease, kidney failure, and depression (Joshi, Song, & Lee, 2017). Chronically ill people may consider suicide when they experience a loss of independence, dignity and/or pleasure in life (Fässberg, et al., 2016). Poor quality of life is associated with an increased risk of suicidal ideation and attempt in those with POTS (Pederson & Brook, 2017a). In those with multiple physical illnesses, poor quality of life was also linked with increased risk of death by suicide (Wei & Mukamal, 2019).

PREVENTING SUICIDE IN CHRONICALLY ILL POPULATIONS

There are opportunities to identify and help chronically ill patients at high-risk for suicide before they make an attempt. Of those who attempt suicide, 64% visited a healthcare practitioner in the month before the attempt, and 38% visited the week prior (Ahmedani, et al., 2015). Therefore, suicide prevention training for primary care staff is critical in reducing suicide attempts in chronically ill patients (Nakagami, et al., 2018). By practicing compassionate care, screening for suicide risk, and developing a protocol to address suicidal risk and/or behavior when it is discovered, healthcare practitioners can take positive steps toward reducing suicide attempts in this population (Pederson, 2018). Uncovering and more aggressively treating physical symptoms like sleep disturbances (Pederson & Brook, 2017b), pain (Racine, 2017), depression, and fatigue (Dutta, et al., 2017) can decrease suicide risk in chronically ill patients.

Public health policies can reduce suicide risk. Decreasing the stigma associated with suicide, as well as increasing accessibility to suicide prevention resources for families and healthcare practitioners is a good first step (Anestis, et al., 2017). Providing contact information for local counselors and support groups sensitive to the specific vulnerabilities of the chronically ill population, as well as more general, free resources like the National Suicide Prevention Lifeline (1-800-273-TALK) or Hopeline (741741 and text "start") could be helpful. Additionally, training mental health staff to address issues surrounding perceived burdensomeness, thwarted belongingness and hopelessness experienced by the chronically ill could also decrease suicide risk (Pederson & Brookings, 2018). Furthermore, advocating for proper firearm security, reduction of medication that is potentially lethal in overdose, and managing other important means of suicide can reduce the likelihood of an attempt (Manuel, Crowe, Inder, & Henaghan, 2018). Finally, teaching children strategies that help them to tolerate distress and cope with their emotions has the potential to protect their mental health and decrease future suicide risk (Anestis, et al., 2017).

Psychological factors associated with suicide risk in chronic illness can be altered by targeted intervention (Racine, et al., 2017), giving practitioners the opportunity to prevent suicide. Mental health practitioners can use a variety of approaches to decrease the psychological aspects of chronic illness related to burdensomeness, hopelessness, and depression, such as cognitive-behavioral therapy and acceptance and commitment therapy. In order to specifically treat suicidal tendencies, dialectical behavior therapy and collaborative assessment and management of suicidality can be helpful (Pederson, Gorman-Ezell, & Hochstetler-Mayer, 2017). If perceived burdensomeness is a major factor, identifying individuals at risk and working with caretakers to make interactions more positive might decrease suicide risk (Pederson, et al., 2017).

Quality social support that nurtures optimism can decrease hopelessness (Beedie & Kennedy, 2002) and reduce the risk of suicide (Chang, et al., 2018). Increasing social connections can decrease suicidal ideation in invisible illness communities (Van Orden & Deming, 2018). Online support groups may provide understanding and companionship as well as increasing social connections and belonging, especially when the patient is home or bedbound (Pederson, et al., 2017). Increasing positive connections with friends and family in an accessible environment is also an important tool in the battle against suicidal ideation. Providing positive life events, such as playing board games, making a favorite snack, or sharing a movie at home, that require minimal energy expenditure and increase social belonging can decrease both perceived burdensomeness and suicide risk (Chang, Muyan, & Hirsch, 2015).

Due to the invisible nature of these illnesses, it is important to believe people when they describe their experience with chronic invisible illness. In recent years, physical anomalies have been detected that authenticate these as "real" illnesses. For example, autoantibodies and other physical markers have been identified for CFS/ME (Loebel, et al., 2016), fibromyalgia (Jeong, et al., 2019), chronic Lyme disease (Arvikar, et al., 2017), and POTS (Ruzieh, et al., 2017). The demonstrated presence of autoantibodies indicates that these chronic invisible illnesses may actually be part of the autoimmune illness family (Ruzieh, et al., 2017), and not psychosomatic in nature.

In this population, suicidal thinking is sometimes a symptom of depression, often a response to physical suffering, and frequently a practical mechanism to permanently relieve both physical and emotional misery (Alderson, et al., 2012). Taking a longitudinal perspective can be helpful: Chronically ill people perceive themselves as a burden to others, which leads to depression and, ultimately, may increase suicide risk (Pederson & Brookings, 2018). Recognizing and treating the physical and psychological issues in the chronically ill population is critical to decreasing their suicide risk.

REFERENCES

Ahmedani, B. K., Peterson, E. L., Hu, Y., Rossom, R. C., Lynch, F., Lu, C. Y. ... & Simon, G. E. (2017). Major physical health conditions and risk of suicide. *American Journal of Preventive Medicine*, *53*, 308-315.

Ahmedani, B. K., Stewart, C., Simon, G. E., Lynch, F., Lu, C. Y., Waitzfelder, B. E. ... & Williams, K. (2015). Racial/Ethnic differences in health care visits made before suicide attempt across the United States. *Medical Care*, *53*, 430-435.

Alderson, S. L., Foy, R., Glidewell, L., McLintock, K. & House, A. (2012). How patients understand depression associated with chronic physical disease--a systematic review. *BMC Family Practice*, *13*, 41.

Alderson, S. L., Foy, R. & House, A. (2015). Understanding depression associated with chronic physical illness: a Q-methodology study in primary care. *British Journal of General Practice*, *65*(635), e401-408. D.

Anestis, M. D., Law, K. C., Jin, H., Houtsma, C., Khazem, L. R. & Assavedo, B. L. (2017). Treating the capability for suicide: a vital and understudied frontier in suicide prevention. *Suicide & Life-Threatening Behavior*, *47*, 523-537.

Arout, C. A., Sofuoglu, M., Bastian, L. A. & Rosenheck, R. A. (2018). Gender differences in the prevalence of fibromyalgia and in concomitant medical and psychiatric disorders: a National Veterans Health Administration study. *Journal of Women's Health*, *27*, 1035-1044.

Arvikar, S. L., Crowley, J. T., Sulka, K. B. & Steere, A. C. (2017). Autoimmune arthritides, rheumatoid arthritis, psoriatic arthritis, or peripheral spondyloarthritis following Lyme disease. *Arthritis & Rheumatology*, *69*, 194-202.

Bagai, K., Peltier, A. C., Malow, B. A., Diedrich, A., Shibao, C. A., Black, B. K. & Raj, S. R. (2016). Objective sleep assessments in patients with postural tachycardia syndrome using overnight polysomnograms. *Journal of Clinical Sleep Medicine*, *12*, 727-733.

Bagai, K., Song, Y., Ling, J. F., Malow, B., Black, B. K., Biaggioni, I. & Raj, S. R. (2011). Sleep disturbance and diminished quality of life in postural tachycardia syndrome. *Journal of Clinical Sleep Medicine*, *7*, 204-210.

Bateman, L., Sarzi-Puttini, P., Burbridge, C. L., Landen, J. W., Masters, E. T., Bhadra Brown, P. & Pauer, L. R. (2016). Burden of illness in fibromyalgia patients with comorbid depression. *Clinical & Experimenta Rheumatology*, *34*, (2 Suppl 96), S106-113.

Bauer, B. W., Martin, R. L., Allan, N. P., Fink-Miller, E. L. & Capron, D. W. (2019). An investigation into the acquired capability for suicide. *Suicide & Life-Threatening Behavior*, *49*, 1105-1118.

Beedie, A. & Kennedy, P. (2002). Quality of social support predicts hopelessness and depression post spinal cord injury. *Journal of Clinical Psychology in Medical Settings*, *9*, 227-234.

Benrud-Larson, L. M., Dewar, M. S., Sandroni, P., Rummans, T. A., Haythornthwaite, J. A. & Low, P. A. (2002). Quality of life in patients with postural tachycardia syndrome. *Mayo Clinic Proceedings*, *77*, 531-537.

Blitshteyn, S., Brinth, L., Hendrickson, J. E. & Martinez-Lavin, M. (2018). Autonomic dysfunction and HPV immunization: an overview. *Immunological Research*, *66*, 744-754.

Boris, J. R. & Bernadzikowski, T. (2018). Demographics of a large paediatric postural orthostatic tachycardia syndrome program. *Cardiology in the Young*, *28*, 668-674.

Bransfield, R. C. (2017). Suicide and Lyme and associated diseases. *Neuropsychiatric Disease & Treatment*, *13*, 1575-1587.

Bransfield, R. C. (2018). Neuropsychiatric Lyme Borreliosis: an overview with a focus on a specialty psychiatrist's clinical practice. *Healthcare (Basel)*, *6*(3), online.

Burke, T. A., Ammerman, B. A., Knorr, A. C., Alloy, L. B. & McCloskey, M. S. (2018). Measuring acquired capability for suicide within an ideation-to-action framework. *Psychology of Violence*, *8*, 277-286.

Burr, E. M., Rahm-Knigge, R. L. & Conner, B. T. (2018). The differentiating role of state and trait hopelessness in suicidal ideation and suicide attempt. *Archives of Suicide Research*, *22*, 510-517.

Bénistan, K. & Martinez, V. (2019). Pain in hypermobile Ehlers-Danlos syndrome: new insights using new criteria. *Americal Journal of Medical Genetics A*, *179*, 1226-1234.

Calandre, E. P., Navajas-Rojas, M. A., Ballesteros, J., Garcia-Carrillo, J., Garcia-Leiva, J. M. & Rico-Villademoros, F. (2015). Suicidal ideation in patients with fibromyalgia: a cross-sectional study. *Pain Practice*, *15*, 168-174.

Caneo, C., Marston, L., Bellón, J. & King, M. (2016). Examining the relationship between physical illness and depression: is there a difference between inflammatory and non inflammatory diseases? A cohort study. *General Hospital Psychiatry*, *43*, 71-77.

Cederlöf, M., Larsson, H., Lichtenstein, P., Almqvist, C., Serlachius, E. & Ludvigsson, J. F. (2016). Nationwide population-based cohort study of psychiatric disorders in individuals with Ehlers-Danlos syndrome or hypermobility syndrome and their siblings. *BMC Psychiatry*, *16*, 207.

Chang, E. C., Chang, O. D., Martos, T., Sallay, V., Li, X., Lucas, A. G. & Lee, J. (2018). Does optimism weaken the negative effects of being lonely on suicide risk? *Death Studies*, *42*, 63-68.

Chang, E. C., Muyan, M. & Hirsch, J. K. (2015). Loneliness, positive life events, and psychological maladjustment: when good things happen, even lonely people feel better. *Personality & Individual Differences*, *86*, 150-155.

Cheung, G. & Sundram, F. (2017). Understanding the progression from physical illness to suicidal behavior: a case study based on a newly developed conceptual model. *Clinical Gerontology*, *40*, 124-129.

De Leo, D., Scocco, P., Marietta, P., Schmidtke, A., Bille-Brahe, U., Kerkhof, A. J. & Bjerke, T. (1999). Physical illness and parasuicide: evidence from the European Parasuicide Study Interview Schedule (EPSIS/WHO-EURO). *International Journal of Psychiatry in Medicine*, *29*, 149-163.

Deb, A., Morgenshtern, K., Culbertson, C. J., Wang, L. B. & DePold Hohler, A. (2015). A survey-based analysis of symptoms in patients with postural orthostatic tachycardia syndrome. *Baylor University Medical Center Proceedings*, *28*, 157-159.

Devendorf, A. R., McManimen, S. L. & Jason, L. A. (2018). Suicidal ideation in non-depressed individuals: the effects of a chronic, misunderstood illness. *Journal of Health Psychology*, 1359105318785450.

Drapeau, C. W., Nadorff, M. R., McCall, W. V., Titus, C. E., Barclay, N. & Payne, A. (2019). Screening for suicide risk in adult sleep patients. *Sleep Medicine Reviews*, *46*, 17-26.

Dutta, R., Ball, H. A., Siribaddana, S. H., Sumathipala, A., Samaraweera, S., McGuffin, P. & Hotopf, M. (2017). Genetic and other risk factors for suicidal ideation and the relationship with depression. *Psychological Medicine*, *47*, 2438-2449.

Fedorowski, A. (2019). Postural orthostatic tachycardia syndrome: clinical presentation, aetiology and management. *Journal of Internal Medicine*, *285*, 352-366.

Fässberg, M. M., Cheung, G., Canetto, S. S., Erlangsen, A., Lapierre, S., Lindner, R. & Wærn, M. (2016). A systematic review of physical illness, functional disability, and suicidal behaviour among older adults. *Aging & Mental Health*, *20*, 166-194.

Gould, R., Miller, B. L., Goldberg, M. A. & Benson, D. F. (1986). The validity of hysterical signs and symptoms. *Journal of Nervous & Mental Disease*, *174*, 593-597.

Horton, S. M., Poland, F., Kale, S., Drachler, M. E. L., de Carvalho Leite, J. C., McArthur, M. A. & Nacul, L. (2010). Chronic fatigue syndrome/myalgic encephalomyelitis (CFS/ME) in adults: a qualitative study of perspectives from professional practice. *BMC Family Practice*, *11*, 89.

Hvidberg, M. F., Brinth, L. S., Olesen, A. V., Petersen, K. D. & Ehlers, L. (2015). The health-related quality of life for patients with myalgic encephalomyelitis/chronic fatigue syndrome (ME/CFS). *PLoS One*, *10*(7), e0132421.

Jaiswal, S. V., Faye, A. D., Gore, S. P., Shah, H. R. & Kamath, R. M. (2016). Stressful life events, hopelessness, and suicidal intent in patients admitted with attempted suicide in a tertiary care general hospital. *Journal of Postgraduate Medicine*, *62*, 102-104.

Jason, L. A., Corradi, K., Gress, S., Williams, S. & Torres-Harding, S. (2006). Causes of death among patients with chronic fatigue syndrome. *Health Care for Women International*, *27*, 615-626.

Jeong, J., Kim, D. H., Park, G., Park, S. & Kim, H. S. (2019). Clinical significance of anti-dense fine speckled 70 antibody in patients with fibromyalgia. *Korean Journal of Internal Medicine*, *34*, 426- 433.

Joiner, T. E. (2005). *Why people die by suicide*. Cambridge, MA: Harvard University Press.

Joshi, P., Song, H. B. & Lee, S. A. (2017). Association of chronic disease prevalence and quality of life with suicide-related ideation and suicide attempt among Korean adults. *Indian Journal of Psychiatry*, *59*, 352-358.

Kanzler, K. E., Bryan, C. J., McGeary, D. D. & Morrow, C. E. (2012). Suicidal ideation and perceived burdensomeness in patients with chronic pain. *Pain Practice*, *12*, 602-609.

Kavi, L., Nuttall, M., Low, D. A., Opie, M., Nicholson, L. M., Caldow, E. & Newton, J. L. (2016). A profile of patients with postural tachycardia syndrome and their experience of healthcare in the UK. *British Journal of Cardiology*, *23*(1), 1-6.

Khazem, L. R. (2018). Physical disability and suicide: recent advancements in understanding and future directions for consideration. *Current Opinion in Psychology*, *22*, 18-22.

Koenig, J., Thayer, J. F. & Kaess, M. (2016). A meta-analysis on pain sensitivity in self-injury. *Psychological Medicine*, *46*, 1597-1612.

Legarreta, M., Bueler, E., DiMuzio, J., McGlade, E. & Yurgelun-Todd, D. (2018). Suicide behavior and chronic pain: an exploration of pain-related catastrophic thinking, disability, and descriptions of the pain experience. *Journal of Nervous & Mental Disease*, *206*, 217-222.

Loebel, M., Grabowski, P., Heidecke, H., Bauer, S., Hanitsch, L. G., Wittke, K. & Scheibenbogen, C. (2016). Antibodies to β adrenergic and muscarinic cholinergic receptors in patients with chronic fatigue syndrome. *Brain Behavior & Immunity*, *52*, 32-39.

Manuel, J., Crowe, M., Inder, M. & Henaghan, M. (2018). Suicide prevention in mental health services: a qualitative analysis of coroners' reports. *International Journal of Mental Health Nursing*, *27*, 642-651.

Martín, J., Torre, F., Aguirre, U., Padierna, A., Matellanes, B. & Quintana, J. M. (2017). Assessment of predictors of the impact of fibromyalgia on health-related quality of life 12 months after the end of an interdisciplinary treatment. *Journal of Affective Disorders*, *208*, 76-81.

May, A. M. & Victor, S. E. (2018). From ideation to action: recent advances in understanding suicide capability. *Current Opinion in Psychology*, *22*, 1-6.

McManimen, S. L., McClellan, D., Stoothoff, J. & Jason, L. A. (2018). Effects of unsupportive social interactions, stigma, and symptoms on patients with myalgic encephalomyelitis and chronic fatigue syndrome. *Journal of Community Psychology*, *46*, 959-971.

Miranda, N. A., Boris, J. R., Kouvel, K. M. & Stiles, L. (2018). Activity and exercise intolerance after concussion: identification and management of postural orthostatic tachycardia syndrome. *Journal of Neurologic Physical Therapy*, *42*(3), 163-171.

Mu, W., Muriello, M., Clemens, J. L., Wang, Y., Smith, C. H., Tran, P. T. & Bodurtha, J. (2019). Factors affecting quality of life in children and adolescents with hypermobile Ehlers-Danlos syndrome/hypermobility spectrum disorders. *American Journal of Medical Genetics A, 179*, 561-569.

Muriello, M., Clemens, J. L., Mu, W., Tran, P. T., Rowe, P. C., Smith, C. H. & Kline, A. D. (2018). Pain and sleep quality in children with non-vascular Ehlers-Danlos syndromes. *American Journal of Medical Genetics A*, *176*, 1858-1864.

Nakagami, Y., Kubo, H., Katsuki, R., Sakai, T., Sugihara, G., Naito, C. & Kato, T. A. (2018). Development of a 2-h suicide prevention program for medical staff including nurses and medical residents: a two-center pilot trial. *Journal of Affective Disorders*, *225*, 569-576.

Newton-John, T. R. O. (2014). Negotiating the maze: risk factors for suicidal behavior in chronic pain patients. *Current Pain & Headache Reports*, *18*(9), 1-7.

Nicholas, M. (2011). Depression in people with pain: there is still work to do. *Scandinavian Journal of Pain*, *2*(2), 45-46.

Owen-Smith, A. A., Ahmedani, B. K., Peterson, E., Simon, G. E., Rossom, R. C., Lynch, F. L. & Braciszewski, J. M. (2019). The mediating effect of sleep disturbance on the relationship between nonmalignant chronic pain and suicide death. *Pain Practice*, *19*, 382-389.

Pederson, C. L. (2018). The importance of screening for suicide risk in chronic invisible illness. *Journal of Health Science & Education*, *2*(4), 1-5.

Pederson, C. L. & Brook, J. B. (2017a). Health-related quality of life and suicide risk in postural tachycardia syndrome. *Clinical Autonomic Research*, *27*(2), 75-81.

Pederson, C. L. & Brook, J. B. (2017b). Sleep disturbance linked to suicidal ideation in postural orthostatic tachycardia syndrome. *Nature & Science of Sleep*, *9*, 109-115.

Pederson, C. L. & Brookings, J. B. (2018). Suicide risk linked with perceived burdensomeness in postural tachycardia syndrome. *Journal of Health Science & Education*, *2*(1), 1-8.

Pederson, C. L., Gorman-Ezell, K. & Hochstetler-Mayer, G. (2017). Invisible illness increases risk of suicidal ideation: the role of social workers in preventing suicide. *Health & Social Work*, *42*(3), 183-186.

Pederson, C. L., Gorman-Ezell, K. & Mayer, G. H. (2018). Assessing depression in those who are chronically ill. *Counseling Today*, *60*(9), 38-43.

Porras-Segovia, A., Perez-Rodriguez, M. M., Lopez-Esteban, P., Courtet, P., Barrigon, M. L., Lopez-Castroman, J. & Baca-Garcia, E. (2019). Contribution of sleep deprivation to suicidal behaviour: a systematic review. *Sleep Medicine Reviews*, *44*, 37-47.

Qiu, T., Klonsky, E. D. & Klein, D. N. (2017). Hopelessness predicts suicide ideation but not attempts: a 10-year longitudinal study. *Suicide & Life-Threatening Behavior*, *47*, 718-722.

Racine, M. (2017). Chronic pain and suicide risk: a comprehensive review. *Progress in Neuro-Psychopharmacology and Biological Psychiatry*, *87*, 269-280.

Racine, M., Sanchez-Rodriguez, E., Galan, S., Tome-Pires, C., Sole, E., Jensen, M. P. & Choiniere, M. (2017). Factors associated with suicidal ideation in patients with chronic non-cancer pain. *Pain Medicine*, *18*, 283-293.

Raj, V., Opie, M. & Arnold, A. C. (2018). Cognitive and psychological issues in postural tachycardia syndrome. *Autonomic Neuroscience*, *215*, 46-55.

Ranque-Garnier, S., Eldin, C., Sault, C., Raoult, D. & Donnet, A. (2019). Management of patients presenting with generalized musculoskeletal pain and a suspicion of Lyme disease. *Médicine & Maladies Infectieuses*, *49*, 157-166.

Ribeiro, J. D., Huang, X., Fox, K. R. & Franklin, J. C. (2018). Depression and hopelessness as risk factors for suicide ideation, attempts and death: meta-analysis of longitudinal studies. *British Journal of Psychiatry*, *212*, 279-286.

Ruzieh, M., Batizy, L., Dasa, O., Oostra, C. & Grubb, B. (2017). The role of autoantibodies in the syndromes of orthostatic intolerance: a systematic review. *Scandinavian Cardiovascular Journal*, *51*, 243-247.

Schmaling, K. B. & Betterton, K. L. (2016). Neurocognitive complaints and functional status among patients with chronic fatigue syndrome and fibromyalgia. *Quality of Life Research*, *25*, 1257-1263.

Smith, M. T., Edwards, R. R., Robinson, R. C. & Dworkin, R. H. (2004). Suicidal ideation, plans, and attempts in chronic pain patients: factors associated with increased risk. *Pain*, *111*, 201-208.

Smith, W. R., Noonan, C. & Buchwald, D. (2006). Mortality in a cohort of chronically fatigued patients. *Psychological Medicine*, *36*, 1301-1306.

Stiles, L. E., Cinnamon, J. & Balan, I. (2018). The patient perspective: what postural orthostatic tachycardia syndrome patients want physicians to know. *Autonomic Neuroscience*, *215*, 121-125.

Strand, E. B., Mengshoel, A. M., Sandvik, L., Helland, I. B., Abraham, S. & Nes, L. S. (2019). Pain is associated with reduced quality of life and functional status in patients with myalgic encephalomyelitis/chronic fatigue syndrome. *Scandinavian Journal of Pain*, *19*, 61-72.

Triñanes, Y., González-Villar, A., Gómez-Perretta, C. & Carrillo-de-la-Peña, M. T. (2015). Suicidality in chronic pain: predictors of suicidal ideation in fibromyalgia. *Pain Practice*, *15*, 323-332.

Tucker, R. P., Hagan, C. R., Hill, R. M., Slish, M. L., Bagge, C. L., Joiner, T. E. & Wingate, L. R. (2018). Empirical extension of the interpersonal theory of suicide: investigating the role of interpersonal hopelessness. *Psychiatry Research*, *259*, 427-432.

Van Orden, K. & Deming, C. (2018). Late-life suicide prevention strategies: current status and future directions. *Current Opinion in Psychology*, *22*, 79-83.

Wei, M. Y. & Mukamal, K. J. (2019). Multimorbidity and mental health-related quality of life and risk of completed suicide. *Journal of the American Geriatric Society*, *67*, 511-519.

Wilson, K. G., Kowal, J., Caird, S. M., Castillo, D., McWilliams, L. & Heenan, A. (2017). Self-perceived burden, perceived burdensomeness, and suicidal ideation in patients with chronic pain. *Canadian Journal of Pain*, *1*, 127-136.

Wolfe, F., Smythe, H. A., Yunus, M. B., Bennett, R. M., Bombardier, C., Goldenberg, D. L. & Clark, P. (1990). The American College of Rheumatology 1990 criteria for the classification of fibromyalgia. Report of the Multicenter Criteria Committee. *Arthritis & Rheumatology*, *33*, 160-172.

Wolfe, K. L., Nakonezny, P. A., Owen, V. J., Rial, K. V., Moorehead, A. P., Kennard, B. D. & Emslie, G. J. (2019). Hopelessness as a predictor of suicide ideation in depressed male and female adolescent youth. *Suicide & Life-Threatening Behavior*, *49*, 253-263.

You, S., Van Orden, K. A. & Conner, K. R. (2011). Social connections and suicidal thoughts and behavior. *Psychology of Addictive Behaviors*, *25*, 180-184.

Zimmerman, M., Ellison, W., Young, D., Chelminski, I. & Dalrymple, K. (2015). How many different ways do patients meet the diagnostic criteria for major depressive disorder? *Comprehenive Psychiatry*, *56*, 29-34.

Zullo, L., Horton, S., Eaddy, M., King, J., Hughes, J., Diederich, A. & Stewart, S. (2017). Adolescent insomnia, suicide risk, and the interpersonal theory of suicide. *Psychiatry Research*, *257*, 242-248.

In: Understanding Suicidal Ideation
Editor: David Lester
ISBN: 978-1-53616-999-7

Chapter 7

"MY LIFE IS FALLING APART, AND THINGS WILL NEVER GET ANY BETTER": THE CONTENT AND PROCESS OF SUICIDAL IDEATION

James C. Overholser, Eleanor Beale, Stephanie Gomez and Liliana Varman

ABSTRACT

Suicidal ideation is a complex problem with many potential causes. Suicidal ideation typically develops within a foundation of depression. Then, in a vulnerable person, the dysfunctional reaction may extend into a suicidal crisis. The content of suicidal ideation can focus on ruminative thoughts about current problems, and the present chapter discusses five domains: financial, interpersonal, loss and isolation, medical problems, and experiences with death. No matter the content of suicidal thoughts, the cognitive process involved is highly disruptive to the individual, but suicidal ideation derives from extremist views of negative life events. The subjective reactions are created by the perceived magnitude and anticipated durability of the negative event, resulting in the belief that the problems can never be solved. At the core of the suicide process is a view that life is bad now (despair), and there is no reason to expect they will get any better (hopelessness). By confronting these assorted issues, the rates of desperation and suicidal behavior may begin to decline. It may be helpful to promote psychosocial strategies that enhance interpersonal connections, feelings of competence, and ultimately cultivate a sense of hope for a better future.

Suicide rates in the United States are high and continuing to rise. Death by suicide in the United States has risen by 31% from a rate of 10.7 per 100,000 in 2001 to a rate of 14.0 per 100,000 in 2017 (NIMH, 2019). As of 2017, suicide was the tenth leading cause of death overall, the second leading cause of death in individuals aged 10 to 34, and the fourth leading cause of death in individuals aged 35 to 54 (NIMH, 2019). Part of the problem in successfully treating suicidal individuals lies in understanding the progression of suicide and teasing apart how suicidal ideation evolves into suicidal action. Worldwide, approximately 9.2% of individuals report experiencing suicidal ideation, and 2.7% report a past suicide attempt (Nock et al., 2008). Of those individuals with suicidal ideation, 34% made a suicide plan, of whom 72% completed a suicide attempt. In 2015, approximately 4% of adults in the U.S. had experienced serious thoughts of suicide (Piscopo, Lipari, Cooney, & Glasheen, 2016). These rates fail to account for those individuals who do not disclose experiencing suicidal ideation or having a suicide attempt.

Suicide is a complex issue with many potential causes. It is useful to rely on a comprehensive approach for understanding suicide risk by incorporating biological factors, psychological processes, and social or cultural concerns. Distinguishing between risk factors for suicidal ideation versus suicide attempts may help to clarify when and how to intervene (Klonsky & May, 2014). Additionally, suicidal ideation, suicidal intent, and suicidal behaviors are complex terms that carry different meanings for various clinicians and researchers. Although efforts have been made to make the terms more consistent (O'Carroll, et al., 1996; Silverman, Berman, Sanddal, O'Carroll, & Joiner, 2007), there remains discontinuity in how concepts like suicidal ideation are defined and used. This ambiguity impacts how suicidal ideation is measured, researched and treated (Klonsky, May, & Saffer, 2016). The current chapter will use the term suicidal ideation to refer to any thoughts about or consideration of wishing to be dead or taking suicidal action and the term suicide attempt to mean any step or action taken with the intent to cause harm to the self that will result in death.

A recent meta-analysis looked at risk factors for suicide across research from 1965 until 2015 (Franklin, et al., 2017). In order of importance, the top risk factors for suicidal ideation included hopelessness, diagnosis of depression, any history of abuse, and diagnosis of anxiety. Depression, hopelessness, and impulsivity are consistently shown to relate to suicidal thoughts and behaviors (O'Connor & Nock, 2014). However, while depression and hopelessness are important factors to attend to when gauging risk of suicide, they do not always distinguish between individuals with suicidal ideation and individuals who attempt suicide (May & Klonsky, 2016). Not being able to identify the nuances between these two groups is an important current limitation in the field of psychology. The qualities that are often viewed as predicting or relating to the risk of a suicide attempt may actually be targeting suicidal ideation (Klonsky, et al., 2016).

The patterns of suicidal ideation are variable. In a study of 997 Hong Kong residents who were interviewed at baseline as well as 12 months later (Zhang, Law, & Yip, 2011), 30.9% reported experiencing suicidal ideation throughout their lifetime, 6.2% reported that suicidal ideation persisted at the 12-month follow-up, and 1.9% reported a new onset of suicidal ideation during the follow-up period. Anxiety and reasons for living were the only factors found to be significantly associated with incidence of suicidal ideation over the 12-month follow up. Average life distress was shown to be the strongest predictor of suicidal ideation persistence 12 months later, while hope was shown to be the strongest protective factor. The relationship between average life distress and persistence of suicidal ideation was partially mediated by depression.

Understanding the subjective experience of suicidal clients is important. A simple screening measure for suicidal ideation is likely to result in incorrect categorizations, with a high rate of false positive and false negative prediction errors. For example, among cancer patients who had endorsed suicidal thoughts on an intake questionnaire, follow-up evaluations revealed that one-third of suicidal patients denied the presence of suicidal ideation, and another third admitted to experiencing vague thoughts of death but with no suicidal intent (Walker, et al., 2011). Other studies have documented poor agreement between structured interview and clinician insight when estimating suicide risk. When comparing a research assessment to a clinical assessment of 201 adult inpatient women experiencing a major depressive episode, interrater agreement was only moderate when assessing past suicide attempts (kappa = 0.595) and low when assessing suicidal ideation (kappa = 0.250), with 29.7% of cases identified during research assessment being missed by clinical assessors (Bongiovi-Garcia, et al., 2009). The biggest difference between the two methods was that the research inquiry was much more structured than that completed within the context of the clinical assessment. Assessment may require a better understanding of the process and context of suicidal ideation in order to more accurately capture the experience of the individual.

Available assessments targeting suicidal ideation are generally lacking. Ghasemi, Shaghaghi, and Allahverdipour (2015) conducted a systematic review spanning 1974 through 2008 and found 15 scales meant to assess suicidal ideation. The scales ranged from 4 to 36 items, including both self-report and interview methods. Despite the variety of scales available, there was no gold standard that stood out as the best way to assess suicidal ideation. There may be an important difference in terms of risk between having thoughts of killing oneself and having a wish for death. Endorsing both of these factors results in the highest rates of lifetime suicide attempts when compared to endorsement of either one in isolation (Baca-Garcia, et al., 2011). Assessment is at the core of proper case conceptualization and diagnosis. Without a gold standard for measuring suicidal ideation, there is a major gap in clinically targeting this construct.

The risk posed by suicidal ideation is muddled by the unclear path that leads from having suicidal thoughts to taking suicidal actions. While having suicidal ideation at all puts an individual at higher risk for suicide, this higher risk does not appear to be statistically different than the risk seen in individuals who attempt suicide (May & Klonsky, 2016). The presence of a psychiatric disorder, including depression, is ineffective in distinguishing ideators from attempters (Baca-Garcia, et al., 2011). When it comes to passive versus active suicidal ideation, passive ideators have been shown to score similarly on measures of depression, hopelessness, and suicidality, with both types of ideators scoring significantly higher than non-ideators (May, Overholser, Ridley, & Raymond, 2015). However, the severity of suicidal ideation was found to be effective in discriminating suicide attempters from non-attempters (Park, Hong, Jon, Hong, & Jung, 2017). In a sample of Malaysian adult psychiatric patients, individuals with baseline suicidal ideation were at greater risk of transitioning to a suicide attempt when they were in a lower social class, had a previous psychiatric hospitalization, and had more severe suicidal ideation at baseline (Chan, Shamsul, & Maniam, 2014). One study looking at the trajectory of suicidal ideation over time found two distinct classes: moderate severity decreasing over time and high severity remaining stable over time (Batterham et al., 2019). Individuals in the high severity remaining stable over time trajectory were more likely to be unemployed and to have higher levels of perceived burdensomeness. The progression of suicidal ideation and the state or trait-like qualities of this construct are important targets of future research.

Many factors are involved in the process whereby depression evolves into suicidal ideation and onto suicidal acts (Klonsky, et al., 2016). Suicidal ideation tends to be consistent across depressive episodes. In a prospective study of 69 community adults with history of major depressive disorder who were followed over a 12-month span (Williams, Crane, Barnhofer, Van der Does, & Segal, 2006), 56% of the participants experienced a new depressive episode during the follow-up period. Suicidal ideation tended to occur in a consistent manner across the depressive episodes.

Depression severity is related to the intensity of suicidal ideation (Gensichen, Teising, König, Gerlach, & Petersen, 2010; Hawton,

Comabella, Haw, & Saunders, 2013; Keilp, et al., 2012). However, some research suggests that the overlap between depression severity and suicidal ideation arises from the inclusion of suicidal thoughts as a component of self-report measures of depression (Keilp, et al., 2012). The core features of depression that appear to be related to suicidal ideation include those relating to mood disturbance, such as sadness, pessimism, loss of interest, appearance, and guilt (Keilp, et al., 2012). A recent meta-analysis found that anhedonia was significantly higher in individuals with current suicidal ideation, even after controlling for depression and other psychiatric diagnoses (Ducasse, et al., 2018). The qualities of a depressed mood may carry a particular degree of influence depending on the content of suicidal ideation.

When it comes to suicidal ideation, the risk is not always obvious, and understanding these thoughts requires self-disclosure from the individual. In a general population sample from the Netherlands, 48% of individuals reported experiencing suicidal ideation but not reporting it to anyone (Mérelle, et al., 2018). Adults reporting non-disclosure of suicidal ideation were more likely to have fewer social contact and to be older, while they were less likely to have poor health, frequent suicidal ideation, or severe psychological distress. Suicidal ideation may have a negative health-related impact for individuals beyond the obvious risk of suicide. Experiencing any suicidal ideation puts individuals at 2.1 times higher risk of all-cause mortality, with that number almost doubling when suicidal ideation was experienced daily (Cain & Loprinzi, 2018).

The identification and treatment of suicide risk is complicated by the mental health system's approach to the care of major depression. Depression often goes untreated, even by mental health professionals (Olfson, Blanco, & Marcus, 2016). Over the past number of years, there has been a nationwide tendency whereby many distressed adults have become less likely to seek psychological treatments and more likely to seek pharmacological treatments for depression (Marcus & Olfson, 2010; Olfson & Marcus, 2010). Over-reliance on biological treatment of depression may overlook important modifiable factors associated with suicidal ideation that can be targeted in a psychological treatment context.

The assessment and treatment of suicidal ideation can become hidden behind the mental health system approach to depression. Prescription medications are used to treat depression, anxiety, and panic. Even when effective in suppressing symptoms, these drugs only have their medicinal effects as long as the patient continues taking their prescribed dose. Even when following prescription orders accurately, the effectiveness of many antidepressant medications tends to wane over time, and patients either need a strong dose or a trial on a different antidepressant. Some research suggests that the widespread use of prescription antidepressants can help to lower the suicide rate (Gibbons, Hur, Bhaumik, & Mann, 2005). However, there has been some concern that antidepressant medications can increase the tendency for suicidal thoughts (Healy & Aldred, 2005). Furthermore, there is evidence that most antidepressant medications rely heavily on patient expectations and nonspecific therapy factors to bring about emotional relief (Ankarberg & Falkenström, 2008). In many cases, antidepressant medications have their effects through a placebo reaction (Kirsch, 2014), especially in cases of moderate or less depression (Fournier, et al., 2010). More importantly, the strong reliance on antidepressant medications conveys the message that moods are dysfunctional, and the physician is prepared to treat an emotional problem as if it were a medical illness. An overreliance on medication treatments for depression can convey a message that negative moods are dysfunctional, and sadness is a disease. Instead, a psychosocial perspective helps to highlight the real and magnified life problems that have been encountered by the client.

Medications work only to temporarily suppress some symptoms, but they fail to address the assorted areas of conflict, worry or loss. Thus, for many depressed clients, the impact of medications will be short-lived, and it risks leaving the person in a worse condition, feeling that their problems are beyond the scope of even proper medical/psychiatric treatment. There is a risk that, when it becomes apparent that medications have not helped to resolve life difficulties, the depressed individual may begin to feel hopeless about the future.

A more detailed exploration of suicidal thoughts and ideation may shed light on the core features of suicide risk. The present review will confront two primary issues that underlie suicidal ideation: the severity of negative life events compounded by the perceived duration or unsolvable nature of their problems. The present chapter will explore several factors that could help to explain the onset of suicidal ideation, focusing on factors that might create a bastion for higher levels of depression, despair and hopelessness, thereby elevating the risk for suicidal acts.

"My Life Is Falling Apart": The Content of Suicidal Ideation

Many factors can initiate suicidal thoughts and feelings in an individual and the specifics of how and why a person experiences suicidality remain unclear. However, certain life domains may initiate the process toward suicidal ideation. Five central life problem domains are proposed as common triggers that may initiate suicidal thoughts and a desire to die. The first domain is based on financial problems. Suicidal thoughts can focus on recent job problems, current unemployment, and the subsequent financial crisis that often ensues. The second domain relates to various interpersonal struggles. Suicidal thoughts can focus on social isolation and loneliness, whether a lifetime of social difficulties or the recent end of an intimate relationship. The third domain focuses on important areas of loss or isolation. In a manner that is aligned with the first two domains, suicidal thoughts can focus on a recent experience of loss, shame, rejection or humiliation. The fourth domain is connected to the health problems experienced by the individual. Suicidal thoughts can focus on severe or chronic medical problems, especially in cases of terminal illness or chronic pain. Finally, the fifth domain of suicidal ideation content relates to thoughts about death and dying. Suicidal thoughts can focus on a person's prior exposure to death and dying in a loved one, sometimes viewing death in a romanticized view of a peaceful end to life struggles. In a large scale study of depression and suicidal thoughts in community adults (Zhang, et al., 2011), the strongest predictor of suicidal thoughts was a subjective feeling of life distress arising from recent stressful events. These subjective feelings of life distress may be triggered by one or more of these five core domains, thus making up the content of suicidal ideation.

Financial Factors

One of the main factors that can contribute to suicidal ideation is financial problems. Poverty, unemployment, job loss, low wages, and loss of a home are all examples of how individuals experience financial hardship in their lives. Current financial problems can play a central role in depression (Butterworth, Rodgers, & Windsor, 2009). In addition, economic strain can increase the risk for suicide (Stack & Wasserman, 2007). For example, in a study of 62 adults who had died by suicide, Stack and Wasserman found high levels of economic strain, especially as it related to poor wages, unemployment and potential loss of car or home.

Job Loss and Unemployment

When considering suicide as an option, clients are frequently troubled by recent job loss and the subsequent financial crisis that often ensues. National suicide rates are influenced by a mixture of social and economic factors (Yang & Lester, 1995), including the national economy (dos Santos, Tavares, & Barros, 2016). For example, countries that have experienced economic recessions also experience subsequent increases in suicide rates (Oyesanya, Lopez-Morinigo, & Dutta, 2015). In fact, a recent study found linkage between the 2008-2010 economic recession in England and increased suicide rates during those same years (Barr, Taylor-Robinson, Scott-Samuel, McKee, & Stuckler, 2012). The impact of unemployment on suicide rates may not be immediate but can be delayed by 3-5 years (Fountoulakis, Koupidis, Siamouli, Grammatikopoulos, & Theodorakis, 2013). This time lag makes sense, as the individual may seek alternate employment, rely on personal savings, and eventually give up hope due to the expanding financial debt and endless employment rejection. Suicide rates are influenced by a country's level of unemployment (Lin, 2006), especially in countries with higher income levels (Noh, 2009). However, the impact of unemployment on suicide rates can be minimized if adequate unemployment benefits are available (Cylus, Glymour, & Avendano, 2014).

Job loss and the subsequent financial distress are related to increased suicide risk, especially in middle-aged adults (Hempstead & Phillips, 2015). Suicidal thoughts may develop when a person experiences job termination, career setbacks, lay-offs, and the subsequent burden of financial stress that looms over many areas of their life. Unemployment and the subsequent financial problems contribute significantly to the risk of death by suicide (Coope, et al., 2015), especially for men (Chan, Yip, Wong, & Chen, 2007). While some houses may have two working spouses or parents, it is possible that the responsibility of financial support falls all onto one individual. In a world where money often relates to privileges like healthcare, education or just daily needs being met, it follows that financial struggles may intensify a state of hopelessness about accessing these resources and eventually lead to suicidal ideation.

Poverty and Low Wages

There are economic challenges facing many people today. Minimum wage is often inadequate to support most adults, and the wage disparity between the rich and the poor only magnifies the struggles experienced by the masses. Individuals with higher incomes have been shown to live longer and healthier lives compared to those with lower incomes (Braveman, Cubbin, Egerter, Williams, & Pamuk, 2010). Additionally, poverty is related to higher rates of suicide (Bantjes, et al., 2016) and suicide rates are influenced by income inequality (Machado, Rasella, & Dos Santos, 2015). In fact, a 2019 study investigating the relationship between state minimum wages and suicide rates in the U.S. from 2006-2016 found that every dollar increase in the minimum wage resulted in a 1.9% decrease in the annual suicide rate (Gertner, Rotter, & Shafer, 2019).

This is evidence that low wages are a crucial factor when it comes to suicide and that policy changes regarding the minimum wage could help decrease suicide rates.

When living at the poverty level, a mixture of stressors can easily accumulate (Evans & English, 2002). Limited finances can create difficulties paying for basic essentials, such as groceries, rent, gas, or even going to the doctor. The financial cost of hospitalization may deter a suicidal client from seeking professional help (Yaniv, 2001). Furthermore, financial restrictions can cause a reduction in socialization, for example, no longer being able to afford dinner or other social activities with friends. Finally, financial restrictions can create conflict and frequent arguments with a person's spouse or teenage children, especially when combined with social comparison (i.e., seeing social media reports of others who are able to afford a new car, a bigger house or an exotic vacation). Individuals may be inclined to drink alcohol to cope with financial stressors, as it was found that poverty rates were positively associated with alcohol involvement in suicides for men and women aged 45-64 years (Kerr, et al., 2017). Additionally, during the economic recession of 2008-2011, alcohol-related suicides increased by 7% compared to those from 2005-2007 (Kaplan, et al., 2015), indicating that alcohol may be used more frequently as a coping mechanism. The increased stress that results from living in poverty sets the scene for no longer wanting to live with such unstoppable pressures.

Loss of Housing

Unemployment and job loss can be perceived as major life crises. The financial problems can result in restricted personal finances and can culminate in housing foreclosure. Foreclosure and loss of housing can be a significant personal crisis that increases the risk of suicide (Fowler, Gladden, Vagi, Barnes, & Frazier, 2015). Home eviction and foreclosure are significant risk factors related to suicide (Fowler, et al., 2015), especially among middle aged adults (Houle & Light, 2014) and white males (Houle & Light, 2017).

In a study of almost 22,000 Swedish households, Rojas and Stenberg (2016) found that those who were served with an eviction order during 2009-2012 were four times more likely to die by suicide compared to those who had not had that experience. Loss of housing can be associated with feelings of shame, guilt, or inadequacy, all of which are common factors in suicidal ideation.

Interpersonal Factors

Suicide risk is associated with a broad spectrum of interpersonal problems. Many depressed and suicidal clients report social isolation and loneliness, whether a lifetime of social difficulties or the recent end of an intimate relationship. Furthermore, social withdrawal is predictive of suicidal ideation (Cheatle, Wasser, Foster, Olugbodi, & Bryan, 2014). Even worse, when a person becomes socially isolated, there may be no one nearby to talk the suicidal individual out of a dangerous action, no one to notice that a suicide attempt has occurred, and no one to initiate rescue when emergency medical services are needed.

Technology has improved everyday life in many ways, but it has also created a societal shift that seems to exacerbate social disconnectedness throughout modern society. A lack of social connection plays a central role in the development of depression (Cruwys, Haslam, Dingle, Haslam, & Jetten, 2014). Isolation and loneliness can add to the feeling of being overwhelmed, as individuals may find they have no one with whom to share their burden, express their emotions, or lean on during trying times. It has long been known that social isolation, interpersonal rejection, and loneliness can increase suicide risk. Poor social connections have been associated with higher mortality rates across a wide range of causes of death (Holt-Lunstad, Smith, & Layton, 2010). The impact of lack of social connection on suicidal ideation may be exacerbated by the indirect nature of social connectedness today through social media and other phone applications, resulting in a higher quantity, but a lower quality of social interactions.

Marital Status

Conflict within a romantic relationship is a risk factor for subsequent suicidal thoughts and behaviors, although interpersonal conflict may affect individuals differently based on gender. Individuals who die by suicide are likely to be single and living alone, especially among male suicides (Heikkinen, Isometsä, Marttunen, Aro, & Lönnqvist, 1995). Marital separation has a more powerful impact on suicide risk for men than women (Kõlves, Ide, & De Leo, 2010). Widowhood among older men leads to a lack of social belonging (McLaren, Gomez, Gill, & Chesler, 2015). Interpersonal conflict, with a romantic partner or others, tends to be higher in suicidal patients (Baca-Garcia, et al., 2007). When the reliability of a stable romantic relationship is threatened or removed, it can have detrimental effects on an individual's ability to cope.

Divorce can be a potent risk factor for suicide in the United States (Stack & Scourfield, 2015) as well as in Japan (Andrés, Halicioglu, & Yamamura, 2011), possibly in part due to cultural norms of marriage expectations. Kposowa (2000) argued that Western societies emphasize the importance of having a strong marriage, and that individuals who divorce may experience shame, guilt, hurt and disorientation as a result. Among separated individuals, those experiencing suicidal ideation were found to have significantly higher levels of internalized shame compared to their non-suicidal counterparts (Kõlves, et al., 2010). Even if the stress of the relationship was worse than its ending, there may be important societal pressures that view divorce as equivalent to failure. If these expectations are internalized as core beliefs in a person who is divorced, he or she may ruminate on this failure and worry about never finding another partner or spouse.

Rejection, Harassment and Bullying

Another effect of the increased use of technology today is the alteration of the social sphere in ways that can increase social comparison, peer rejection, online bullying and feelings of isolation. Among youth, being victimized by cyber-bullying is related to both suicidal ideation and suicide attempts, even more strongly than victimization through traditional bullying (Van Geel, Vedder, & Tanilon, 2014). The negative impact of peer victimization on depression (Bauman, Toomey, & Walker, 2013), suicidal thoughts, and suicidal attempts is especially important for adolescent females (Klomek, Sourander, & Gould, 2010). In one recent study (Bauman, et al., 2013), among males, cyber bullying was associated with suicide attempts, whereas among females, cyber victimization was associated with depression.

Sexual Identity

Young adults who identify as sexual minorities may be especially vulnerable to suicidal thoughts and behaviors. LGBTQ youth may experience discrimination and even harassment, by friends or family members based on their sexual identity. This can result in social isolation or feelings of rejection which may lead to depression or suicidal ideation. Experiencing interpersonal microaggressions significantly increased odds of attempted suicide amongst a sample of LGBTQ youth, while resilience acted as a protective factor (Woodford, et al., 2018). Due to prejudice and stigma surrounding transgender individuals, they are at an increased risk for both suicide and depression (Tebbe & Moradi, 2016). However, the risk of suicide among transgender youth can be reduced by adequate support from friends (Tebbe & Moradi, 2016).

Loss and Isolation

In close alignment with the first two domains, feelings of loss and isolation can lead to suicidal ideation usually after recent experiences of shame, humiliation or rejection. Feelings of shame can be defined as when someone feels bad about themselves or who they are as a person, while feelings of humiliation are when someone feels degraded or devalued by other people (Hartling, Rosen, Walker, & Jordan, 2004). Both shame and humiliation can lead to feelings of rejection by others, which may interrupt an individual's ability to maintain social relationships, resulting in perceived loss and isolation. These are all factors that can lead to depression and suicidal ideation.

Victims of childhood physical or sexual violence often feel shame, humiliation and rejection after their abuse. Experiences of abuse can also be very isolating, as the victims may not want to tell others about what happened, or they may feel that it is their own fault. Childhood physical and sexual abuse both increase the risk for suicidal ideation (Obikane, Shinozaki, Takagi, & Kawakami, 2018). All types of severe violence (including both physical and sexual) were associated with trauma-related shame and guilt in a study of the general Norwegian population, and these emotions were both independently associated with mental health problems (Aakvaag, et al., 2016). Feelings of shame or humiliation can lead to social disengagement and a desire to withdraw from others, leading to social isolation (Chao, Cheng, & Chiou, 2011). Depressed women with a history of childhood sexual abuse had an increased risk of suicidal ideation, and the risk was even greater for those women with higher levels of shame-proneness (You, Talbot, He, & Conner, 2012). Social isolation poses as a risk for suicidal ideation through the lack of support, as well as tendencies for rumination and self-blame about the isolation.

Veterans often experience loss and isolation after returning home from combat. They can feel shame or guilt for a variety of reasons, such as not performing well enough in combat or surviving combat while a fellow service member was seriously injured or killed (Elliott, 2018). In a sample of military personnel in an outpatient mental health clinic, those who had a history of suicidal ideation had higher levels of guilt and shame, and both guilt and shame were associated with more severe current suicidal ideation (Bryan, Morrow, Etienne, & Ray-Sannerud, 2013). These results support a cyclical interaction between suicidal ideation and guilt or shame. Trauma-related guilt had direct effects on suicidal ideation in a sample of U.S. veterans (Cunningham, et al., 2017). There may be different types of guilt that, when unprocessed, fester into feeling unworthy of life.

Another group of people who experience isolation and rejection, especially from the general community, are convicted felons who rejoin society after serving a jail sentence. Many felons report feeling like "outsiders" once they rejoin society (Uggen, Manza, & Behrens, 2004), which can put barriers to them building new relationships and even getting a job. This feeling of overall rejection can contribute to feeling isolated and may lead to mental health problems. Current, recent and prior incarcerations are significantly associated with major depression, and this association heavily depends on both economic and social factors relating to their reintegration into society (Turney, Wildeman, & Schnittker, 2012). A previous incarceration of greater than one year during young adulthood predicted suicidal thoughts during adulthood (Barnert, et al., 2017). Additionally, women released from prison are 14.2 times more likely, and men 4.8 times more likely, to die by suicide than the general population (Spittal, Forsyth, Pirkis, Alati, & Kinner, 2014). Thus, societal groups that feel separate from the general public are at risk for feeling isolated and desperate.

Medical Problems

A recent serious injury or illness has been found to predict a future suicide attempt (Chan, et al., 2014). Suicide risk has been associated with severe or chronic medical problems, especially in cases of terminal illness or chronic pain.

Terminal Illness

Individuals with terminal illness are at greater risk for both depression and suicide than healthy controls. A study of terminal cancer patients who died by suicide found multiple vulnerability factors across the decedents, such as loss or fear of losing autonomy as well as a feeling of being a burden on others (Filiberti, et al., 2001). Older adults with a terminal illness may begin to see suicide as a rational choice. Older terminal cancer patients who died by suicide were less likely to have a depression diagnosis or past contact with mental health services than patients whose cancer is curable, suggesting members of the former group may have chosen to end their lives to avoid future suffering (Cheung, Douwes, & Sundram, 2017).

A diagnosis of cancer increases the tendency to think about suicide, especially during the first year after receiving the diagnosis (Lu, et al., 2013). Indeed, the first weeks following a cancer diagnosis appear to be a particularly stressful period for newly diagnosed individuals. Patients receiving a cancer diagnosis have an elevated relative risk of suicide within 12 weeks of being diagnosed (Fang, et al., 2012). This risk elevation decreases rapidly over time but remains elevated beyond the first year post-diagnosis compared to cancer-free individuals. A poor prognosis is associated with increased suicide risk, and the highest relative risk was associated with esophageal, liver, and pancreatic cancers, followed by lung cancer (Fang, et al., 2012).

Chronic Pain

Even individuals without a terminal diagnosis, such as those experiencing chronic pain, are more likely to experience increased suicidality compared to the general population (Anguiano, Mayer, Piven, & Rosenstein, 2012). Chronic pain is associated with suicide risk, though risk seems to differ based on pain location (Misono, Weiss, Fann, Redman, & Yueh, 2008). For example, back pain has been shown to be more strongly associated with suicidality than neuropathic pain (Hassett, Aquino, & Ilgen, 2014).

The relationship between chronic pain and death by suicide remains unclear. Experiencing chronic pain can affect one's quality of life and result in psychiatric comorbidity and, therefore, subsequent elevated risk for suicide (Nock, et al., 2008). Individuals with chronic pain are five times more likely to express a desire for death than those experiencing acute pain (Fishbain, Bruns, Disorbio, & Lewis, 2009). Pain severity also seems to be related to suicidal death. A study of veteran patients found that those experiencing severe or very severe pain were more likely to die by suicide compared to those experiencing moderate or less pain, a relationship that held even after controlling for demographic factors and psychiatric characteristics (Ilgen, et al., 2010). It is possible that chronic pain is an independent contributor to an individual's overall suicide risk (Hassett, et al., 2014). The unbearable nature of pain may impact an individual's normal coping ability and may lead to hopelessness that the problem has any solution, both resulting in an increase in suicidal ideation.

When considering terminal illness and chronic pain, the factors of perceived burdensomeness and thwarted belongingness, constructs in the interpersonal theory of suicide, may play a role. Perceived burdensomeness refers to one's belief that they impose on others and that others would be better off if they were not around, while thwarted belongingness refers to a lack of feeling connected to others (Joiner, 2007). When tested among individuals with chronic pain, the interpersonal theory of suicide was supported. Individuals with chronic pain who perceive themselves as a burden and who experienced stress in their interpersonal relationships were more likely to experience suicidal ideation above and beyond demographic characteristics, depression and pain characteristics (Wilson, Kowal, Henderson, McWilliams, & Péloquin, 2013). The dependence associated with these health states, paired with the isolation of the experience of pain, may further promote hopelessness about change in these populations.

Experience with Death

Suicidal thoughts may take the form of visual images portraying acts of death and dying (Hales, Deeprose, Goodwin, & Holmes, 2011). Suicidal ideation can be increased by personal exposure to the death of a loved one. Loss of a close relative increases risk of suicide and psychiatric illness for at least ten years after the death, but particularly within the first year (Guldin, et al., 2017). A common situation that occurs for individuals who have lost loved ones to terminal illness is that they served as a caregiver shortly before the death (Molina, et al., 2019). This role can be stressful for the individual and may affect their mental health during bereavement. Factors such as place of death and the quality of life of the deceased loved one have an impact on the caregiver's quality of life during bereavement and increase the risk of developing psychiatric disorders (Wright, et al.,

2008, 2010). The experience of losing a loved one can lead someone to romanticize death as a peaceful end to life struggles.

Suicide risk may be higher among individuals living in communities where the act is considered acceptable or expected. When asked to indicate what they thought were the most likely precipitants of suicide in older adults, health problems were most commonly endorsed (Winterrowd, Canetto, & Benoit, 2017). Furthermore, adult suicide was seen in a more favorable light when the suicide was precipitated by health problems versus other stressors such as financial problems or bereavement. Suicide resulting from poor health was viewed as more rational, courageous and acceptable than suicide resulting from other conditions (Winterrowd, et al., 2017). Permissive attitudes toward suicide are related to higher levels of suicidal intent (Jeon, Park, & Shim, 2013). Acceptance of suicidal acts could put someone at risk of considering suicide as a more reasonable option in times of stress.

Perceived stigma is an important factor to consider amongst those who have experienced the death of loved one. The individual may perceive negative attitudes of those around them regarding the death, which may interfere with help-seeking and other social supports (Molina, et al., 2019). Causes of death such as drug overdoses, HIV/AIDS, and suicide are shown to have high levels of stigma associated with them (Molina, et al., 2019). Those with a higher level of perceived stigma regarding their loved one's death, whether the death be suicide or non-suicide, are at increased risk of suicidal thoughts and attempts (Pitman, Osborn, Rantell, & King, 2016). Additionally, of those who felt suicidal after bereavement, high levels of perceived stigma differentiated those who considered suicide versus those who attempted suicide (Pitman, Rantell, Marston, King, & Osborn, 2017). The clinical implications of this are crucial, as perceived stigma could be addressed by clinicians with bereaving patients to assess suicide risk and provide intervention. In the context of discussing death, the taboo of suicide may have been broken, increasing the importance of addressing these topics in a direct and non-judgmental manner.

"Things Will Never Get Better:" The Process of Suicidal Ideation

A suicidal crisis involves a series of progressive changes, creating a dark cloud that engulfs the client. Depressive thoughts can grow into suicidal ideation in certain individuals. The process seems to involve a simple multiplication, whereby a negative situation is multiplied by the hopelessness of the event. These nihilistic thoughts pose a large problem for suicide risk. Depressed individuals may see their feelings of despair expand into a desire for death. Current struggles may be seen as impossible to deal with and too much to bear. The mixture combines the view that life is bad with the anticipation that their current situation is unlikely to improve.

A sense of hopelessness about the future can lead one to believe that the only viable solution to their problems is to end their life. Hopelessness has been found to be predictive of the severity of suicidal thoughts one month after discharge from a psychiatric hospital (Links, et al., 2012). In a prospective study of 997 community adults, hopelessness was related to the presence and persistence of suicidal thoughts at the 12-month re-assessment (Zhang, et al., 2011). A lack of hope seems to influence not only the presence of suicidal thoughts but their duration as well. Hopelessness also appears to be a risk factor for eventual death by suicide. In a prospective study of 6,891 psychiatric outpatients (Brown, Beck, Steer, & Grisham, 2000), hopelessness (BHS scores > 8) was found to be predictive of eventual death by suicide across the 20-year follow-up period. The relationship between hopelessness and suicide is pivotal in understanding the process of suicidal ideation. The initial stressor is important to recognize, but the ongoing interpretation, thinking patterns, and beliefs that continue to feed ideation about dying serves as the target of intervention. Therapists cannot change life circumstances, but they can help clients to change their perspectives about them.

A tendency to interpret a life problem negatively may lead one down the path to thinking about death. Perceiving a problem as negative can keep one from finding solutions and can lead one to think that death is the only solution. Suicidal thoughts often derive from the estimated magnitude of a problem. When viewed as severe, a life stressor will become a major problem deemed a personal catastrophe. Suicidal thoughts can be related to the estimated complexity of a life problem, seeing the problem as unsolvable, and believing that a positive resolution is impossible. Indeed, the anticipated emotional reaction to a problem can be overwhelming. Suicidal thoughts are often also related to the perceived permanence of the problem. When a major life stressor is viewed as chronic or perpetually recurrent, the patient may want to give up since there does not seem to be a clear end in sight.

Beliefs about a person's ability to cope with life can help to suppress suicidal ideation (Bakhiyi, Calati, Guillaume, & Courtet, 2016). Someone who feels they are unable to cope with life stress is not likely to feel capable of resolving his or her problems and is more susceptible to feeling hopeless about the future. As a result, these individuals may be more likely to experience suicidal thoughts. Conversely, individuals who believe they are able to cope with life's challenges are less likely to experience suicidal thoughts because they are less likely to see their difficult situation as enduring and without solution. A belief in one's ability to cope is a natural barrier to needing suicide as a potential solution to the problem at hand.

Factors outside of depression may be predictive of suicidal ideation. A study found that, after controlling for depression and psychiatric disorders, there remained a significant association between anhedonia and suicidal ideation (Ducasse, et al., 2018). Anhedonia refers to decreased pleasure obtained from experiences as well as decreased motivation (Treadway & Zald, 2011). Anhedonia was higher in individuals with suicidal ideation compared to those no experiencing suicidal thoughts, suggesting a specific relationship between the two for individuals over the age of 30 (Ducasse, et al., 2018). Experiential avoidance, or the tendency to avoid unpleasant emotions, is a maladaptive coping strategy that could lead to suicidal thoughts or an exacerbation of negative emotions and a suppression of positive ones. The resulting suicidal thoughts could be a dysfunctional experiential avoidance strategy resulting from an excess of pain compared to pleasant emotions and motivation. Suicidal thoughts can be expressed in the form of decreased motivation as well as a desire to avoid pain, both of which could be factors predicting suicidal behavior (Xie, et al., 2014). These results suggest the potential for different risk factors for suicidal ideation based on age, as well as the potential for different pathways of suicidal ideation for individuals in different age groups.

Thinking about suicide may serve the purpose of creating the illusion of control or choice. Considering suicide allows an individual to feel like he or she is making an active choice about what to do and permits him or her to feel like there is some small semblance of control to be had over an otherwise uncontrollable negative life circumstance. Thinking about suicide may provide some type of emotional relief for people who may feel trapped in their current situations. Someone may be ruminating over multiple psychosocial stressors and not know how to deal with them, but considering suicide allows them to feel like there is a way out if things do not improve. For many people, suicidal ideation allows them to have a last resort escape plan, even if they do not intend on acting on the thoughts. However, even though many people truly do not have intent on acting on their suicidal thoughts in the beginning, over time these thoughts can turn into plausible actions. When viewing suicidal ideation as serving this purpose, there are natural targets for clinical intervention that present themselves. The suicidal individual must be reminded of other options to choose from and given other avenues of being in control. However, these tools will be more powerfully initiated when they come from the clients themselves, with collaboration from the therapist, rather than directly from the therapist. There must be personal relevance to the suicidal individual or there will be no meaningfulness.

Whether the content of suicidal thoughts is focused on financial worries, interpersonal struggles, social isolation, medical illness, or exposure to death, individuals can find support in the therapeutic relationship and guidance from the therapist in discovering alternative paths to moving past the problem. Recognizing that death avoids the problem at hand, but does not eliminate it, will be important for debunking suicide as a viable choice. Building and reinforcing autonomy in the decision to take action or change thinking patterns about non-suicide related options will enhance a feeling of control over the stressful situation. In a therapeutic context when working with a suicidal client, the therapist must carry some of the burden for decreasing hopelessness and building hope in the client. The client presents with suicidal ideation because he or she truly believes that the current despair has no hope of remitting. Through support, delicate questioning, and honesty the therapist must guide the suicidal client to a place of hope.

CONCLUSION

Suicide is a complex problem that deserves a thoughtful approach (Conejero, Lopez-Castroman, Giner, & Baca-Garcia, 2016). Many different factors play a role in suicide risk. No one case of suicide can serve of the definition of them all. The risk of suicide is best examined through a comprehensive and multidisciplinary perspective that includes an appreciation for biological factors, psychological processes, and social or cultural forces. Flexibility and personalization of treatment to the client's particular content of despair is crucial.

At the center of suicidal ideation lies a nihilistic foundation based on feelings of despair and hopeless attitudes. There may be several indirect pathways that move a client toward suicidal acts, but the process often begins with a severe or chronic form of depression, that makes the person vulnerable to risky behaviors (see Figure 7.1). Then, despair over current life struggles can provoke an attitude of hopelessness, as the person begins to lose hope for a better future. This combination of despair and hopelessness can create a desire to die.

Without hope, death seems like a reasonable alternative to a desperate situation. The individual may feel engulfed in feelings of emotional despair, and unable to step outside of their own current struggles. Hopelessness is central component in suicidal ideation and is related to the presence as well as the duration of suicidal ideation (Smith, Alloy, & Abramson, 2006). The strength of one's hopelessness is related to the intensity of suicidal thoughts. Hopelessness is higher in suicidal ideators and attempters compared to nonsuicidal depressed patients (Qiu, Klonsky, & Klein, 2017). Higher levels of hopelessness are associated with a strong risk for ongoing suicidal thoughts (Zhang, et al., 2011) as well as eventual death by suicide (Hawton, et al., 2013). Despite the prominence of hopelessness, we know essentially nothing about what creates these nihilistic expectations. When hopelessness begins to lift, suicidal ideation is likely to subside (Sokero, et al., 2006). The present chapter has attempted to explore the main components of suicidal ideation that create a hopeless view of one's personal future.

Suicide rates may be reduced by improving local access to treatments for depression (Székely, et al., 2013). Furthermore, intervention strategies can be improved by specifically targeting an individual's feelings of hopelessness. Helping an individual who is actively experiencing suicidal thoughts often involves helping them to see their situation as less permanent than expected. A more balanced view could help to prevent suicidal patients from seeing death as the only solution to their problems. Therapy can be used to teach specific coping strategies, thus allowing clients to see their life situation in a more positive light. A mixture of coping options can help prevent patients from experiencing the multiplication of negative thoughts leading to suicidal ideation. Individuals at risk for suicidal ideation can benefit from learning coping strategies at a young age to help instill a sense of capability in one's problem solving abilities.

When working with suicidal clients, cultivating hope for a better future is essential. Treatment for suicidal clients can include attempts to understand the person's subjective experience, help them cope with major life struggles, conduct a thoughtful assessment of assorted risk factors, and take steps to protect the person from their own self-destructive urges. When working with suicidal clients, the therapist must find a way of maintaining a complex balance, being supportive but sometimes fairly directive. In most situations, the therapist can try to discuss a client's suicidal thoughts in a somber and objective manner, without rashly denying their presence or minimizing the risk. However, the therapist can also express concern and support, showing a sincere understanding for the client's severe level of distress. Throughout the conversation, the therapist can demonstrate a willingness to discuss a sensitive, and often taboo, topic. Despite concern and sensitivity, the therapist must take care to avoid elevating the magnitude of the thoughts beyond the level of thoughts at which level they have no power or ability to control the client's actions. At times of crisis, the therapist may need to take a strong lead, directing the client toward safe actions and away from self-destructive tendencies, including social isolation or coping with emotional pain through alcohol or drugs. Social isolation is often a central concern in cases of suicide risk, and unfortunately the therapist may serve as the only source of social interaction and influence. Therapists must help individuals experiencing suicidal ideation find meaning in their lives that is personally valid and sustainable.

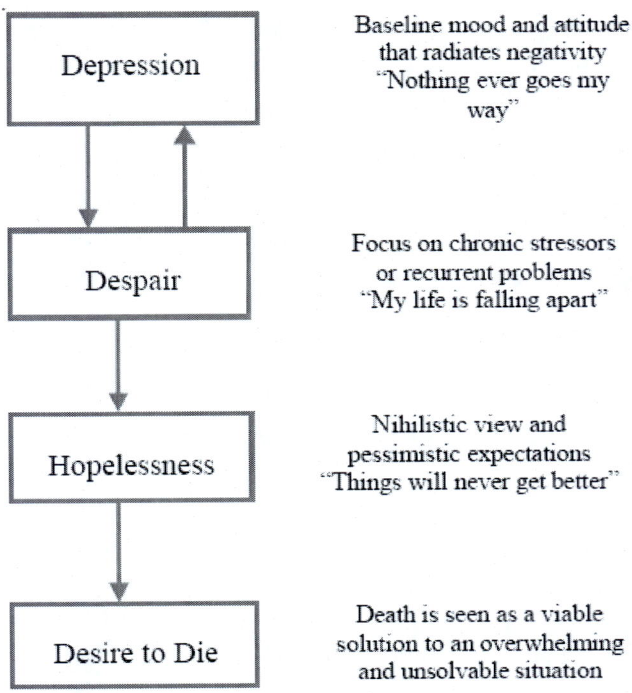

Figure 7.1. Pathways that move a client toward suicidal acts.

Unfortunately, society does not always respect mental illness at the same level as medical illness. Many clients discontinue therapy prematurely because they lack insurance coverage to help defray the cost. Patients may refuse hospitalization because of the cost or the limited time permissible away from their job. Treatment is often focused on short-term crisis management with minimal attention to long-term recovery. Medical and mental health professionals rely too heavily on antidepressant medications for a cost-efficient approach to treatment that sadly fails to address the real-life problems or subjective feelings of hopelessness that likely drive the suicidal urges.

The core of suicidal ideation lies in two dimensions, the feeling of despair captured by the view that that things are bad now, and the attitude of hopelessness, captured by the view that things will never get any better in the future. The combination of despair and hopelessness is likely to promote a desire to die. Suicide risk is a process that develops over time. The problem begins with life stressors that can trigger depression, loneliness, and feelings of despair. If severe or chronic, hopelessness can create an insidious path toward suicidal thoughts. If left unchecked, the suicidal thoughts can move toward suicidal actions, and sometimes result in the unfortunate death of the desperate individual. Thankfully, if stopped early, through identification and intervention, the person can be redirected toward more effective coping strategies, positive social engagement, life meaning, and a more balanced approach to life problems.

REFERENCES

Aakvaag, H. F., Thoresen, S., Wentzel-Larsen, T., Dyb, G., Røysamb, E., & Olff, M. (2016). Broken and guilty since it happened: A population study of trauma-related shame and guilt after violence and sexual abuse. *Journal of Affective Disorders, 204*, 16-23.

Andrés, A. R., Halicioglu, F., & Yamamura, E. (2011). Socio-economic determinants of suicide in Japan. *Journal of Socio-Economics, 40*, 723-731.

Anguiano, L., Mayer, D. K., Piven, M. L., & Rosenstein, D. (2012). A literature review of suicide in cancer patients. *Cancer Nursing, 35*(4), E14-E26.

Ankarberg, P., & Falkenström, F. (2008). Treatment of depression with antidepressants is primarily a psychological treatment. *Psychotherapy: Theory, Research, Practice, Training, 45*, 329-339.

Baca-Garcia, E., Perez-Rodriguez, M. M., Oquendo, M. A., Keyes, K. M., Hasin, D. S., Grant, B. F., & Blanco, C. (2011). Estimating risk for suicide attempt: Are we asking the right questions?: Passive suicidal ideation as a marker for suicidal behavior. *Journal of Affective Disorders, 134*, 327-332.

Baca-Garcia, E., Parra, C. P., Perez-Rodriguez, M. M., Sastre, C. D., Torres, R. R., Saiz-Ruiz, J., & de Leon, J. (2007). Psychosocial stressors may be strongly associated with suicide attempts. *Stress & Health, 23*, 191-198.

Bakhiyi, C. L., Calati, R., Guillaume, S., & Courtet, P. (2016). Do reasons for living protect against suicidal thoughts and behaviors? A systematic review of the literature. *Journal of Psychiatric Research, 77*, 92-108.

Bantjes, J., Iemmi, V., Coast, E., Channer, K., Leone, T., McDaid, D., Palfreyman, A., Stephens, B., & Lund, C. (2016). Poverty and suicide research in low-and middle-income countries: Systematic mapping of literature published in English and a proposed research agenda. *Global Mental Health, 13*(3), e32.

Barnert, E. S., Dudovitz, R., Nelson, B. B., Coker, T. R., Biely, C., Li, N., & Chung, P. J. (2017). How does incarcerating young people affect their adult health outcomes? *Pediatrics, 139*(2), e20162624.

Barr, B., Taylor-Robinson, D., Scott-Samuel, A., McKee, M., & Stuckler, D. (2012). Suicides associated with the 2008-10 economic recession in England: Time trend analysis. *BMJ, 345*, e5142.

Batterham, P. J., van Spijker, B. A., Mackinnon, A. J., Calear, A. L., Wong, Q., & Christensen, H. (2019). Consistency of trajectories of suicidal ideation and depression symptoms: Evidence from a randomized controlled trial. *Depression & Anxiety, 36*, 321-329.

Bauman, S., Toomey, R. B., & Walker, J. L. (2013). Associations among bullying, cyberbullying, and suicide in high school students. *Journal of Adolescence, 36*, 341-350.

Bongiovi-Garcia, M. E., Merville, J., Almeida, M. G., Burke, A., Ellis, S., Stanley, B. H., Posner, K., Mann, J. J., & Oquendo, M. A. (2009). Comparison of clinical and research assessments of diagnosis, suicide attempt history and suicidal ideation in major depression. *Journal of Affective Disorders, 115*, 183-188.

Braveman, P. A., Cubbin, C., Egerter, S., Williams, D. R., & Pamuk, E. (2010). Socioeconomic disparities in health in the United States: What the patterns tell us. *American Journal of Public Health, 100*(S1), S186-S196.

Brown, G. K., Beck, A. T., Steer, R. A., & Grisham, J. R. (2000). Risk factors for suicide in psychiatric outpatients: A 20-year prospective study. *Journal of Consulting & Clinical Psychology, 68*, 371.

Bryan, C. J., Morrow, C. E., Etienne, N., & Ray-Sannerud, B. (2013). Guilt, shame, and suicidal ideation in a military outpatient clinical sample. *Depression & Anxiety, 30*, 55-60.

Butterworth, P., Rodgers, B., & Windsor, T. D. (2009). Financial hardship, socio-economic position and depression: Results from the PATH Through Life Survey. *Social Science & Medicine, 69*, 229-237.

Cain, D. S., & Loprinzi, P. D. (2018). Suicidal ideation and all-cause mortality risk. *Best Practices in Mental Health, 14*(2), 1-8.

Chan, L. F., Shamsul, A. S., & Maniam, T. (2014). Are predictors of future suicide attempts and the transition from suicidal ideation to suicide attempts shared or distinct: A 12-month prospective study among patients with depressive disorders. *Psychiatry Research, 220*, 867-873.

Chan, W. S., Yip, P. S., Wong, P. W., & Chen, E. Y. (2007). Suicide and unemployment: What are the missing links? *Archives of Suicide Research, 11*, 327-335.

Chao, Y. H., Cheng, Y. Y., & Chiou, W. B. (2011). The psychological consequence of experiencing shame: Self-sufficiency and mood-repair. *Motivation & Emotion, 35*, 202.

Cheatle, M. D., Wasser, T., Foster, C., Olugbodi, A., & Bryan, J. (2014). Prevalence of suicidal ideation in patients with chronic non-cancer pain referred to a behaviorally based pain program. *Pain Physician, 17*(3), e359-367.

Cheung, G., Douwes, G., & Sundram, F. (2017). Late-life suicide in terminal cancer: A rational act or underdiagnosed depression? *Journal of Pain & Symptom Management, 54*, 835-842.

Conejero, I., Lopez-Castroman, J., Giner, L., & Baca-Garcia, E. (2016). Sociodemographic antecedent validators of suicidal behavior: A review of recent literature. *Current Psychiatry Reports, 18*(10), number 94.

Coope, C., Donovan, J., Wilson, C., Barnes, M., Metcalfe, C., Hollingworth, W., Kapur, N., Hawton, K., & Gunnell, D. (2015). Characteristics of people dying by suicide after job loss, financial difficulties and other economic stressors during a period of recession (2010–2011): A review of coroners' records. *Journal of Affective Disorders, 183*, 98-105.

Cruwys, T., Haslam, S. A., Dingle, G. A., Haslam, C., & Jetten, J. (2014). Depression and social identity: An integrative review. *Personality & Social Psychology Review, 18*, 215-238.

Cunningham, K. C., Farmer, C., LoSavio, S. T., Dennis, P. A., Clancy, C. P., Hertzberg, M. A., Collie, C. F., Calhoun, P. S., & Beckham, J. C. (2017). A model comparison approach to trauma-related guilt as a mediator of the relationship between PTSD symptoms and suicidal ideation among veterans. *Journal of Affective Disorders, 221*, 227-231.

Cylus, J., Glymour, M. M., & Avendano, M. (2014). Do generous unemployment benefit programs reduce suicide rates? A state fixed-effect analysis covering 1968–2008. *American Journal of Epidemiology, 180*, 45-52.

dos Santos, J. P., Tavares, M., & Barros, P. P. (2016). More than just numbers: Suicide rates and the economic cycle in Portugal (1910–2013). *SSM - Population Health, 2*, 14-23.

Ducasse, D., Loas, G., Dassa, D., Gramaglia, C., Zeppegno, P., Guillaume, S., Olié, E., & Courtet, P. (2018). Anhedonia is associated with suicidal ideation independently of depression: A meta-analysis. *Depression & Anxiety, 35*, 382-392.

Elliott, B. (2018). Understanding guilt, shame, and moral injury in veteran patients. *MedSurg Matters, 27*(6), 10-12.

Evans, G. W., & English, K. (2002). The environment of poverty: Multiple stressor exposure, psychophysiological stress, and socioemotional adjustment. *Child Development, 73*, 1238-1248.

Fang, F., Fall, K., Mittleman, M. A., Sparén, P., Ye, W., Adami, H.-O., & Valdimarsdóttir, U. (2012). Suicide and cardiovascular death after a cancer diagnosis. *New England Journal of Medicine, 366*, 1310-1318.

Filiberti, A., Ripamonti, C., Totis, A., Ventafridda, V., De Conno, F., Contiero, P., & Tamburini, M. (2001). Characteristics of terminal cancer patients who committed suicide during a home palliative care program. *Journal of Pain & Symptom Management, 22*, 544-553.

Fishbain, D. A., Bruns, D., Disorbio, J. M., & Lewis, J. E. (2009). Risk for five forms of suicidality in acute pain patients and chronic pain patients vs pain-free community controls. *Pain Medicine, 10*, 1095-1105.

Fountoulakis, K. N., Koupidis, S. A., Siamouli, M., Grammatikopoulos, I. A., & Theodorakis, P. N. (2013). Suicide, recession, and unemployment. *Lancet, 381*, 721-722.

Fournier, J. C., DeRubeis, R. J., Hollon, S. D., Dimidjian, S., Amsterdam, J. D., Shelton, R. C., & Fawcett, J. (2010). Antidepressant drug effects and depression severity: A patient-level meta-analysis. *Journal of the American Medical Association, 303*, 47-53.

Fowler, K. A., Gladden, R. M., Vagi, K. J., Barnes, J., & Frazier, L. (2015). Increase in suicides associated with home eviction and foreclosure during the US housing crisis: Findings from 16 national violent death reporting system states, 2005–2010. *American Journal of Public Health, 105*, 311-316.

Franklin, J. C., Ribeiro, J. D., Fox, K. R., Bentley, K. H., Kleiman, E. M., Huang, X., Musacchio, K. M., Jaroszewski, A. C., Chang, B. P., & Nock, M. K. (2017). Risk factors for suicidal thoughts and behaviors:

A meta-analysis of 50 years of research. *Psychological Bulletin, 143*, 187.

Gensichen, J., Teising, A., König, J., Gerlach, F. M., & Petersen, J. J. (2010). Predictors of suicidal ideation in depressive primary care patients. *Journal of Affective Disorders, 125*, 124-127.

Gertner, A. K., Rotter, J. S., & Shafer, P. R. (2019). Association between state minimum wages and suicide rates in the US. *American Journal of Preventive Medicine, 56*, 648-654.

Ghasemi, P., Shaghaghi, A., & Allahverdipour, H. (2015). Measurement scales of suicidal ideation and attitudes: A systematic review article. *Health Promotion Perspectives, 5*, 158-168.

Gibbons, R. D., Hur, K., Bhaumik, D. K., & Mann, J. J. (2005). The relationship between antidepressant medication use and rate of suicide. *Archives of General Psychiatry, 62*, 165-172.

Guldin, M. B., Ina Siegismund Kjaersgaard, M., Fenger-Grøn, M., Thorlund Parner, E., Li, J., Prior, A., & Vestergaard, M. (2017). Risk of suicide, deliberate self-harm and psychiatric illness after the loss of a close relative: A nationwide cohort study. *World Psychiatry, 16*, 193-199.

Hales, S. A., Deeprose, C., Goodwin, G. M., & Holmes, E. A. (2011). Cognitions in bipolar affective disorder and unipolar depression: Imagining suicide. *Bipolar Disorders, 13*), 651-661.

Hartling, L. M., Rosen, W., Walker, M., & Jordan, J. V. (2004). Shame and humiliation: From isolation to relational transformation. In J. V. Jordan, M. Walker & L. M. Hartling (Eds.) *The Complexity of Connection* (pp. 103-128). New York: Guilford.

Hassett, A. L., Aquino, J. K., & Ilgen, M. A. (2014). The risk of suicide mortality in chronic pain patients. *Current Pain & Headache Reports, 18*(8), number 436.

Hawton, K., Comabella, C. C., Haw, C., & Saunders, K. (2013). Risk factors for suicide in individuals with depression: A systematic review. *Journal of Affective Disorders, 147*, 17-28.

Healy, D., & Aldred, G. (2005). Antidepressant drug use & the risk of suicide. *International Review of Psychiatry, 17*, 163-172.

Heikkinen, M. E., Isometsä, E. T., Marttunen, M. J., Aro, H. M., & Lönnqvist, J. K. (1995). Social factors in suicide. *British Journal of Psychiatry, 167*, 747-753.

Hempstead, K. A., & Phillips, J. A. (2015). Rising suicide among adults aged 40–64 years: The role of job and financial circumstances. *American Journal of Preventive Medicine, 48*, 491-500.

Holt-Lunstad, J., Smith, T. B., & Layton, J. B. (2010). Social relationships and mortality risk: A meta-analytic review. *PLoS Medicine, 7*(7), e1000316.

Houle, J. N., & Light, M. T. (2014). The home foreclosure crisis and rising suicide rates, 2005 to 2010. *American Journal of Public Health, 104*, 1073-1079.

Houle, J. N., & Light, M. T. (2017). The harder they fall? Sex and race/ethnic specific suicide rates in the US foreclosure crisis. *Social Science & Medicine, 180*, 114-124.

Ilgen, M. A., Zivin, K., Austin, K. L., Bohnert, A. S., Czyz, E. K., Valenstein, M., & Kilbourne, A. M. (2010). Severe pain predicts greater likelihood of subsequent suicide. *Suicide & Life-Threatening Behavior, 40*, 597-608.

Jeon, H. J., Park, J.-H., & Shim, E. J. (2013). Permissive attitude toward suicide and future intent in individuals with and without depression: Results from a nationwide survey in Korea. *Journal of Nervous & Mental Disease, 201*, 286-291.

Joiner, T. (2007). *Why people die by suicide*. Cambridge, MA: Harvard University Press.

Kaplan, M. S., Huguet, N., Caetano, R., Giesbrecht, N., Kerr, W., & McFarland, B. (2015). Economic contraction, alcohol intoxication and suicide: Analysis of the National Violent Death Reporting System. *Injury Prevention, 21*, 35-41.

Keilp, J. G., Grunebaum, M. F., Gorlyn, M., LeBlanc, S., Burke, A. K., Galfalvy, H., Oquendo, M. A., & Mann, J. J. (2012). Suicidal ideation and the subjective aspects of depression. *Journal of Affective Disorders, 140*, 75-81.

Kerr, W. C., Kaplan, M. S., Huguet, N., Caetano, R., Giesbrecht, N., & McFarland, B. H. (2017). Economic recession, alcohol, and suicide rates: Comparative effects of poverty, foreclosure, and job loss. *American Journal of Preventive Medicine, 52*, 469-475.

Kirsch, I. (2014). Antidepressants and the placebo effect. *Zeitschrift für Psychologie, 222*(3), 128-134.

Klomek, A. B., Sourander, A., & Gould, M. (2010). The association of suicide and bullying in childhood to young adulthood: A review of cross-sectional and longitudinal research findings. *Canadian Journal of Psychiatry, 55*, 282-288.

Klonsky, E. D., & May, A. M. (2014). Differentiating suicide attempters from suicide ideators: A critical frontier for suicidology research. *Suicide & Life-Threatening Behavior, 44*, 1-5.

Klonsky, E. D., May, A. M., & Saffer, B. Y. (2016). Suicide, suicide attempts, and suicidal ideation. *Annual Review of Clinical Psychology, 12*, 307-330.

Kõlves, K., Ide, N., & De Leo, D. (2010). Suicidal ideation and behaviour in the aftermath of marital separation: Gender differences. *Journal of Affective Disorders, 120*(, 48-53.

Kposowa, A. J. (2000). Marital status and suicide in the National Longitudinal Mortality Study. *Journal of Epidemiology & Community Health, 54*, 254-261.

Lin, S. J. (2006). Unemployment and suicide: Panel data analyses. *Social Science Journal, 43*, 727-732.

Links, P., Nisenbaum, R., Ambreen, M., Balderson, K., Bergmans, Y., Eynan, R., Harder, H., & Cutcliffe, J. (2012). Prospective study of risk factors for increased suicide ideation and behavior following recent discharge. *General Hospital Psychiatry, 34*, 88-97.

Lu, D., Fall, K., Sparén, P., Ye, W., Adami, H.-O., Valdimarsdóttir, U., & Fang, F. (2013). Suicide and suicide attempt after a cancer diagnosis among young individuals. *Annals of Oncology, 24*, 3112-3117.

Machado, D. B., Rasella, D., & Dos Santos, D. N. (2015). Impact of income inequality and other social determinants on suicide rate in Brazil. *PLoS One, 10*(4), e0124934.

Marcus, S. C., & Olfson, M. (2010). National trends in the treatment for depression from 1998 to 2007. *Archives of General Psychiatry, 67*, 1265-1273.

May, A. M., & Klonsky, E. D. (2016). What distinguishes suicide attempters from suicide ideators? A meta-analysis of potential factors. *Clinical Psychology: Science & Practice, 23*, 5-20.

May, C. N., Overholser, J. C., Ridley, J., & Raymond, D. (2015). Passive suicidal ideation: A clinically relevant risk factor for suicide in treatment-seeking veterans. *Illness, Crisis & Loss, 23*, 261-277.

McLaren, S., Gomez, R., Gill, P., & Chesler, J. (2015). Marital status and suicidal ideation among Australian older adults: The mediating role of sense of belonging. *International Psychogeriatrics, 27*, 145-154.

Mérelle, S., Foppen, E., Gilissen, R., Mokkenstorm, J., Cluitmans, R., & Van Ballegooijen, W. (2018). Characteristics associated with non-disclosure of suicidal ideation in adults. *International Journal of Environmental Research & Public Health, 15(5)*, e943.

Misono, S., Weiss, N. S., Fann, J. R., Redman, M., & Yueh, B. (2008). Incidence of suicide in persons with cancer. *Journal of Clinical Oncology, 26*, 4731-4738.

Molina, N., Viola, M., Rogers, M., Ouyang, D., Gang, J., Derry, H., & Prigerson, H. G. (2019). Suicidal ideation in bereavement: A systematic review. *Behavioral Sciences, 9*(5), e53.

NIMH. (2019). *Suicide rate estimates, age-standardized estimates by country.* Retrieved from https://www.nimh.nih.gov/health/statistics/suicide.shtml.

Nock, M. K., Borges, G., Bromet, E. J., Cha, C. B., Kessler, R. C., & Lee, S. (2008). Suicide and suicidal behavior. *Epidemiologic Reviews, 30*, 133-154.

Noh, Y. H. (2009). Does unemployment increase suicide rates? The OECD panel evidence. *Journal of Economic Psychology, 30*, 575-582.

O'Carroll, P. W., Berman, A. L., Maris, R. W., Moscicki, E. K., Tanney, B. L., & Silverman, M. M. (1996). Beyond the Tower of Babel: A nomenclature for suicidology. *Suicide & Life-Threatening Behavior, 26*, 237-252.

O'Connor, R. C., & Nock, M. K. (2014). The psychology of suicidal behaviour. *Lancet Psychiatry, 1*(1), 73-85.

Obikane, E., Shinozaki, T., Takagi, D., & Kawakami, N. (2018). Impact of childhood abuse on suicide-related behavior: Analysis using marginal structural models. *Journal of Affective Disorders, 234*, 224-230.

Olfson, M., Blanco, C., & Marcus, S. C. (2016). Treatment of adult depression in the United States. *JAMA Internal Medicine, 176*, 1482-1491.

Olfson, M., & Marcus, S. C. (2010). National trends in outpatient psychotherapy. *American Journal of Psychiatry, 167*, 1456-1463.

Oyesanya, M., Lopez-Morinigo, J., & Dutta, R. (2015). Systematic review of suicide in economic recession. *World Journal of Psychiatry, 5*(2), 243-254.

Park, E.-H., Hong, N., Jon, D.-I., Hong, H. J., & Jung, M. H. (2017). Past suicidal ideation as an independent risk factor for suicide behaviours in patients with depression. *International Journal of Psychiatry in Clinical Practice, 21*(1), 24-28.

Piscopo, K., Lipari, R. N., Cooney, J., & Glasheen, C. (2016). Suicidal thoughts and behavior among adults: Results from the 2015 National Survey on Drug Use and Health. In *NSDUH Data Review*. 2016. Washington, DC: SAMHSA.

Pitman, A., Rantell, K., Marston, L., King, M., & Osborn, D. (2017). Perceived stigma of sudden bereavement as a risk factor for suicidal thoughts and suicide attempt: Analysis of British cross-sectional survey data on 3387 young bereaved adults. *International Journal of Environmental Research & Public Health, 14*(3), e286.

Pitman, A. L., Osborn, D. P., Rantell, K., & King, M. B. (2016). The stigma perceived by people bereaved by suicide and other sudden deaths: A cross-sectional UK study of 3432 bereaved adults. *Journal of Psychosomatic Research, 87*, 22-29.

Qiu, T., Klonsky, E. D., & Klein, D. N. (2017). Hopelessness predicts suicide ideation but not attempts: A 10-year longitudinal study. *Suicide & Life-Threatening Behavior, 47*, 718-722.

Rojas, Y., & Stenberg, S.-Å. (2016). Evictions and suicide: A follow-up study of almost 22 000 Swedish households in the wake of the global financial crisis. *Journal of Epidemiology & Community Health, 70*, 409-413.

Silverman, M. M., Berman, A. L., Sanddal, N. D., O'Carroll, P. W., & Joiner, T. E. (2007). Rebuilding the tower of babel: A revised nomenclature for the study of suicide and suicidal behaviors part 1: Background, rationale, and methodology. *Suicide & Life-Threatening Behavior, 37*, 248-263.

Smith, J. M., Alloy, L. B., & Abramson, L. Y. (2006). Cognitive vulnerability to depression, rumination, hopelessness, and suicidal ideation: Multiple pathways to self-injurious thinking. *Suicide & Life-Threatening Behavior, 36*, 443-454.

Sokero, P., Eerola, M., Rytsälä, H., Melartin, T., Leskelä, U., Lestelä-Mielonen, P., & Isometsä, E. (2006). Decline in suicidal ideation among patients with MDD is preceded by decline in depression and hopelessness. *Journal of Affective Disorders, 95*, 95-102.

Spittal, M. J., Forsyth, S., Pirkis, J., Alati, R., & Kinner, S. A. (2014). Suicide in adults released from prison in Queensland, Australia: A cohort study. *Journal of Epidemiology & Community Health, 68*, 993-998.

Stack, S., & Scourfield, J. (2015). Recency of divorce, depression, and suicide risk. *Journal of Family Issues, 36*, 695-715.

Stack, S., & Wasserman, I. (2007). Economic strain and suicide risk: A qualitative analysis. *Suicide & Life-Threatening Behavior, 37*, 103-112.

Székely, A., Thege, B. K., Mergl, R., Birkás, E., Rózsa, S., Purebl, G., & Hegerl, U. (2013). How to decrease suicide rates in both genders? An effectiveness study of a community-based intervention (EAAD). *PLoS One, 8*(9), e75081.

Tebbe, E. A., & Moradi, B. (2016). Suicide risk in trans populations: An application of minority stress theory. *Journal of Counseling Psychology, 63*, 520-533.

Treadway, M. T., & Zald, D. H. (2011). Reconsidering anhedonia in depression: Lessons from translational neuroscience. *Neuroscience & Biobehavioral Reviews, 35*, 537-555.

Turney, K., Wildeman, C., & Schnittker, J. (2012). As fathers and felons: Explaining the effects of current and recent incarceration on major depression. *Journal of Health & Social Behavior, 53*, 465-481.

Uggen, C., Manza, J., & Behrens, A. (2004). Less than the average citizen: Stigma, role transition and the civic reintegration of convicted felons. In *After crime and punishment: Pathways to offender reintegration* (pp. 261-293). Portland, OR: Willan Publishing.

Van Geel, M., Vedder, P., & Tanilon, J. (2014). Relationship between peer victimization, cyberbullying, and suicide in children and adolescents: A meta-analysis. *JAMA Pediatrics, 168*, 435-442.

Walker, J., Hansen, C. H., Butcher, I., Sharma, N., Wall, L., Murray, G., & Sharpe, M. (2011). Thoughts of death and suicide reported by cancer patients who endorsed the "suicidal thoughts" item of the PHQ-9 during routine screening for depression. *Psychosomatics, 52*, 424-427.

Williams, J., Crane, C., Barnhofer, T., Van der Does, A., & Segal, Z. (2006). Recurrence of suicidal ideation across depressive episodes. *Journal of Affective Disorders, 91*, 189-194.

Wilson, K. G., Kowal, J., Henderson, P. R., McWilliams, L. A., & Péloquin, K. (2013). Chronic pain and the interpersonal theory of suicide. *Rehabilitation Psychology, 58*, 111-115.

Winterrowd, E., Canetto, S. S., & Benoit, K. (2017). Permissive beliefs and attitudes about older adult suicide: A suicide enabling script? *Aging & Mental Health, 21*, 173-181.

Woodford, M. R., Weber, G., Nicolazzo, Z., Hunt, R., Kulick, A., Coleman, T., Coulombe, S., & Renn, K. A. (2018). Depression and attempted suicide among LGBTQ college students: Fostering resilience to the effects of heterosexism and cisgenderism on campus. *Journal of College Student Development, 59*, 421-438.

Wright, A. A., Keating, N. L., Balboni, T. A., Matulonis, U. A., Block, S. D., & Prigerson, H. G. (2010). Place of death: correlations with quality of life of patients with cancer and predictors of bereaved caregivers' mental health. *Journal of Clinical Oncology, 28*, 4457-4464.

Wright, A. A., Zhang, B., Ray, A., Mack, J. W., Trice, E., Balboni, T., Mitchell, S. L., Jackson, V. A., Block, S. D., & Maciejewski, P. K. (2008). Associations between end-of-life discussions, patient mental health, medical care near death, and caregiver bereavement adjustment. *Journal of the American Medical Association, 300*, 1665-1673.

Xie, W., Li, H., Luo, X., Fu, R., Ying, X., Wang, N., Yin, Q., Zou, Y., Cui, Y., & Wang, X. (2014). Anhedonia and pain avoidance in the suicidal mind: behavioral evidence for motivational manifestations of suicidal ideation in patients with major depressive disorder. *Journal of Clinical Psychology, 70*, 681-692.

Yang, B., & Lester, D. (1995). Suicide, homicide and unemployment. *Applied Economics Letters, 2*, 278-279.

Yaniv, G. (2001). Suicide intention and suicide prevention: An economic perspective. *Journal of Socio-Economics, 30*, 453-468.

You, S., Talbot, N. L., He, H., & Conner, K. R. (2012). Emotions and suicidal ideation among depressed women with childhood sexual abuse histories. *Suicide & Life-Threatening Behavior, 42*, 244-254.

Zhang, Y., Law, C. K., & Yip, P. S. (2011). Psychological factors associated with the incidence and persistence of suicidal ideation. *Journal of Affective Disorders, 133*, 584-590.

In: Understanding Suicidal Ideation
Editor: David Lester
ISBN: 978-1-53616-999-7

Chapter 8

DEPRESSION AND SUICIDE IDEATION IN THE VIRTUAL WORLDS OF YOUTH

Jennifer Laffier

ABSTRACT

This study explored how suicidal ideation may be expressed in virtual worlds such as social media sites. To accomplish this, a qualitative case study was conducted on ten youth suicide cases in the United States and Canada. A checklist of signs and symptoms of suicidal ideation guided the content analysis of the data sources related to these cases, such as media reports and social media postings. The findings from this case study provide several insights, such as that both words and images can hint at signs and symptoms of suicidal ideation, and that engaging in social media may solicit negative or positive support for a person experiencing depression. Recommendations for further research and intervention programs on suicide for youth are discussed.

Suicide is a worldwide problem that affects people of all ages and cultures. Youth, in particular, may be at risk of suicide. It is the second leading cause of death for youth in Canada and the third leading cause of death for youth in the United States (Canadian Mental Health Association, 2014). Identified warning signs and symptoms for suicidal ideation help in the development of suicide prevention and intervention programs (American Association of Suicidology, 2010; Canadian Mental Health Association, 2011). It is the early recognition of these warning signs that is essential to preventing suicide (Sakinofsky, & Webster, 2010).

Over the last decade, it has become apparent that social media, such as Snapchat, Twitter, Facebook and YouTube, may act as a vehicle for youth to communicate signs and symptoms of mental health distress and suicidal ideation (Luxton, June, & Fairall, 2012). There is an increased amount of self-disclosure online because adolescents report they are better able to express themselves authentically online perhaps due to the anonymity they feel (Lenhart, Rainie, & Lewis, 2001). Thus, social media have become a key expressive tool for youth in which they may express signs and symptoms of depression and suicidal ideation. The media has covered numerous cases of youths who have died by suicide and communicated their mental health distress through social media such as Facebook, Twitter, Tumblr, and YouTube (Curry, 2012). For example, Jayah Ram Jackson, a 15-year old, communicated suicidal ideation on Facebook prior to jumping to her death (Farrell, 2014).

In a previous study, the present author explored how four youths who died by suicide in Canada and the United States had communicated signs and symptoms on their social media sites (Laffier, 2013). The results of this small case study indicated that the youths displayed numerous escalating signs and symptoms of suicide ideation in their virtual world. However, there is a need for further exploration of how suicidal ideation and mental health distress is communicated online, especially through social media sites. Awareness of how suicidal ideation is expressed in a virtual world can inform the development of intervention and prevention programs for youth suicide. Therefore, the present study explores how youths communicate signs and symptoms of suicidal ideation on social media sites using a larger sample and cross-case comparison to determine informative themes of online behavior. Ten youth suicide cases were explored in the media to examine how social media was used during times of mental health distress. Content analysis of media reports, public interviews, and online communication was used to reveal themes of suicidal ideation. The research questions for this study were identified as: (1) how do signs and symptoms of suicide ideation present within the context of social media for youth suicide cases, (2) what are the common features of online behaviors that are related to suicidal ideation, and (3) how can this information guide intervention and prevention programs.

LITERATURE REVIEW

Global statistics for youth suicide (15-19 yrs. old) indicate that suicide is the second most common cause of death after road-traffic accidents (Wasserman, Cheng, & Jiang 2005). According to the Centers for Disease Control and Prevention (2017), suicide in the United States is the third leading cause of death in young people between the ages of 10 and 24. In the United States, there has been a significant increase in emergency department visits for self-inflicted, non-fatal injuries among children and young adults. There was a 5.7% increase in visits per year from 2008 to 2015 with female tweens and young teens leading the way in this troubling trend (Mercado-Crespo, Holland, Leemis, Stone, Deborah & Wang, 2017). In Canada, youth are among the highest risk populations for suicide, and suicide is the second leading cause of death for youths 10-24 years old (Youth Mental Health Canada, 2019). However, current statistics may be a gross underestimate considering the number of suicide attempts every year that are not recorded (Skinner & McFaull, 2012) and the misclassification of suicide in young people (Hawton, Saunders, & O'Connor, 2012).

There are a number of identified risk factors for suicidal ideation in youth, including social factors such as bullying or break-ups, pre-existing mental health problems, alcohol or drug abuse, stressful life events, exposure to suicide behavior by others, and a family history of suicide (Center for Disease Control and Prevention, 2014, 2017; Child Trends Data Bank, 2012). Depression and loneliness were recognized as the two most influential risk factors for adolescent suicide (American Foundation for Suicide Prevention, 2012; Apter, 2010). Researchers speculate that these two risk factors have a reciprocal relationship, resulting in increased negative impacts on mental health (Lasgaard, Goossens, & Elklit, 2011). Depression is associated with social withdrawal and self-perceived social failure, which can increase the risk of loneliness, in turn causing greater depression (Lasgaard et al., 2011). Unfortunately, many people tend to respond negatively to people suffering from depression, thereby increasing their isolation and feelings of loneliness (Bertera, 2007). They may feel *thwarted belongingness,* a sense that one does not belong to or feel connected with a valued group or relationship, causing both loneliness and anger (Lasgaard et al., 2011).

Additional signs and symptoms of suicide behavior are often classified into three categories: behavioral, cognitive, and emotional. Behavioral signs and symptoms are the visible behaviors and actions that identify suicidal thoughts or feelings. This may include (a) giving possessions away, (b) getting affairs in order (bank accounts, wills), (c) excessive crying, (d) isolating oneself, (e) writing good bye letters, (f) sleeping problems, (g) directly or indirectly expressing a wish to die, and (h) developing a plan for suicide. Emotional signs and symptoms of suicidal ideation may include (a) depression, (b) a sense of hopelessness, (c) emotional pain, and (d) feeling out of control or helplessness. Cognitive signs and symptoms of suicidal ideation include the mental processes and may include (a) negative or pessimistic thoughts, (c) imagining oneself as worthless, and (d) memory and concentration difficulties.

These signs and symptoms may progress in intensity and duration as a person moves towards suicide ideation (Hawton, et al., 2012). According to Wenzel and Beck (2008), the more an individual exhibits negative cognitive content and maladaptive information processing biases, the more likely it is that suicide-relevant cognitive processes will be triggered in response to stressful life events, thus spurring the development of suicidal thoughts. (Burke, et al., 2016). According to this cognitive model of suicide, suicidal acts occur when an individual reaches his or her threshold for tolerating the pain associated with a suicidal crisis. A person may have occasional thoughts of suicide with no real intent if they still have positive thoughts and memories. However, as the events become more painful (increased signs and symptoms) and their thoughts become more biased and increasingly negative (hopeless and helpless) the person may begin to think extensively about suicide.

Recently researchers have noted the role that social media has in adolescents' lives, and thus a potential role in mental health, including suicidal ideation (Luxton, et al., 2012). As children age, there is an increased participation in social media-related activities which is consistent with developmental literature that suggests social connection becomes more important as they move from childhood to the teen years. Between Grade 4 and Grade 11, reading others' profiles increases from 18% to 72%, tweeting increases from 5% to 42%, following friends/family on Twitter rises from 8% to 39%, posting on one's own profile rises from 19% to 50%, and following celebrities on Twitter rises from 5% to 32%. Girls are more likely than boys to report using social media to communicate with family and friends: 45% posted on their own social networking site, compared with 36% of boys (Johnson, 2013). Social networking sites such as Snapchat, Instagram, Facebook, Twitter, blogs, are particularly popular among young people (Zakik & Park, 2013).

Social media represents a new facet of young people's environments; a place where they spend time exploring their identities, expressing themselves, and communicating with friends (Robertson, Skegg, Poore, Williams, & Taylor, 2012). Adolescents are able to experiment with social skills, identities, and receiving support that is less risky than in a face-to-face context (Sun & Hui, 2007). They may be able to present themselves as more "stereotypically desirable" (Fu, Cheng, Wong, & Yip, 2013 pg 2). However, there may be negative effects of this increased self-disclosure and social experimenting. Communicating with known others was found to have more of a beneficial impact while communicating with strangers was found to have more of a negative impact on relationship quality (Blais, Craig, Peplar, & Connolly, 2008). For instance, some people may provide hurtful or antagonizing feedback to vulnerable people online. This may have a negative impact on youths who are communicating signs and symptoms of mental health distress.

Patterns of suicide communication are changing due to the advent of the Internet, especially the use of social media sites (Fu, et al. 2013). There are two views on the link between social media and adolescent suicide: (1) social media increases the risk for youth suicides (Biddle et al., 2008; Lenhart et al., 2012), and (2) social media can be a protective factor against youth suicide (Luxton et al., 2012; Skinner & McFaull, 2012). The first view argues that social media can increase the risk of suicide in several ways. First, social media can offer a 'how to' dictionary for youths considering suicide. Some internet sites promote suicide by offering ideas or support for following through with suicidal acts (Apter, 2010; Hawton et al., 2012). Second, social media can cause suicide contagion; when others learn and mimic suicide behavior through social modelling (Biddle et al., 2008). Social media may allow for the rapid spread of information and rumors within communities, thereby influencing more people (Luxton et al., 2012).

The other view is that social media can act as a protective factor against suicide (Hawton, et al., 2012; Luxton, et al., 2012; Robertson, et al., 2012; Skinner & McFaull, 2012). Social media may provide adolescents a social and expressive outlet, thereby reducing mental health distress (Zazik & Park, 2010). Additionally, social media may act as a prevention aid by offering online support groups or crisis center information (Skinner & McFaull, 2012). However, studies that explore how these sites and information are supportive for people at risk are needed (Hawton, et al., 2012). Another possible benefit of social media is the ability to screen people at risk (Robertson et al., 2012). The monitoring of information by social media sites could facilitate the detection of conversations about suicide. Key words could be identified as high risk when typed into computers, allowing site administrators to send supportive messages to the user. Some social media sites such as Twitter and Facebook are already engaging in such activities (Curry, 2010). However, difficulties such as the differentiated words used to signify suicidal ideation may cause barriers to these strategies. Screening can also come from friends and family members if they were properly trained to identify signs and symptoms of suicidal ideation.

The risks and benefits of social media related to suicide warrants further investigation for a number of gaps have been identified (Skinner & McFaull, 2012). First, although there are avenues for reporting risk factors and presence of suicide ideation, there are still major problems in the objective assessment of suicidal adolescents (Bertera, 2007). Second, there is a need to understand the time sequence that affects suicidal ideation, including how individuals escalate from minor thoughts to frequent ideation (Apter, 2010). Third, there is a need for greater understanding of the factors that contribute to suicide in young people (Hawton, et al., 2012). Lastly, and the gap this study tries to address, there is a need to understand the role that social media plays in the communication of suicidal ideation by adolescents (Hawton, et al., 2012; Luxton, et al., 2012). Further exploration of these gaps could assist in the development of effective prevention and intervention programs for youth.

METHODOLOGY

In order to accomplish this research, which was to explore themes of suicidal ideation in social media communication by youth, a qualitative case study was used with ten public cases of adolescent suicides. A case study design was conducive to describing context and illustrating participants' realities and actions; both essential to fulfilling the purpose of this study (Yin, 2011). Using a small sample size such as ten allowed for detailed descriptions that can uncover patterns of meanings that might be lost with much larger sample sizes (Eisenhart & Graebner, 2007). Additionally, detailed data from ten cases allowed for comparison.

Purposeful sampling was applied in this study in order to select participants who could provide insight and in-depth information about the phenomenon of central importance (Fletcher & Plakoyiannaki, 2010). Selection criterion included: (1) current or prominent cases in the media to increase the available data sources on each case, (2) adolescents similar in age in order to increase the reliability of cross-case comparisons, and (3) adolescents who used social media. Based on these criteria ten cases were selected for this exploratory study. The ten cases involved high school students ranging in ages from 14 years old to 19 years old. All of the adolescents were from Canada and the United States.

In order to understand how the ten adolescents used social media to communicate signs and symptoms of suicidal ideation, public data were collected. This included news archives (online, radio, television, print), public interviews with family and friends, and recorded online social media communications. Unfortunately, access to the social media pages of the youth was limited since many of the sites were shut down following their deaths. Information was available through many media outlets. These data sources were collected, labelled, and put into chronological order to create a time line of events for each youth.

Content analysis, a qualitative data reduction method that attempts to identify core themes and meanings from text or images, was used as it provided the opportunity to understand the adolescents' social reality in a subjective, but scientific, manner (Zhang & Wildemuth, 2009). In particular, a directed content analysis approach was used in which theories and relevant research findings related to suicidal ideation guided the initial coding (Yin, 2009). This involved using a checklist of common signs of symptoms of suicidal ideation created from the literature to guide a review of the data (see Table 8.1).

Each sign/symptom from the checklist was defined as a potential theme (i.e., depression or loneliness). The data was coded by going through each data source and reviewing what the adolescent did on social media sites; including what they wrote, posted, liked, created or browsed. Once a theme was identified from their use of words, images or behaviors it was coded and then entered into a construct table that contained columns for each theme, case and date (Zhang & Wildemuth, 2009; Berg & Lune, 2011). Any new repetitive themes, not fitting the checklist, were also recording in order to expand or extent our understanding of suicidal ideation and social media use. Lastly, conclusions were made from the data; first on a case-by-case basis, and then using a cross case comparison.

Table 8.1. Content Analysis Themes of Suicidal ideation

Emotional	Cognitive	Behavioral
i. depression	i. perceptions of thwarted belongingness	i. social isolation
ii. emotional numbness or pain	ii. hopelessness	ii. sleeping difficulties
iii. feeling out of control or helpless	iii. negative or pessimistic thoughts	iii. giving possessions away
iv. anger	iv. feelings of worthlessness	iv. getting affairs in order (bank accounts, wills)
v. lack of emotional regulation or inability to cope	v. unfounded guilt or shame	v. excessive crying
vi. loneliness	vi. low self-esteem	vi. writing good bye letters,
vii. desperation	vii. memory and concentration difficulties	vii. directly or indirectly expressing a wish to die
	viii. perceptions of lack of supports	viii. developing a plan for suicide
		ix. risky behavior

Theme: the escalation process- represents the increased intensity, frequency and duration of symptoms, increased combination of signs and symptoms.

Sources: American Foundation for Suicide Prevention, 2012; Apter, 2010; Canadian Mental Health Association, 2012; Hawton et al., 2012). American Association of Suicidology, 2010;

RESULTS

The results of this analysis are first presented as individual case studies, and then a cross-case comparison is highlighted. These results are followed by a discussion and recommendations.

Individual Case Presentations

Case 1: Amanda Todd

Amanda, a Grade 10 student from British Columbia, had suffered mental health issues, including anxiety, depression and eating disorders, as well as peer victimization prior to her suicide in October 2012 (Grenoble, 2012). A series of events involving harassment, physical assaults, and cyber-bullying lead to Amanda attempting suicide (Shaw, 2013). Derogatory remarks and insults were left on Amanda's Facebook page after her suicide attempt (Shaw, 2013). During this time, Amanda engaged on social media sites such as chat-rooms, Facebook, and YouTube as a means of expressing herself (National Post, 2012; Todd, 2012). One month prior to her death, she posted a nine-minute video clip to YouTube titled *My Story: Struggling, bullying, suicide and self-harm* (National Post, 2012). In the video she used flashcards, without any verbal communication, to tell of her ordeal. Amanda hinted at feeling *lonely* in one of her slides ("I have no one") (Todd, 2012). She demonstrated a *wish to die* by stating, "I wanted to die so bad," and describing her previous attempt ("When he brought me home, I drank bleach") (Todd, 2012). Amanda's posts also demonstrated hopelessness, depression, perception of lack of supports, inability to cope, and a suicide plan.

Case 2: Jamie Hubley

Jamie, a Grade 10 student from Ottawa, Canada, was openly gay and took his own life in 2011 after years of bullying, depression, and loneliness (CBC, 2011). Jamie often engaged with social media sites. He had his own blog page on Tumblr and used YouTube to post comments or videos of himself (Tumblr, 2011). Early on-line communications from Jamie were positive. He discussed his love for music and hoped to meet others (CTV, 2011). However, over time, his posts became more negative. He expressed frustration and *anger* for being the only open gay male at his school and wanting to find a boyfriend. "I hate being the only open gay guy in my school… It f***ing sucks" (Burke, 2011). Indirect *wishes to die* were expressed several times in his blogs: "I really want it to end," "I am tired of life," and "Maybe in my next life I will be a flying squirrel" (Tumblr, 2011). Jamie's posts also demonstrated hopelessness, depression, anger, pessimistic views, isolation, and escalating behaviors.

Case 3: Felicia Garcia

Felicia was from New York and took her own life in October 2012 by jumping in front of a subway train in front of her classmates (Pow, 2012). Felicia experienced bullying and harassment due to rumors that she slept with members of the football team. This caused her to suffer depression and isolation (Driskill, 2012). Felicia liked to use social media sites such as Twitter, Facebook, Instagram, and YouTube. Although Felicia was described as a private and tough person (Pow, 2012) she demonstrated signs and symptoms of depression and suicide ideation on these sites. She posted a photo of herself on Instagram that demonstrated *depression;* the photo was of her smiling, but the word *depressed* was cut and pasted across her eyes. The caption read, "Just because someone is smiling does not make them happy" (Driskill, 2012).). Two days before Felicia died by suicide, she posted her last tweet saying, "I cant, im done, I give up" (Pow, 2012). The message communicated a *wish to die*, *hopelessness,* and *inability to cope*. Felicia's posts also demonstrated pessimistic views, escalating behaviors, and low self-esteem.

Case 4: Amanda Cummings

Amanda, also from New York, died by jumping in front of a city bus with a suicide note in her pocket two days after Christmas (Chapman & Boyle, 2012). Speculation about the causes of Amanda's death focused on bullying, a history of depression, self-injurious behaviors, and heartbreak over boys (Mackenzie, 2012). For weeks leading up to her death, Amanda posted messages on Facebook chronicling her feelings and thoughts. Signs of *depression* were evident in several posts: "worst sat. nite evr I cnt believe this is happening what did I do to deserve this?", "im spending this sat nite alone in my room crying", and "I am so tired......... fml depressed mood too" (Chapman & Boyle, 2012). Amanda demonstrated *desperation* for help through her Facebook message posted 11 days before her death.

"When I say Im ok I want that one person to look me in the eye, hug me, and say no you are not." On the day she died, she posted a message on Facebook: Nd, I'll die tonight crying over you (Chapman & Boyle, 2012). Amanda's posts also demonstrated anger, pessimistic views, a wish to die, anxiety, isolation, desperation, shame and guilt, low self-esteem, and loneliness, and perception of lack of alternative choices.

Case 5: Rebecca Sedwick

Rebecca, from Lakeland, Florida, died by jumping off a building when just 12-years-old. She was terrorized on her social media sites causing her severe anguish, ultimately leading to her death (Tampa Bay Times, 2013). For example, up to fifteen girls told Rebecca to "commit suicide" on her Facebook page (Daily News, 2013). Rebecca communicated warning signs about a *planned suicide.* For example, she searched websites to see how many Advil tablets she would need to die (Tampa Bay Times, 2013). She demonstrated a *wish to die* by changing her messenger name on 'Kik' to '*that dead girl.*' Hours before jumping off a building, Rebecca messaged a boy she had met on a social media website indicating a *severe sense of hopelessness.* She wrote she was "*dead*" and wrote "*I'm jumping, I can't take it anymore*" (Tampa Bay Times, 2013). Rebecca also demonstrated a wish to die, a plan for suicide, and desperation.

Case 6: Olivia Liv Penpraze

Olivia, 19-yrs. old, was taken off life support in April 2012 after a suicide attempt left her in the hospital with irreversible absence of brain activity (BlogHer, 2012). She suffered mental health problems including depression and anxiety. "I have been severely depressed since 2007 (Penpraze, 2012)). Olivia posted numerous videos on social media sites such as YouTube, Vblog, and Veimo announcing her *sense of hopelessness.* For example, she wrote: "The last few weeks everything is just going down and down, like how I feel," and "I've been trying so hard to be happy, but I just can't anymore." In her videos and vblogs, she revealed a *lack of support.* "None of my friends know anything about me, they fall for my fake smiles and laughs, they believe I am FINE." In her videos, she communicates she is *unable to cope*: "I just can't do it anymore," "I can't hide it anymore," and "don't know what to do anymore" (Penpraze, 2012). Olivia demonstrated all of the signs of suicidal ideation, such as not being able to imagine the future, anger, a wish to die, a suicide plan, anxiety, escalation of emotional pain, and low self-esteem.

Case 7: Adrian Alvaresz

Adrian, a 15-year-old from Austin, Texas, died by a self -inflicted gunshot wound. He shot himself in front of classmates at school. On the day he died, Adrian posted a photo of himself on Facebook holding a gun to his face with a caption that indicated that he was planning on taking his own life (Farrell, 2013). Hours before his death, Adrian posted a suicide note on Facebook: "I Just Whant To Say I Am Taking My Life Away, Not For My Ex but Cause I Am Tired Of Being Who I Am....Also I Am Taking My Life Away Because Everyone Has Always Put Me To the Side" (Farrell, 2013). Beyond these direct *expressions of wanting to die* and a *suicide plan*, he demonstrated feelings of *isolation* and *desperation, perceptions of lack of supports*, and *negative thoughts* in several comments: "I'm taking my life away cause everyone has always put me to the side, I had try asking for help. My life hasn't been easy," and "I'm taking my life away...because of I'm tired of being who I am" (Farrell, 2013). Adrian also demonstrated signs of not being able to imagine the future, perception of lack of supports, negative attitude, getting affairs in order, and making amends with people.

Case 8: Jayah Ram Jackson

Jayah, a 15-year-old living in New York City, jumped to her death after suffering online bullying on her social media sites. Her peers wrote comments on Facebook such as "petition for Jayah to either get prettier, smarter, or dead" (Stieber, 2014). Jayah's wrote a response to this: "i am actually just going to wait for someone to make a petition for me to kill myself because it's inevitable...like, we all see it coming". This message indicates feelings of *isolation, desperation, hopelessness.* This message was posted two days before she took her life. Jayah wrote frequent comments on Facebook and Ask.fm that demonstrated a severe sense of *hopelessness*; “I used to have the intense desire to be respected, or at least liked....It rarely ever worked out. I don’t care anymore”. She expressed her *wish to die* by writing comments such as “Its been six months since I have cut my arms, and because it has been so long I have been considering suicide a lot more frequently” (Farrell, 2014). Jayah also demonstrated signs of not being able to imagine the future, perception of lack of supports, pessimism/negative attitude, desperation, and low self-esteem.

Case 9: Maddie Yates

Maddie from Kentucky died by unknown methods in April 2014. She suffered from depression and anxiety for which she was taking medication (Clayton, 2014). Maddie was very active on social media sites such as YouTube and Teen Ink, posting make-up tutorials and poems. Her postings and videos started to escalate in volume and intensity, demonstrating severe *hopelessness* and *negative attitudes*: “I just can’t do it anymore,” and “I just don’t see how this is a bad idea because it’s like someone’s on the 12th floor, and the room behind them is on fire. And they’re standing on the window ledge and they have a choice whether or not to jump and get away from the fire or just stay and die a slow, excruciating death. It feels like that” (Clayton, 2014). In her poem entitled *Falling Asleep*, she wrote, “My heart is gone, My mind is blown. This is over, It will not grow” (Teen Ink, n.d). In her online biography, Maddie wrote, “none should blame you for walking out early”, indicating a *wish to die*. Maddie also demonstrated signs of not being able to imagine the future, lack of alternative choices, making amends with people, escalated emotions, and personal shame/guilt.

Case 10: Jam Rodemyer

Jam was a 14-year-old boy from Williamsville, New York. Jamey was openly gay and suffered from severe online bullying from peers at his school. His peers left him messages on his Formspring account such as; "JAMIE IS STUPID, GAY, FAT ANND [sic] UGLY. HE MUST DIE!", and "I wouldn't care if you died. No one would. So just do it.” Jamey advocated for gay rights via You Tube videos, and blogging. His main You Tube video which was titled "It Gets Better Project," was intended to reassure LGBT youth that life improves and gets better. This video was posted in May 2011, and Jamey took his own life on September 18, 2011, after posting a final goodbye message on his Tumblr blog; expressing the wish to see his grandmother who had recently died. Prior to this on September 8 2012, Jamey made it evident that he *wished to die* as he posted lyrics to a song that included the line, "I just wanna say good bye, disappear with no one knowing. ... I don't wanna live this lie, smiling to the world unknowing" (ABC News, 2011). Jamey also demonstrated signs of anger, pessimism/negative attitude, and desperation.

A Cross-Case Comparison

A cross-case comparison was conducted to identify common themes in the ten cases. The most common and notable symptoms of mental health distress and suicide ideation expressed by the teenagers were depression, emotional pain, loneliness, thwarted belongingness, and hopelessness. These symptoms were expressed in direct words, phrases, or pictures by the youths. All the youths showed a combination of these symptoms to varying degrees.

Final good-bye messages were written on the social media sites by seven of the ten youths: Amanda Cummings on Facebook, Jamie on his blog, Felicia on Twitter, Rebecca on an unknown SMS, Adrian on Facebook, Jayah on Facebook, and Maddie on You Tube. Within two days of these messages being posted, five of the seven youths took their life; Amanda, Jamie, Felicia, Adrian, and Maddie.

Bullying was a common factor in the lives of eight of the ten youths: Felicia, Jamie, Amanda Todd, Amanda Cummings, Rebecca, Olivia, Jayah, and Jamey. Six of the adolescents, Amanda Todd, Amanda Cummings, Felicia, Rebecca, Jayah, and Jamey experienced cyberbullying and harassment through their social media sites. The very sites they used to express themselves became a vehicle in which others could post derogatory remarks about their death and personal character. Two of the three male cases were openly gay. Both of these youths, Jamie Hubley and Jamey Rodemeyer, suffered severe bullying due to their sexual orientation. Three of the ten youths, Amanda Todd, Maddie and Jamey, spoke out against bullying through social media: Amanda Todd creating a Prezi presentation, Maddie posted poems and remarks on her sites, and Jamey posted to his blog about National Suicide Prevention Week and bullying.

Reaching out for help on social media was performed by nine of the ten youths, either directly or indirectly. In some cases, specific requests for help were made. For example, Amanda Todd wrote on a card shown in her YouTube video, "I need someone." Amanda Cummings wrote, "when I say I am okay, I want one person to look me in the eye, hug me, and say no your not" on Facebook. The one youth described as 'tough,' Felicia, did not make any requests or appeals for help. She often portrayed emotions of anger and no indications of trouble in her life. Seven of the nine youths who did reach out for help online received negative comments from individuals on their social media sites.

The youths varied in their use of social media; some posting more regularly than the others. The two teenagers described as 'sensitive', Jamie Hubley and Amanda Cummings, used their social media sites more frequently and expressed more private emotions and thoughts. Thus, their escalation process was easier to detect. Key words were detected in the cross-case comparison such as 'tired,' 'lonely,' and 'can't.' Five of the ten youths, Felicia, Jamie, Rebecca, Olivia, and Maddie used the phrase "I can't" close to the end of their life.

Conclusion and Recommendations

Several insights as to the role social media plays in youth suicide were gained from this exploratory study. As researchers noted, social media can play an active role in revealing the mental health state of youth (Luxton et al., 2012). Social media can reveal moods, cognitive processes and symptoms. The most common and notable symptoms of mental health distress and suicide ideation expressed by these ten youths online were *depression, emotional pain, loneliness, thwarted belongingness and hopelessness*. These symptoms were expressed in the direct words, phrases, or pictures that the youths posted or made evident by their browsing and commenting activities. It is the growing combination and intensity of these symptoms that contributes to the escalation process. As Wenzel and Beck (2008) suggested, the individual develops biased and distorted cognitions leading to increased symptoms and risk of suicide. These symptoms should be highlighted in suicide programs, specifically the ways they can be expressed in an online environment. For example, hopelessness may be conveyed through written words, such as 'why bother?' or 'nothing ever changes', or be apparent in personal pictures, images or memes that a person posts or browses. Intervention programs should also focus on addressing the cognitive distortions that lead to symptom intensity and frequency. Effective treatments such as cognitive behavior therapy or mindfulness training can be utilized (Mental Health Commission of Canada, 2014).

It is evident that social media sites can record information similar to a personal journal, revealing mood patterns and activities over time. Such online journals can be useful for detecting any escalation of mental health problems, such as depression or suicidal ideation. When experiencing thoughts of suicide, death or emotional pain becomes more frequent; the person has fewer good days and becomes preoccupied with their symptoms (Living Works Education, 2012). They begin to view and interpret the world in a negative manner due to information processing biases (Burke et al., 2016). This was particularly evident for Jamie Hubley and Amanda Cummings whose negative posts escalated over time. However, the findings from this study suggest that personality characteristics may affect the amount of time a person uses social media sites and the amount of personal or sensitive information that someone shares. For example, Jamie Hubley and Amanda Cummings were described as 'sensitive' and posted more often. When in emotional distress people may post more often because they feel better able to express themselves due to the anonymity of social media (Lenhart, Rainie, & Lewis, 2001). Individuals who do not use social media as much may not demonstrate a clear escalation process of symptoms over time for others to detect. Awareness about the escalation process of suicide ideation should be a part of suicide prevention programs particularly designed to address online environments.

Personality characteristics and conflict management styles may also affect the way a person reacts to feelings of thwarted belongingness, depression or loneliness. Some teenagers may convey sadness due to being left out, whereas others convey anger. This difference was evident between Felicia Garcia and Amanda Todd. Although Felicia was distressed due to the things happening in her life, she hid it with anger or indifference. We often assume that people will clearly show sadness or depression, and that is not always the case. Research shows that people may present as happy or unaffected by negative experiences (the outward signs), yet they are still experiencing symptoms (MHCC, 2014). Differences in personality, defense mechanisms, conflict resolution styles and covert vs. overt signs and symptoms should be discussed in intervention programs for youth suicide.

Unfortunately, social media may act as a double edge sword for people experiencing depression. It can provide support or cause pain. Researchers have suggested that communicating with known others may have a beneficial impact, while communicating with strangers may have a negative impact on relationship quality (Blais, et al., 2008). This contradiction was evident in several cases, especially in the case of Amanda Todd. Her social media sites became a channel for strangers to follow and harass her. After she posted her YouTube video clip, she received numerous derogatory and hurtful remarks on her Facebook page and YouTube comments section (Grenoble, 2012). In addition, Amanda Cummings continued to receive negative messages from strangers on her social media sites even after her death. The more they presented depression or needing help, the more they risked isolation from their peer group. This may be because people tend to isolate others showing depression (Lasgaard, et al., 2011; Sun & Hui, 2007). The greater vulnerability people show online to strangers, the more of a target they may be for harassment. Suicide prevention programs should include this information in order to inform youth of the importance of privacy settings online and how or where they can reach out for help.

Bullying was a common factor in the lives of seven of the ten youth. Bullying may not have been the key trigger for their suicides, but bullying could have been a contributing factor (Sun & Hui, 2007). All of the seven youths expressed concerns about being bullied, and their social media sites became a way for others to bully them at all hours and in all of their environments. The inability to escape can lead to feelings of hopelessness and helplessness which contribute to depression (MHCC, 2014). Awareness programs should discuss cyber-bullying as a risk factor for suicide escalation and encourage others to act as empathic bystanders. Specific strategies for addressing the online bullying should be presented, since many youths say that they do not intervene because they do not know what to do or that they think it will not help.

Many social media sites such as Snapchat, Facebook, Instagram, YouTube, and Tumblr allow users create videos, pictures, collages or personal pictures. Choices in pictures and creative displays can reveal emotions, according to research in the field of creative therapies (Malchiodi, 2011). Feelings of loneliness and depression can be communicated through images such as the way Felicia Garcia communicated her feelings of depression in her photo of herself with the word depression cut and pasted over her eyes. Most suicide intervention and awareness programs do not consider online adaptations of signs and symptoms of suicide or severe depression, especially for visual presentations such as videos and pictures. Methods of reviewing photos for signs or symptoms of suicide or depression should be explored, especially for social media sites geared towards youths who are exploring their creative instincts (Malchiodi, 2011).

Posting suicide notes on social network sites in place of hand-written notes is a recent phenomenon (Ruder, Hatch, Ampanozil, Thalil, & Fischer, 2011). In the cases presented in this study, social media offered a venue for seven of the ten youths to leave a suicide note or a final message. Viewers should take these notes seriously, especially since this study found that five of the seven youths took their life within 48 hours of their final messages. This suggests a short time-span for intervention. Therefore, crisis intervention methods for online use should be discussed in awareness programs. Currently Facebook, Instagram, and Twitter have methods for people to report concerns for suicidal behavior, and this information could be reviewed.

In addition, posting a suicide note or goodbye message on a public site may give more pressure for teens to follow through with their actions. A hand-written note can be kept private and discarded if the teenagers change their mind, but messages on social media sites remain forever once posted. Teenagers, who value toughness or credibility, may feel they need to 'walk the walk' among their peer groups. If final messages posted online point to an immediate crisis and crucial timeline, then immediate crisis responses need to be explored in training.

The words we choose are often a reflection of our current cognitive and emotional states. Several key words were identified in this study. The word *can't* was used by five of the ten youths close to the end of their lives. The word *can't* is associated with a feeling of *no alternative* (Oxford Dictionary, 2010). This word may signal feelings of hopelessness and helplessness. Such key words should be highlighted in suicide programs to identify an escalation of symptoms and desperation that may require crisis intervention.

Awareness of signs and symptoms, risk factors and intervention methods in an online environment are key aspects for the intervention and prevention of suicide. To do this effectively, further research is needed on how signs and symptoms of suicide can be communicated online, especially with larger sample sizes and a study of mediating factors such as age, gender, culture and personality. The virtual world is where many of our youths live today. In order to be supportive and protective of them as educators, guardians or community workers we need to enter and understand that virtual world.

REFERENCES

ABC News. (2011). *Gay Buffalo Teen Commits Suicide on Eve of National Bullying Summit.* Retrieved May 2, 2012 from http://abcnews.go.com/Health/gay-buffalo-teen-commits-suicide-evenational-bullying/story?id=14571861.

American Foundation for Suicide Prevention. (2014). *Risk factors for suicide.* Retrieved from https://www.afsp.org/understanding-suicide/risk-factors-and-warning-signs.

American Foundation of Suicide Prevention (2012). About suicide: Facts and figures. Retrieved from http://www.afsp.org/index.cfm?page_id=04EA1254-BD31-1FA3-C549D77E6CA6AA37.

American Association of Suicidology. (2010). *Stats & tools: Warning signs.* Retrieved from www.suicidology.org/web/guest/stats-and-tools/warningsigns.

Anon. (2012). *The cry for help the web didn't answer*. Retrieved March 19, 2014 from http://www.blogher.com/cry-help-web-heard-and-didnt-answer.

Apter, A. (2010). Suicidal behavior in adolescence. *Canadian Journal of Psychiatry*, 55, 271-273.

Berg, B. L., & Lune, H. (2011). *Qualitative research methods for the social sciences* (8th ed.). Las Angeles, CA: Allyn & Bacon.

Bertera, E. M. (2007). The role of positive and negative social exchanges between adolescents, their peers and family as predictors of suicide ideation. *Child & Adolescent Social Work Journal, 24,* 523-538.

Biddle, L., Donovan, J., Hawton, K., Kapur, N., & Gunnell, D. (2008). Suicide and the Internet. *British Medical Journal, 336*, 800–802.

Blais, J. J., Craig, W. M., Peplar, D., & Connolly, J. (2008). Adolescents online: The importance of internet activity choices to salient relationships. *Journal of Youth & Adolescence, 37*, 522–536.

BlogHer. (2012 May 16). *The cry for help the web didn't answer.* Retrieved May 2, 2014 from http://www.blogher.com/cry-help-web-heard-and-didnt-answer

Boyle, L. (2013). *I'm taking my life away because I am tired of who I am: Tragic final Facebook post of student 16, who killed himself in front of his school class.* Retrieved February 18th, 2014, from http://www.dailymail.co.uk/news/article-2464117/Adrian-Alvarez-Teen-killed high-school-wrote-suicide-note-Facebook.html.

Brown, K., Cassidy, W., & Jackson, M. (2006). Cyber-bullying: Developing policy to direct responses that are equitable and effective in addressing this special form of bullying. *Canadian Journal of Educational Administration & Policy, 57*. 1-36.

Burke, A. (2011, October 18). Gay Ottawa teen who killed himself was bullied. *CBC News, Ottawa*. Retrieved from http://www.cbc.ca/news/canada/ottawa/story/2011/10/18/ottawa-teen-suicide-father.html

Burke, T. A., Connolly, S. L., Hamilton, J. L., Stange, J. P., Abramson, L. Y., & Alloy, L. B. (2016). Cognitive risk and protective factors for suicidal ideation. *Journal of Abnormal Child Psychology*, *44*, 1145–1160.

Canadian Broadcasting Centre (2011). Gay Ottawa teen who killed himself was bullied. Retrieved from http://www.cbc.ca/news/canada/ottawa/story/2011/10/18/ottawa-teen-suicide-father.html.

Canadian Mental Health Association. (2014). *Fast facts about mental health.* Retrieved May 6 2014 from http://www.cmha.ca/media/fast-facts-about-mental-illness/.

Canadian Mental Health Association (2012). Mental Health First Aid Manual. Ottawa: Author.

Canadian Psychiatric Research Foundation (2005). *When something is wrong: Ideas for teachers*. Toronto, Canada: The Walsh Group.

Canadian Journal of Educational Administration and Policy, *57*. Retrieved September 20, 2011 from .http://umanitoba.ca/publications/cjeap/articles/brown_jackson_cassidy.html

Centre for Addictions and Mental Health (2010). *Suicide Prevention and Assessment Handbook*. Toronto: Author.

Centers for Disease Control and Prevention (2017). *Preventing Suicide*. Retrieved from https://www.cdc.gov/violenceprevention/suicide/fastfact.html.

Chapman, B. & Boyle, C. (2012, January 3). Staten Island teen Amanda Cummings kills self by jumping in front of bus after being bullied. *The New York Daily News.* Retrieved from http://www.nydailynews.com/new-york/staten-island-teen-kills-jumping-front-bus-family-cites-bullies-article-1.1000243.

Chapman, B., Kemp, J., Siemasko, C., & Tasch, J. (2012, October 25). Tormented 15-year-old Felicia Garcia jumped to death in front of train after bullying over sex with football players. *Daily News*. Retrieved from http://www.nydailynews.com/new-york/15-year-old-throws-front-train-staten-island-article-1.1191808.

Child Trends Databank. (2012). *Teen homicide, suicide, and firearm death: Indicators on children and youth.* Retrieved May 2, 2014 from http://www.childtrends.org/?indicators=suicidal-teens.

Clayton, T. (2014). *A high school student committed suicide after posting a message of her intent on YouTube.* Retrieved on April 20, 2014 from http://www.buzzfeed.com/tracyclayton/ahigh-school-student-committed-suicide-after-posting-a-mess.

CTV News (2011, October 7). Ottawa teen details final suicidal thoughts on blog. Retrieved rom http://www.ctvnews.ca/ottawa-teen-details-final-suicidal-thoughts-on-blog-1.712337.

Curry, C. (2012, March 29). Facebook taking proactive stance against suicides. ABC news, 29 March. Retrieved from http://abcnews.go.com/US/facebook-social-media-sites-working-offer-suicide-sers/story?id=16029673#.ULg3cYP4KSo.

Daily News, (2013). *Rebecca Sedwick case: Both suicide victim and bully grew up in 'disturbing' family environments, cop says*. Retrieved on May 2, 2014 from http://www.nydailynews.com/news/national/rebecca-sedwick-case-suicide-victim-bullygrew-disturbing-family-homes-article-1.1496991.

Driskill, K. (2012, October 28). Another tragic result of bullying, Felicia Garcia jumps in front of train. *The Examiner.* Retrieved from http://www.examiner.com/article/another-tragic-result-of-bullying-felicia-garcia-jumps-front-of-train.

Eisenhart, K. M., & Graebner, F. E. (2007). Theory building from cases: Opportunities and challenges. *Academy of Management Journal*, 50(1), 25-32.

Farrell, P. (2014). *Photos Jayah Ram Jackson the gifted nyc girl who jumped to her death*. Retrieved March 19, 2014 from http://www.heavy.com/news/2014/02/jayah-ram-jackson photos-pics-facebook-ask-fm/14/.

Farrell, P. (2013). *Teen father commits suicide at high school: 5 fast faces you need to know*. Retrieved February 17, 2014, from http://www.heavy.com/news/2013/10/adrian-alvaresz student-suicide-lanier-high-school-austin/.

Fletcher, M., & Plakoyiannaki, E. (2010). *Sampling in case study research: Encyclopedia of case study research.* Thousand Oaks, CA: Sage Publications,

Fu. K., Cheng, Q., Wong, P., & Yip, P. (2013). Responses to a self-presented suicide attempt in social media. *Crisis*, 34, 406-412.

Greenwood, H., Leach, C., Lucock, M., & Noble, R. (2007). The process of long-term art therapy: A case study combining artwork and clinical outcome. *Psychotherapy Research, 17*, 588-599.

Grenoble, R. (2012, October 11). Amanda Todd: Bullied Canadian teen commits suicide after prolonged battle online and in school. *The Huffington Post*. Retrieved from http://www.huffingtonpost.com/2012/10/11/amanda-todd-suicide-bullying_n_1959909.html?utm_hp_ref=amanda-todd#slide=1637677.

Guba, E. G., & Lincoln, Y. S. (1994). Competing paradigms in qualitative research. In N. K. Denzin & Y. S. Lincoln (Eds.), *Handbook of qualitative research* (pp. 105-117). Thousand Oaks, CA: Sage.

Hawton, K., Saunders, K. E. A., & O'Connor, R. (2012) Self-harm and suicide in adolescents. *Lancet, 379*, 2373-2383.

Johnson, D. (2013). The online lives of Canadian youth. Retrieved June 8, 2019 from https://vanierinstitute.ca/online-lives-canadian-youth/.

Kaplan, A., & Haenlein, M. (2009). Users of the word unite! The challenges and opportunities of social media. *Business Horizons. 53,* 59-68.

Laffier, J. (2013). Exploring how youth communicate signs and symptoms of suicidal ideation through social media. In Michel Walrave et al. (Eds), *Youth 2.0: Social Media and Adolescence, Connecting, Sharing, and Empowering*, Toronto, Canada: Springer.

Livingworks Education (2012). *Suicide intervention trainer manual.* Calgary, Canada: Author.

Lasgaard, M., Goossens, L., & Elklit, A. (2011). Loneliness, depressive symptomatology, and suicideideation in adolescence: Cross-Sectional and longitudinal analyses. *Journal of Abnormal Child Psychiatry, 39,* 137-150.

Lenhart, A., Rainie, L., & Lewis, O. (2001). *Teenage life online: The rise of the instant- message generation and the internet's impact on friendships and family relationships.* Washington, DC: Pew Internet and American Life Project.

Luxton, D., June, J. & Fairall, J. (2012). Social media and suicide: A public health perspective. *American Journal of Public Health, 102*(S2), 195-200.

Mackenzie, C. (2012, January 7). Heartbreak for family at funeral of 15-year-old who killed herself because of bullying- and are still bombarded with hate messages on tribute page. *The Daily Mail.* Retrieved from http://www.dailymail.co.uk/news/article-2083504/Amanda-Cummings-suicide-Hate-messages-Facebook-tribute-page.html#axzz2JhfcgBnC.

Malchiodi, C. (2011). *Handbook of Art Therapy*. New York: Guildford.

McKenzie, C. & Keneally, M. (2012, January 17) Bullying NOT the reason why 15-year-old girl jumped in front of the bus even though her death was taunted online. Retrieved from http://www.dailymail.co.uk/news/article-2087854/Amanda-Cummings-suicide-Bullying-NOT reason-15-year-old-jumped-bus.html#ixzz2fg9ay9sJ.

Mercado-Crespo, M., Holland, K., Leemis, R., Stone, D., & Wang, J. (2017). Trends in Emergency Department visits for nonfatal self-inflicted injuries among youth aged 10 to 24 years in the United States, 2001-2015. *Journal of the American Medical Association, 318,* 1931-1933.

Mitchell, K., &Ybarra, M. (2009). Social networking sites: Finding a balance between their risks and benefits. *Archives of Pediatric Adolescent Medicine, 163*, 87–89.

Mydeathspace (2012, January 7) *Amanda Cummings (15) jumped in front of a bus after posting suicide threats on Facebook.* Retrieved from http://mydeathspace.com/article/2012/01/07/Amanda_Cummings_%28 15%29_jumped_in_front_of_a_bus_after_posting_suicide_threats_on_ Facebook.

National Post. (2012, October 12). *Weeks after posting haunting* YouTube video on her years of torment at classmates' hands, 15-year-old B.C. girl commits suicide. Retrieved from .http://news.nationalpost.com/ 2012/10/12/amanda-todd-suicide-2012/.

Ortiz, E. (2013). Texas teen who committed suicide at school posted Facebook warning. Retrieved February 17th 2014, from http://www. nydailynews.com/news/national/texas teen-posted-facebook-warning-school-suicide-article-1.1488343.

Park, B., Im, J., & Ratcliff, K. (2013). Rising youth suicide and changing culture context in South Korea. *Crisis*, 35, 102-109.

Penpraze, O. (April, 2012) *Olivia Penpraze tells her story*. [Video file]. Retrieved http://www.youtube.com/watch?v=RzjFf8ywk3c.

Penpraze., O. (December 2012). Olivia Penpraze video. [Video file] Retrieved http://www.youtube.com/watch?v=ed026xgAOE4.

Portzky, G., & Heerington, K. (2006). Suicide prevention in adolescents: a controlled study of the effectiveness of a school-based psycho-educational program. *Journal of Child Psychology & Psychiatry 47*, 910–918.

Pow, H. (2012, October 25). 'I can't. I'm done. I give up': Bullied teen jumps to her death in front of train as schoolmates look on in horror just days after harrowing tweet. *The Daily Mail.* Retrieved from http://www.dailymail.co.uk/news/article-2223133/Felicia-Garcia-suicide-Bullied-teen-jumps-death-train-schoolmates-look-horror-just-days-harrowing-tweet.html#axzz2JhfcgBnC.

Robinson., J., Cox, G., Malone, A., Williamson. M., Baldwin, G., Fletcnher, K., O'Brian M. (2013). A systematic review of school-based interventions aimed at preventing, treating, and responding to suicide-related behavior in young people. *Crisis, 34*, 164–182.

Robertson, L., Skegg, K., & Poore, M., Williams, S., & Taylor, B. (2012). An adolescent suicide cluster and the possible role of electronic communication technology. *Crisis, 33*, 239-245.

Ruderi, T. D., Hatch, G. M., Ampanozil, G., Thalil, M. J., & Fischer, N. (2011). Suicide announcement on Facebook. *Crisis, 32*, 280–282.

Sakinofsky, I., & Webster, G. (2010). The epidemiology of suicide in Canada. In J. Cairney & D. L. Streiner (Eds.), *Mental Disorder in Canada: An Epidemiological Perspective*. Toronto, Canada: University of Toronto Press.

Shaw, G. (2013, March 13). Amanda Todd's mother speaks out about her daughter, bullying. *The Vancouver Sun.* Retrieved from http://www.vancouversun.com/news/Amanda+Todd+speaks+about+daughter+death/7384521/story.html.

Skinner, R., & McFaull, S. (2012). Suicide among children and adolescents in Canada: Trends and sex differences, 1998-2008. *Canadian Medical Association Journal 184*, 1029-1034.

Sun, R. C. F., & Hui, E. K. P. (2007). Psychosocial factors contributing to adolescent suicidal ideation. *Journal of Youth & Adolescence, 36*, 775-786.

Stieber, Z. (2013). *Adrian Alvaresz identified as dead Lanier High School student.* Retrieved February 18, 2014, from http://www.theepochtimes.com/n3/319215-student-commits suicide-adrian-alvaresz-identified-as-dead-lanier-high-school-student/?photo=2.

Stieber, Z. (2014). *Jayah Ram Jackson, nyc jumps to her death after bullying (+photos).* Retrieved March 19, 2014, from http://www.theepochtimes.com/n3/508834-jayah-ram jackson-nyc-teen-jumps-to-her-death-after-bullying-photos/.

Tampa Bay Times, (2013). *Lakeland girl commits suicide after being bullied online*. Retrieved March 19th 2014 from http://www.tampabay.com/news/publicsafety/crime/12-year-old girl-bullied-online-commits-suicide/2141435.

Teen Ink, (n.d). *Falling asleep.* Retrieved May 3rd 2014, from http://www.teenink.com/poetry/free_verse/article/360317/Falling-Asleep/.

Todd, A. (September 2012) *Cyber Bullying* [Prezi Presentation]. Retrieved from http://prezi.com/atoa68wrotkm/cyber-bulling/.

Todd, A. (October 2012) Amanda Todd's Story: Struggling, Bullying, Suicide, Self-Harm. (video file). Retrieved from .http://www.youtube.com/watch?v=ej7afkypUsc.

Todd, C. (2012). Amanda Todd Legacy Webpage. Retrieved from http://amandatoddlegacy.org/.

Tumblr (2011). Tumblr tagged Jamie Hubley. Retrieved from http://www.tumblr.com/tagged/jamie-hubley

Vancouver Island Crisis Line. (n.d). *Suicide awareness and response.* Retrieved April 23, 2014 from http://www.vicrisis.ca/facts-about-suicide/.

Warren, L. (2014). *I'm doing the whole world a favor. Heartbreaking farewell video, girl 16 posted to You Tube before committing suicide.* Retrieved April 20 from http://www.dailymail.co.uk/news/article-2607248/Im-doing-world-favor-Heartbreaking farewell-video-girl-16-posted-YouTube-committing-suicide.html.

Wenzel, A., & Beck A.T (2008). A cognitive model of suicidal behavior: theory and treatment. *Applied & Preventive Psychology*, *12*, 189–201.

Wenzel, A., Brown, G. K., & Beck, A. T. (2009). *Cognitive therapy for suicidal patients: Scientific and clinical applications*. Washington, DC: American Psychological Association.

Willig, C. (2008). *Introducing qualitative research in psychology: Adventures in theory and method* (2nd ed.). England: McGraw Hill/Open University Press. Retrieved from http://site.ebrary.com.proxy1.ncu.edu/lib/ncent/docDetail.action?docID=10246330.

Wasserman, D., Cheng, Q., & Jiang G. (2005). Global suicide rates among young people aged 15 to 19. *World Psychiatry*, 4(2), 112-120.

Yin, R. K. (2009). *Case study research: Design and methods.* Los Angeles, CA*:* Sage.

Youth Mental Health Canada, (2019). *Youth mental health stats in Canada.* Retrieved from https://ymhc.ngo/resources/ymh-stats/.

Zhang, Y., & Wildemuth, B. M. (2009). Qualitative analysis of content. In B. Wildemuth (Ed.), *Applications of Social Research Methods to Questions in Information and Library Science* (pp. 308-319). Westport, CT: Libraries Unlimited.

Zazik., M., & Park., M. (2010). To tweet, or not to tweet: Gender differences and potential positive and negative health outcomes of adolescents' social Internet use. *American Journal of Men's Health 4*(1) 77–85.

In: Understanding Suicidal Ideation
Editor: David Lester
ISBN: 978-1-53616-999-7

Chapter 9

MAD DOG AND SONGBIRD: THE (G) FACTOR*

Frank S. Bailey

ABSTRACT

The purpose of this personal experience, narrative investigation is to describe how spirituality and religiosity mitigated suicidal ideation through the lived experiences of two individuals born and raised in the United States. "Mad Dog," a Native American male from a lower economic class, and Songbird, a Caucasian female from a middle economic class, are the primary participants. In separate, serious suicide attempts, Mad Dog consumed drain cleaner, and Songbird ingested non-prescription drugs, exacerbating what they considered unendurable situations. Data collection consisted of documents, interviews, and observations (participatory and non-participatory) over time. A laryngectomy, speech impediment, and dysgraphia impair Mad Dog's communication, so creative non-fiction was employed with negotiated outcomes. Checks were used to confirm the result. The study addresses: (i) how poor self-image and negative framing affected the participants; (ii) how the constructs of religion and spirituality changed their

* An unabridged version of this chapter may be obtained by writing to the author.

perspective following near-fatal suicide attempts; and (iii) how those constructs lift and protect them now. The results illustrate how cognitive reframing through the constructs of fundamental Christianity (e.g., the innate worth of every person, purpose, and hope) can alleviate psychache and suicidal ideation.

I was in a unique position to study issues related to suicidal ideation through the lived experiences of two former suicidal individuals from different walks of life. My role was translator, transcriber, and outcome negotiator recording the impact religiosity and spirituality can have through the lens and utterances of the primary participants. Practical applications are discussed in the unabridged version which is available by request from the author.

The focus is on four common causes of suicidal ideation which presented in coding, how the two individuals developed them, and how they were assuaged. The areas include (bolstering) self-image, (establishing) purpose, (evoking) hope, and (re)framing circumstances. For Mad Dog's story, I employed creative non-fiction because of communication issues; I fact-checked the data, filled in the blanks when I had difficulty making connections, then fact-checked again. For Songbird's story, I kept written interviews verbatim except for some grammatical and punctuation editing so that her voice would feel real. In both case studies, I attempted to achieve what Schwandt (2015) referred to as verisimilitude; factual, yet compelling research.

BACKGROUND

Conceptual Framework

A point of reference for this research was non-classical psychology, the advent of which is generally credited to Vygotsky (Kravstova, 2007). Whereas classical psychology follows the investigative paradigm of the natural sciences (i.e., observable physical phenomenon investigated by scientists), non-classical psychology departs from the paradigm of objective knowledge and is "understood within a metacognitive, metatheoretical framework" (Robbins, 2010, p. 5). Stimulus (S) and Response (R) are terms used in classical psychology that refer to environmental behavioral influencers. Organism (O) refers to self-determined, self-regulated behavior and thought. When noted psychologist Gordon Allport studied how each influenced behavior he observed "a very small S and a very small R and a very, very big O" (Leontiev, 2007, p. 21).

Additionally, according to Nespor (1987) beliefs are immensely powerful, can have a stronger impact on affect than knowledge, and generally operate independently of cognition associated with knowledge. In other words, beliefs may influence why people engage in healthy or unhealthy thinking despite knowledge and sometimes independent of knowledge. Fenstermacher (1979) suggested that applying objective data to personal beliefs may change them, but Nespor (1987) added that, for that to happen, they must be supplanted by alternative or new beliefs. This concept is important because the two participants embraced an alternative belief system that mitigated suicidal ideation. That phenomenon is what I call the God (G) factor.

The following themes surfaced in the analysis. Each appears to have had a significant impact on the participants' battle with suicidal ideation and consequential recovery. Note that previous research confirms the impact each theme has on suicidal ideation.

Self-Esteem

Research indicates that negative self-esteem can play a significant role in suicidal ideation and suicidal behavior among adolescents and young adults (Wilburn & Smith, 2005; Creemers, Scholte, Engels, Prinstein, & Wiers, 2012; Manani & Sharma, 2013). The results are supported by a recent meta-analysis (Soto-Sanz, Piqueras, Rodríguez-Marín, Pérez-Vázquez, Rodríguez-Jiménez, Castellví, & Cebria, 2019). Furthermore, using phenomenological methodology, Rasmussen, Dyregrov, Haavind,

Leenaars, and Dieserud (2018) connected poor self-esteem to suicide among men with no previous attempts or mental health treatment.

Purpose

During World War II, Victor Frankl (1963) spent approximately 18 months enslaved in concentration camps. He endured, and watched others endure, indescribable physical and psychological suffering. During his incarceration, he observed that prisoners who were able to identify a purpose were more apt to overcome thoughts of suicide. He founded *logotherapy* on that observation (Leslie, 1965). Linehan, et al. (1983), studied factors that prevent suicide and, of the six factors they identified, two involved having sense of purpose. Using regression analyses, Heisel and Flett (2004) found that purpose significantly mediated other suicidal risk factors. They concluded that their results validated assessing and addressing existential themes with suicidal persons.

Hope

Extensive research indicates that hopelessness commonly accompanies suicidal ideation (Beck, Brown, & Steer, 1989; Klonsky, Saffer, & Byron, 2018; Minkoff, Bergman, Beck, & Beck, 1973). Shneidman (1996) included hopelessness in the top ten list of common traits that suicidal individuals share. Ellis (2014, p. 143) suggested that hopelessness may be the "best validated risk factor for suicide" and that it is universally addressed in therapy (implicitly or explicitly).

(Re)framing

Seligman and Csikszentmihalyi (2000) formalized modern positive psychology. Positive psychology involves the study and praxis of the systems that influence productive outcomes of individuals, groups, and organizations. According to Peterson (2009), the thrust of positive psychology is fourfold (a) regard experiences positively; (b) explore and promote balanced psychological traits; (c) recognize and reinforce relationships germane to positive psychological positioning; (d) understand the role broader institutions play and advance them.

Practical application of positive psychology can be found in the model of learned helplessness and learned optimism. Seligman (1990) suggested that individuals can overcome negativity by learning to be optimistic. He posited that negativity can be transformed by reframing experiences. The premise is that pessimism and optimism are learned and, therefore pessimism can be unlearned, or converted to optimism. The process of reframing experiences begins in an individual's thought life. Gerber, Reiff, and Ginsberg (1996) credited reframing processes for helping some adults overcome stigmas and practical challenges associated with learning disabilities. The adults in the study who reframed their disabilities emerged more resilient and self-actualized.

MAD DOG'S STORY[1]

Drinking drain cleaner may not have been the best way to kill myself, but a double shot should do it, so I thought. I had *had* it and saw no reason to live. Happiness was a vague memory, and hope had become an abstract concept. My childhood was filled with heartache, my adolescence tumultuous, and my adulthood characterized by rejection and heartache. There was no other way.

I was born in April of 1956 in Gallipolis, Ohio. Like most parents, I imagine that mine were excited to bring me home, but my mother was raised in an orphanage and didn't know much about raising children, while my father had schizophrenia. Complicating matters, I had a speech impediment and at the age of six needed speech therapy. A little-known

[1] These personal accounts have been edited to help readers. For the original transcripts write to the author.

auditory processing condition proved to be the cause of my speech issue and corresponding learning problems, but the diagnosis would not be made until I was 40 years old. Children aren't always kind and understanding toward kids who seem different so, to them, I was just stupid and peculiar. School was traumatic, and I think I burdened and embarrassed my parents. One day, when I was seven, I came home from school and my family was gone. Everything and everybody were gone. My mother, father, and four siblings had packed and moved. They came back late that night and found me with the neighbors and tried to justify how they had forgotten me. It was a preview of things to come.

Legal trouble began when I was eight. Not having enough food, my brothers, sister, and I attempted to steal some plums by hiding them under our armpits. I got caught. Ironically, because speech quirks had rendered me incoherent, the store owners could not understand my explanation, gave up, and let me go. Later that year my mother took what little money we had and the family car, and abandoned us. I was twenty-one before I ever saw her again.

Parenting responsibilities for the five of us fell on the shoulders of my father but, because of mental health issues, he was not capable of providing for our needs. Shortly after my mother fled, the family broke up more. Dad could not afford to keep us together, so my older brother joined the navy, another stayed home, and the rest of us went to an orphanage built for Civil War orphans called the Ohio Soldiers and Sailors Orphanage, in Xenia.

The orphanage was not exclusively Catholic, but mass was held, and we had devotions every night. I remember a story told by the nuns about how a mother hen protected her chicks during a fire and how she sacrificed herself for them. She was referring to how Jesus sacrificed Himself for us. Unfortunately, I was young and didn't remember too much more. I do remember having habitual dreams about driving a lawn mower and pulling other kids behind it on a wagon, a dream that proved prophetic. I spent two and a half years in that orphanage, and things did not get better for a long time.

When I was eleven my dad took my sister, brother, and me back, and six months later my aunt took us all in. During that time, my sister and I broke into several churches looking for money and just for fun. We accidentally burned one down, got caught, and were sent to a group home and eventually to a foster home. Our foster parents were Christians, and I remember them talking about Jesus and how He would let children sit on His lap. I thought they were nuts. Soon after, my sister ran away, and we all ended back home with dad. I was twelve.

Meanwhile my aunt had left, and Dad had remarried. I did not get along with my stepmother, and I got picked on in the neighborhood because of my speech impediment. Frequent fights ensued, and I desperately wanted to move. I reasoned that if the house burned down, we would *have* to move, and I knew how to do that. But after several attempts, I concluded that I couldn't do anything right. Everyone was right. I *was* a loser.

Eventually I got caught and was sent to juvenile detention. Several months later they were going to let me go, but my stepmother did not want me. I was transferred to a Columbus, Ohio, juvenile "lock-up." The main purpose was to relieve society of a threat. Clearly, I was not the type of kid that you wanted as a next-door neighbor, but the staff earnestly tried to determine the cause of my issues. I tried to make the most of it and became a steady worker, earned favor, and was given special privileges. Partly because of my status, other kids wanted to associate with me. It wasn't much but, for the first time in my life, I felt like, if not a winner, then a little less like a loser. Eventually, my dad and stepmother heard that I had become a good worker. They took me in and gave me a homecoming gift - a paintbrush; I was sixteen.

Back in school I was promoted even though I couldn't read or write. I am pretty sure the goal was to get me out ASAP. During the week I would endure school, and the teachers would endure me. On the weekends, I would do drugs. But one thing that I retained from my stint in Columbus was a taste for work. I had no aversion to hard work or long hours. Despite habitual drug abuse, I somehow managed to stay out of trouble for nearly four years, eventually getting a ticket for operating under the influence of liquor. A few months later, I was out drinking with some friends, and we came across a car that had been driven into a lake. Knowing opportunity when it knocked, we took everything worth taking and some things not worth taking. My stature and distinctive Native American features made me highly recognizable, and so it is no wonder that I was apprehended quickly. Add a history of delinquency, and I was an easy catch for the state police. I only got a few days in jail, but the abbreviated incarceration was balanced with an extended probation period that was hung over my head. One mistake, and I would be tossed back in.

Having learned to work, I found employment as a cook and, at 21, I got married. My fiancé and I had dated for three years; most of our dating involved drugs and alcohol use. As the wedding date approached, I had second thoughts, but I didn't want to hurt her or disappoint her family. It was like being on a moving train. As the wedding plans gained speed and momentum, jumping off felt impossible. Looking back, I should not have been so concerned by her feelings. After we got married, our pattern of regularly scheduled (and unscheduled) drug parties continued. I worked, and we partied. Along the way my wife became pregnant twice. Unashamed, we aborted both children. I was working up to seventy hours a week and, when my wife requested that I work less, I looked for a different job. Then she complained I was home too much. It wasn't long before I found out she just wanted more chances to sleep with my friends. Our marriage ended on that note. We were married two years.

From childhood on and through a failed marriage my life was defined by rejection. As a boy we moved constantly, and I was often separated from one sibling or another, from one parent or both. I often felt abandoned, and I *was* abandoned. At 13, I had my first smoke, chugged my first drink, and experienced my first blackout. It became a lifestyle that I pursued relentlessly, and my years were spattered with dreadful (often self-inflicted) chaos. My life had started out roughly and went downhill from there and I had *had* it. My wife's escapades with my friends put me over the edge. I could not stand thinking about it, but it was all I could think about. Rejected again, I experienced sleepless night after sleepless night. In July of 1980, I got up and filled a double shot glass with drain cleaner.

I didn't get it all down before I began puking blood. I ran outside, grabbed the garden hose and put it in my mouth. I spun the valve and turned the water on full blast. Pain and terror enveloped me. The water would not go down because my digestive system was rejecting the acid. My insides were in upheaval. I threw-up drain cleaner, and some of it landed on my arm. The scars are still there. My head was exploding, and my belly was on fire. I was in trouble and it hurt, but the emotional pain was worse. I was not sorry. The emptiness I carried day in and day out, night in and night out, seemed to be inescapable, and I wanted out.

Confident of pending success and imagining it would be more comfortable to die in a hospital, I managed to call for help. I informed the receptionist between chokes, vomiting, and spitting up blood and flesh what I had done and where I was. Not waiting for back-up, the emergency responders rushed to the scene where there was no need to inquire if I were the person they were looking for. They tossed me into the ambulance and rushed to the hospital.

A week later I was still on life support, and my chances of survival were slim to none. I overheard a surgeon tell the staff that I must still be alive for a reason and, to the surprise of everyone, I was released after seven weeks. Nevertheless, the doctor had given up, told my father that I would die, and referred me to someone else to deal with it. I certainly was not trying to live, nor did I care to.

In the hospital I was amply drugged and in my element, so to speak. When I was released, the prescriptions ceased, so the pain increased. My belly had shriveled up and, whenever I ate, by way of a feeding tube in my stomach, I got severe cramps. I dropped to around 95 pounds in a short period of time (my ideal weight is 185). I was greatly disappointed with not getting the job done, and then the dark clouds of depression set it.

The medical staff was working for free. I didn't have money or insurance, but they found the case interesting. The stomach shrinkage was not immediately apparent. It was three months before they figured it out and my stomach was removed. At the same time, the team prepared to replace my esophagus with part of my large intestine. But the surgeons didn't take enough intestine and had to cast-off at my neck just above the clavicle. In other words, I now had an esophagus/intestine dangling from my shoulder. Their goal was to keep my feeding tract open until they figured out what to do. They had entered unchartered territory.

One of the side effects was awful acid reflux. Stomach acid spewed out of the tube, down my shoulder and onto my chest. The purpose of stomach acid is to dissolve what we eat. Because it does not discriminate food from flesh, my chest and shoulder often became its unintended target. But again, to the surprise of many, I gained enough strength to prompt the doctors to attempt a procedure used in Russia. I was told that, in Russia, when unmarked bottles of lye were mistaken for homemade vodka, this kind of thing happened. Tissue was extracted from my shoulder, rolled into a tube, and attached to the makeshift esophagus. The tube ended at the base of my neck. In the meantime, I had become a social liability. In most circles, having stuff spill out your chest and onto the carpet is considered bad manners. In addition, my voice had become deep and gravelly. Dogs became uneasy, and they often growled or hid. I was a freak.

Three years later I was still eating from the feeding tube. The hospital was no longer willing or able to foot the bill which, as you can imagine, had become astronomical. The state was also unwilling to pay for the ongoing medical expense. Compounding the constant physical trauma was intense emotional distress. Looking back, it's kind of funny but, had I not been afraid of guns, I would have ended it all.

In 1982, I went back to my father's house in Gallipolis, lived on welfare and social security, and managed sobriety for about a year. Then I began consuming alcohol by pouring it down my feeding tube. At first, I was amazed at how little it took and was delighted by the economy, but the effects were inconsistent. I absorbed liquid through my intestines and satisfying intoxication often required a case of beer. I remember frequent blackouts. During one episode, I fell backwards and put a hole in the wall with my head. Beer and my life were going down the tubes, but I didn't care. If I died it would have been all right.

In 1986, the closure in my throat opened enough for me to consume food. Ironically the tube would clog—the damage was the result of *drain cleaner* after all! When that happened, I had to stand on my head to clear it. Between welfare and social security, I had enough money to cover some medical expenses, including enlargement of the circumference of my esophagus. I underwent multiple endoscopy procedures to dilate my esophagus, but none of them worked very well.

In 1988, surgeons at the University of Toledo extracted more intestine from my belly, and a small section of the upper "esophagus" was replaced. The surgery took many hours which was longer than it worked. Back on life support and confused from anesthesia, I flipped out and yanked all the tubes, wires, and gizmos I could reach. Alarms sounded, and I tried putting everything back in place but couldn't. Later, I wouldn't let the staff replace the devices. So, they just watched me. Once again, I sunk to the deep depths of despair. I was without purpose. I felt no hope. Self-esteem had died long ago, but once again, I survived.

After I moved to a new city to escape jail time for drug-related activities, I was reaching the critical point again and harboring suicidal thoughts. A psychiatrist at the tribal center asked me to telephone her before I acted on them. After a short time, I made the call. An ambulance transported me to the hospital where I was placed in detox and on suicide watch. I remember observing a man sitting in the hall and noticed that he had not moved for a week. When I walked by, I diverted my eyes, and I remember thinking, "At least *I* have a bed!" Eventually I realized that it was not a man at all. It was a dummy put there as a Halloween prop. I was the real dummy, but that incident played a part in my recovery. I went back to my room, sat on the bed, and contemplated how I had fallen into such a mental and emotional abyss. I thought, "What are you *doing* here?"

After ten days, I was moved 150 miles to a substance abuse unit. A counselor talked me into going to a residential facility for chemically dependent people. I was not enthusiastic, but my options were limited - treatment or death. Making one of the first good decisions in my life, I chose treatment and asked God to help me listen to those trying to support me. Prior to my divorce, my wife and I were visited by a couple from a local church. They shared the message of forgiveness, hope, and purpose in Christ. We realized they had what we were really looking for and prayed that God would forgive us. We did not continue to pursue religion or spiritual things, but the seeds had been sown and, now, the seeds were taking root. A tiny sprout had emerged, and I soon made another prayer. I knew that it was unlikely that I would ever be able to earn a paycheck again, but I asked God to give me a job, any job, so I would have something to live for, a purpose.

Remarkably, I soon found myself sought by other residents at rehab. They began looking to me for guidance and support. The staff even joked that I had a following. Could this be an answer to my prayer? Could this be my purpose, my "job?" My spirits began to lift. My entire life had just been a matter of endurance. As the focus of my attention shifted off myself and onto others, so did my attitude and sense of purpose, which in turn affected my sense of self in a positive way. People began turning to *me* as a role model! If *this* guy could hang in there, if *he* could overcome the things he has, so could they. I looked a wreck, the history of my misery was broadcast every time I spoke, and I owned nothing. I had limped through life trying to "get it" and for the first time, I felt like I had.

I successfully completed the program and my conversations with God have become a regular part of my daily routine. The seeds sown by the church visitors 1979 found fertile ground. The Bible indicates that I am special, that God knit me together in my mother's womb, and that I was made in the image of God. It says that I have a purpose, that He has plans for me, and it gives me hope. My favorite promise of all is from Psalms (139:13); "He will wipe every tear from their eyes. There will be no more death or mourning or crying or pain. All these things are gone forever." I just look at things differently. In addition, I was hired by the same rehab center to transport clients to doctor appointments, court hearings, meetings, and so forth. Do you remember the dreams I had of pulling kids around on a wagon? I like to think there is a connection.

Because of health issues, I may not be here long (I have astounded a lot of people already). As long as the Lord lets me live, I will be an anomaly. I might breathe my last breath tomorrow, but I believe that that breath will precede my first breath in the presence of the Almighty. I look forward to hearing Him saying, "Well done, good and faithful servant," and I especially look forward to singing.

SONGBIRD'S STORY

Songbird was in the bathroom a long time, too long, so I called to her. She had been depressed, struggling with anxiety and sleep issues, eating problems, substance abuse, and serious thoughts of suicide. Two weeks earlier she carried out a near-fatal suicide attempt. When I called, she did not answer, so I forced my way in and found her lying on the cold linoleum floor with her head behind the clothes hamper. *"God, I've lost her!!!"* Rushing over, I lay down and held her, perhaps for the last time.

She was limp and unresponsive, but her skin was warm, and she was breathing! I placed my hand underneath her head and gently raised it. She opened her eyes. A sickening dread engulfed me as I looked around the room to see if this was another suicide attempt. I was beset by a cacophony of emotion, at once grateful she was alive and fearful that she would die in my arms. Multiple suicide attempts are common. One attempt predicts others.

I did not notice anything out of place, so I asked her if she had taken anything, but her eyes were dull. I asked again. With an almost imperceptible shake of the head, she indicated that she had not, but I was far from convinced. To determine if she was coherent, I asked if she knew who I was. Her hesitation made me doubt that she did and, when she did not respond promptly, I repeated the question. This time she nodded, but through cloudy, unfocused eyes. Still not sure that she understood the question, I persisted; "Who am I? Can you tell me who I am?" With considerable effort and in a soft, barely audible tone she reached out. "Daddy*?*"

Home from NICU

Songbird was born two minutes after her fraternal twin sister, Olivia. The girls were carried full-term, but they were small. Of the pair, Songbird was the smallest, weighing just over three pounds. She was transferred to the neonatal intensive care unit at a better equipped hospital, and Olivia came home. We bonded as I took time off from work to rock and feed her. I watched closely as she hovered around three pounds, lost weight, and then slowly gained again. She stabilized without major incident and, soon, Songbird came home to be reunited with her twin sister and get acquainted with her siblings. We were delighted! Songbird joined her former womb-mate, Olivia, a three-year-old sister, and a six-year-old brother. Her homecoming was greatly anticipated. We were relieved and thrilled. Neighbors were constantly asking for updates, and I could not contain my excitement.

Infancy

After a wobbly beginning, Songbird had come home to a promising situation. I was gainfully employed, and my wife focused her energies on being a homemaker. We lived in a modest house in a picturesque town with a unique combination of aesthetic appeal, educational opportunities, and cultural events. For a while, everything was fine.

Smootchable

Songbird could not remember much about her pre-school days. Others described her as happy, affectionate, and well-adjusted. Standard health screenings and regular visits to a pediatrician did not disclose issues of any kind. If anything was amiss, it was not discerned by siblings, relatives, or neighbors. Songbird fit in and was altogether kissable.

Sadly, when the twins were three years old, my wife asked for a divorce, and I was awarded physical custody of the children. The girls were enrolled in kindergarten and assigned to the same teacher. On the first day of school, I watched as they held hands, looked both ways before crossing the street, and skipped across the field toward Tall Oaks Elementary School. The scene repeated itself many times during the year, but I will always remember that first day. I was quite certain that a cuter pair could not possibly exist.

Olivia had an easier go of it, but Songbird held her own. As hoped, Olivia helped and encouraged Songbird academically and, to some extent, socially. Compliments came from school, church, and neighbors about how polite and pleasant the girls were. They were a popular pair and often had friends over to play. Little ones would knock on the door and inquire whether one or the other was available—it didn't matter which. It was unusual if the girls weren't together anyway. The girls negotiated kindergarten without issues, going to school enthusiastically, and coming home happy. Songbird described her teacher with affection:

"She was always so nice to us. She was always in a cheerful mood. She gave us candy and was never mean." Likewise, her teacher remembers Songbird with fondness, "She was fanciful and fit in well."

Songbird attended summer school between second and third grades as part of the Title I program to improve her reading skills. She was eligible for services again in fifth grade, but I declined. Songbird's academic deficits were not pronounced, and I felt that I could help her just as well at home. Songbird liked my decision, stating that she did not want to be labeled or ostracized. Mid-way through elementary school I remarried. Songbird's stepfamily included six children ages three to fourteen and, within a year, a half-brother was added. By December of her fourth-grade year, there were ten children in the household. Three of the girls were in the same grade: Songbird, Olivia, and Ruthie. As improbable as it may seem, the transition was relatively smooth, and the atmosphere at home was warm and happy. Songbird expressed positive feelings about growing up in our large blended family:

"I have a twin, an older sister, and an older brother. We always got along well. I have three stepsisters who I am very close to and love very much. They have always been there for me in my life even though I wasn't always in their lives. I am so blessed. I also have three stepbrothers and a half-brother. Family is family. They are all so important to me. Being a kid, you didn't have to worry about anything, and I played outside a lot. I felt good about myself. I was pretty happy then. I didn't like that I was shy though. I felt like I took longer to grow up than most kids because I was still playing outside when others were playing with make-up. I liked to walk in the woods and play outside. I liked to play with my Beanie Babies and dolls. We had a golden retriever named Daisy who died when I was in 4th grade, I think. I used to dress her up in my clothes. I loved our new dog, but Daisy was my favorite." She did tend to compare herself with others, particularly her twin sister who seemed to be good at everything:

"For the most part I did not feel successful in school. I couldn't even count to 100 in kindergarten and had to attend summer school in 2nd grade. This made me feel less smart than others. Also, my sister would make fun of me and tell me I had a learning disability. I felt like I wasn't as social. I was shy, so I didn't have as many friends as some kids. There were times when I felt insecure, but I also felt unique because I didn't mind being by myself. I felt like I didn't wear the clothes that were 'in' but wore what I wanted, and so it made me feel like I didn't fit in. Also, I wasn't friends with the cool kids as much as Olivia was. She always had more friends than me. But I also felt unique because I didn't mind being by myself. I believed in God and went to Bible camp a lot in the summer."

Middle School

Songbird entered middle school with the exuberance typical of adolescence. She gradually increased her autonomy from Olivia, but they would see each other often, and the three sisters (step and natural) shared various classes, participated in common extra-curricular activities, and mingled at lunchtime and between class periods. Homework was a joint venture that took place at the dining room table.

With the help of her sisters, Songbird maintained average grades in most of her classes. She was behind Olivia and Ruthie academically, but not far behind Ruthie who was a year younger. In eighth grade, I requested that Songbird and Ruthie be placed in the same math class so that they could work together on assignments and study for tests, while Olivia was placed in a more advanced class. This proved to be beneficial. Ruthie guided Songbird through math class, confessing several years later that if she had not given her the answers, Songbird would have flunked.

Songbird was on the cross-country team and participated in choir. YMCA dances were a highlight for all the girls. They took turns primping at home and at their friends' houses before making the scene. Up to that point, there was no indication that Songbird was having serious academic difficulty, social issues, or emotional fluctuations atypical of girls her age. Reports from school were positive. Her behavior and affect at home were appropriate, and she was well received by peers. Her stepmother remembers her as "one of the darlings of the family." She seemed to be navigating puberty successfully and generally maintained an upbeat, positive outlook. This is how she described it:

"Middle school years were the best years of my life. I felt carefree, and I also felt like I had friends. I was pretty much friends with everybody. I loved middle school because I felt like I didn't have to be responsible yet, and I didn't have very many worries. It was exciting to have crushes on boys and gossip with friends. I liked who I was in middle school. I liked to go to YMCA dances and get ready for it at friends' houses. I also loved birthday parties. I enjoyed going for long walks and watching movies like *Lord of the Rings* with Ruthie and my stepbrother. I also liked running cross country. I enjoyed watching basketball games at school." But later in the same interview she confided:

"I compared myself by how outgoing and talkative other people were. While I was quiet and shy, mostly I always wished I wasn't and could talk to people more easily. I also compared myself with people, and I was jealous of the things they had. Some of my friends seemed to get whatever they wanted. I also compared myself with popular girls, and I knew I would never be popular. I felt okay about myself, but I often wished I was more outgoing and social like my friends. I wanted to be popular and hang out with the popular girls in middle school, but I was quiet and not as outgoing as they were, so it didn't last for a long time. We were still friends of course, but we didn't really hang out much. I jumped from friend to friend, but I was friendly with everyone. I was not popular, but I accepted that. Olivia would invite me to hang out with her girlfriends, and

I would tag along sometimes although I felt awkward because I was quieter.

"My favorite subject was social studies because it was mostly book-work, and I was good at that. I also find it interesting. I enjoyed choir as well. I liked it because I enjoyed singing in concerts and being part of something. My least favorite subjects were math and English. I have always been bad at math and usually got bad grades. I didn't like English because I hated grammar and punctuation. I didn't really feel successful in school, but I didn't really care.

"I didn't have a strong relationship with God then. I believed that he sent his son to die for me and that I was a Christian. I prayed, but only for selfish reasons. Like if something was going right, I would thank him. I didn't truly put my trust in him fully as I do now."

High School: Chuggy

Songbird was excited about high school because she "only had four years of school left." The four teenagers shared a vehicle to get to and from school that they nicknamed Chuggy, an ancient Plymouth Voyager with a mismatched door. It was a four-cylinder minivan that could run on three. Every morning, Mary, Songbird's stepmother, would fix breakfast and brown-bag lunches for the seven siblings still at home, and the teens would pile in the van. Chuggy emitted heavy gray-white smoke and left a vapor trail down the street and around the corner, accompanied by a chugging sound. The kids often made fun of the vehicle, but their affection for it was obvious. Years after it was recycled, they reminisced about it with laughter and fondness. But despite the camaraderie, comments from family members, personal observation, and by her own account, it was early in high school that things began to trouble her:

"Growing up, I felt good about myself. I knew I was never popular or had a lot of friends, but I liked and accepted myself. Probably up till the point of 9th grade." Songbird listed her three closest friends during her first years in high school, and her best friend was stepsister Ruthie. Olivia was omitted from her list. They were, "growing apart, but not in a bad way." Songbird admitted to using drugs, and she recalls an auditory processing problem that included significant impairments in consistency of responding to auditory stimuli and in auditory memory (especially recall):

"I was excited because I knew that I had only four years of school left. I never really liked school. I was also excited because high school was different, and I felt more cool and older. I didn't have too big of a social life. My only friends were Ruthie, Dee, and Kerry. I didn't feel like I fit into high school very well because I was quiet and not really outgoing, and so my social life sucked.

"My favorite teacher was Mr. Taz. He was easy going and fun, and his class was easy. My least favorite teacher was my Spanish teacher. She was annoying and would always yell 'Hola' down the hall. I think I failed her class. I liked English best because my teachers were always nice, and I was good at it. Math and foreign languages are hard for me because I am not good at memorizing and would always forget what I just learned.

"Overall, I felt average in school. I didn't feel successful, but I didn't feel like a failure either. If I was trying my hardest, I felt okay. I didn't do a whole lot of extra-curricular things in high school. I liked to read, listen to music, and work out. I had ups and downs about my feelings about myself. I didn't like how I was quiet, and I felt like a loser sometimes. I compared myself too much with others, and that made me feel insecure. I didn't totally dislike myself, but I didn't accept myself for who I was. In high school, I stopped believing in God. I didn't believe Jesus died for me. I had lost my faith.

"The first time I used drugs and alcohol I was 15 and had gone camping with friends. I pretty much passed out on the picnic table. I had only three beers and smoked some pot, but it was my first time. I knew then that I wanted to do it again. I felt cool. All I could think about after that was when I could get more or drink again."

It was during this sensitive period when she received a brutal letter from a close relative with negative comments about her acne, weight, and intelligence. The writer of the letter sent a copy to Friend of the Court, and they forwarded it to me. We sent her on a vacation to visit her grandmother and aunt in Florida for some love and affirmation as we contemplated what to do next.

Back home, relationships became strained and prior to her junior year, Songbird decided she would like to live with her biological mother 2,000 miles away. "I was tired of living in a small town, and I felt there was nothing for me in Crossbridge. I wanted a better life, and I missed my mom. The first days at the new school were very hard. I didn't know anyone, and the school was huge. I floated around lunch tables, and I didn't feel like I fit in with anyone. I don't have very good memories of those first days. I didn't make friends right away."

It was during her first year at the new school that auditory processing disorder (APD) became apparent. "Not many people hear or know about APD. I sure didn't until I was diagnosed with it at age 17. I didn't really notice my brain was slower at processing info until I was diagnosed with APD. After that though, I started noticing how, for example, when someone said a joke and everyone would laugh, I would laugh after everyone was done. Sometimes I just give up when someone is talking too fast and stop listening because I can't keep up with what they are saying. My brain just gets so tired sometimes from studying and processing information that it feels like my head will explode or just shut down. Sometimes it just drains me and sucks up all my energy. I feel embarrassed sometimes and frustrated by my APD. I know I'm not stupid, but it would be nice to be on the same level as everyone. It feels as if I'm hard of hearing sometimes. When someone tells me something, I misinterpret what they say. It's like my brain makes up words, but I just process it wrong.

"My senior year had its ups and downs. I loved the school I was attending, Possibility Institute, and my teachers there were so kind and helpful. When I was going through anorexia, they worked with me so that I could go to treatment and still graduate. Me and my best friend Hilda had fun together and were always hanging out. I was working as a cashier at the grocery store and loved it.

"The low points were my DUI and getting heavy into pills. I don't remember some of my senior year. Going to treatment for anorexia was really tough. Also, my stupid boy-friend was crazy, and I had to deal with him. Another low point was not getting along with my mom and thinking suicidal thoughts. Graduation went well, but ended up bad in the end because I bought pills afterwards and disappointed everybody. The first part of my senior year was happy and exciting but, after I got my DUI, everything went downhill, and it was a nightmare. I was anorexic, suicidal, and couldn't stop doing pills."

Slippery Slide

The downward slide accelerated. Songbird continued to vacillate spiritually, lost her moral compass, sense of purpose, hope, and thoughts of suicide became more frequent:

"I wasn't really optimistic about my future. I wasn't sad about it, but I didn't know what I wanted to do career-wise, and it was frustrating because it seemed liked all of my peers knew what they wanted to do. I honestly didn't think about my future a whole lot. I just went with the flow. Plus thinking about my future always stressed me out.

"I ended up in my first rehab when I was 19, the fall after I graduated high school. My mom said I had to go or find another place to live. I had nowhere else to go, so that's how I ended up there. She had had enough of my pill popping and drinking. It was a 30-day program, but my counselor said that I didn't 'get it,' so I ended up staying another 60 in the extended program. At first, I hated it and I remember that I couldn't even talk. I just cried at first. It was government-funded for a lot of people, and some of them came from the streets. I was scared at first but, once I went to the extended program, we got more freedom and outings. I stayed sober for five months. I still didn't have a relationship with God. I came up with my own concept of God, but obviously, it didn't help!

"My second experience was different from my first. By that point I knew I was an alcoholic after my mom found about ten empty vodka bottles stashed in my closet. I still had my car and didn't get in trouble with the law. I went to a place called Shiloh Hacienda in Glacier, Texas. I really liked it there and worked hard. I was there for about 26 days. I believed that this was it, and I could stay sober for the rest of my life. I was 21 then. I still had my own concept of a higher power, not the Christian God but my own God. Again, it failed or rather, I failed.

"When I got out, I moved into another sober house about 30 minutes away in a small town. There were two other girls living in the same house who I been with in rehab. I went to a lot of meetings and worked at Mama Mia Pizza. I had a sponsor, and we met often. It was a big sober community with a lot of young people. I got along well with all the girls and had my car, and life was pretty good."

Dark Days in Texas

Despite the turbulent journey, Songbird tried to stay connected to family, but not to me. I was unaware of her dark days in Texas:

"I lasted almost six months again after I had my 2nd relapse. I left the sober house and went to visit my uncle for a while in Michigan. I really didn't have any expectations. I was just trying to survive at that point. I guess I wanted to test the waters again, and I thought that this time is going to be different. I can control it. I stopped going to AA meetings, and I felt lonely. At first it was okay, but then it quickly progressed and was worse than it ever was before. I spent all my money, made excuses, and stopped caring about the people and things that were important to me. When I did stop drinking for a few days, I had horrible sweats and cravings. The guilt was too much for me. I had already messed up and had consequences, so I figured what's the use? I just felt so ashamed and felt as if I had failed everyone. I still did not have a relationship with God. I was thinking that my life was hopeless, and there was no way out. I lost my family's trust, and I felt that I couldn't get it back. I felt like a failure. I thought suicide was the answer to my drinking problem. I simply wanted to die and not be on this earth anymore. I didn't have a relationship with God. I didn't really think about Heaven and Hell. I convinced myself there were no such things. I didn't want to be alive anymore. I couldn't stop drinking, and I was a loser, a failure, and a selfish person.

"I had thought about suicide ever since I was a teenager, but I never felt desperate enough to act on it before. I thought about suicide for a long time the night I tried it. I knew that it would be painful, but I didn't care. I also knew that it was selfish but, when you're trapped in addiction, you don't think about how your actions may affect others. I just wanted out of the hellhole I was living in. I saw myself as hopeless, a failure, friendless, worthless, and an ugly person. I saw myself as self-centered with no talents and nothing to live for. I thought others saw me as selfish, irresponsible, and untrustworthy. I didn't want to be alive anymore."

When am I Going Die?

"The night I took the Tylenol, I was in the room next to my bedroom. I was on the computer for a longtime that day looking up ways how to commit suicide on Tylenol. I remember reading stories on Yahoo about people saying that they tried to do it or knew someone who had done it. Everyone said, "Don't try it because it's extremely painful." I had been really depressed for a while and couldn't stop drinking. I was so tired of failing everyone I loved. I honestly didn't think anyone would miss me if I died. I thought I was a big burden to everyone. My uncle knew I was drinking again and so did my mom. I thought it was the end of the world, and I didn't know how to make things right again. It was nighttime when I took the Tylenol, and I had been drinking vodka. My Uncle Billy was in the living room watching TV when I was in the bathroom taking the pills. My thoughts were focused on one thing and that was wanting to die and end my pain. I did not want to be a burden to my Uncle Billy or my mom anymore.

"I don't remember how long it was after I took the Tylenol, but I started throwing up pretty soon. My uncle thought I was throwing up my food, and I remember him yelling, "Cut that out. You're scaring the cats." I still don't know if he knows that I took the Tylenol that day. I threw up all night and didn't really sleep. I eventually was too sick to run to the bathroom, so I just hung my head over the side of the bed and threw up wherever it landed - on the sheets, dresser. I just didn't care about anything anymore at that point. I didn't know who to turn to ask for help. I felt crazier than I ever have in my entire life. I guess I was crazy.

"Eventually I feel asleep and woke up the next morning to my uncle knocking on the door saying, 'It's a new day time for bigger and better things.' He also told me to clean up whatever mess I had going on in my room. I remember the sun was coming through the shades, and it was a beautiful day outside. However, the sunshine didn't help my mood. I felt a dark cloud hovering above me. It was 10:30 am. I just wanted things to be the way they were before I started drinking again at Uncle Billy's. I felt like the hole I had dug was too deep to crawl out of. I didn't leave a suicide note because I didn't really know what to write on it. Plus, I didn't really have the energy. It just wasn't my focus at the time. Suicide notes are too sad. I thought death was the answer for me. I thought people died, and there was no Heaven or Hell. We just didn't exist anymore.

"The day after I tried to kill myself, I didn't do much. I tried to read, but I just felt really sick. I remember thinking, 'When am I going to die?' I was waiting to die. Olivia came over that day, and she wanted to get her shorts. I wished so bad that I was her instead of me. I hated myself. Why couldn't I be smart, happy and have a boyfriend and friends? Why did I have to be such a failure? I hated myself so badly. When was I going to die? It must be soon. That's all I was thinking. I must have gotten scared though or else I wouldn't have told Mary what I did. I didn't tell Uncle Billy because I thought he would be very angry, and I was afraid of how he would react.

I didn't plan to tell Dad right away what I had done. I wasn't really scared. I was feeling so sick and shocked that I didn't feel scared. I wanted to die after all. I waited because I was scared of the reaction - Uncle Billy's reaction anyway. I thought he would be angry and tell me I was stupid. I didn't want him to get mad. I didn't tell Olivia because I didn't want to burden her. I knew she had school and her own life. I didn't want to worry her. I wasn't really scared, but I remember feeling embarrassed, maybe ashamed, for what I had done. I felt so physically sick that I didn't really have any emotional thoughts. Yes, I knew I might die. I thought that this can't be me. This only happens on television. I think I detached myself. I didn't want to think. I thought, "This can't be real." Did I really do this to myself? I had regret and embarrassment about myself."

Second Chances

The day after Songbird took the Tylenol, Uncle Billy suggested that she visit her dad and stepmom up north. Songbird agreed and, after five long years, she came home. Since she had been away, I had not heard from her, but she did not hesitate to phone us to ask for a ride. This is how she described her decision to return to Crossbridge and the trip home:

"I decided to ask after my uncle suggested that maybe I take a trip there and see you. I think he didn't know what to do with me, and I felt happy being around you. I missed you all and knew that it was the right choice to be back with my family. I didn't expect Mary to come and get me so quickly. That made me feel good that you all loved me enough and welcomed me back home with no questions asked. I felt so relieved when Mary said she would come and get me. I even felt a little hopeful.

"The 3-hour ride north where we were meeting Mary was not good. Uncle Billy had to stop the car once because I almost puked. I could hardly eat breakfast, and I felt sick the whole way. I *was* relieved and could hardly wait to get away. It was good seeing Mary. I felt happy to see her. I was glad to be with her and excited to hear about my brothers and sisters.

"I told her in the car. At that point I was very sick. I said that I had taken a lot of Tylenol and that I wasn't feeling well. I was nervous about telling her, but I felt safe doing it. I knew she wouldn't judge me, and I felt very relieved after I told her. She just nodded her head and asked me if I was feeling low when I took them. I said yes, and she kept it at that. She didn't harass me with questions or judge. She was very calm and kind. The rest of the ride she talked about family, and it was pleasant despite my confession and how ill I was feeling. She kept up good conversation which I am thankful for because it was a good distraction. I was thankful to be with Mary and the opportunity I got to tell her. It would have been difficult if it weren't just the two of us. I was thinking how grateful I was to have a caring and loving person like Mary to confess to."

As they talked, my wife drove the 159 miles to Crossbridge and went straight to the emergency room. All the time, I was at hunting camp, and she did not have a way to contact me. Mary called friends who were dairy farmers, and they drove out and found me in my recliner, napping in my underwear. Forgoing formalities, they burst in and, as I grabbed a blanket to cover up, they told me that Songbird was back in Crossbridge. My heart leaped! Then they told me that she was in the emergency room. My heart fell. I was to go to the hospital as soon as possible. That was all they knew. I haphazardly broke camp and headed home, about a three-hour drive, pushing the speed limit.

I went straight to the emergency room, disheveled, unkempt, and smelling like campfire smoke and was escorted to a partitioned room. Songbird was in bed being administered an antidote intravenously while doctors waited for the results of blood tests. Mary was holding her hand. Poison Control had been contacted, and a hepatologist consulted. I got Mary's attention and asked her how serious it was. She began to answer but stammered. I remember thinking how ironic it would be to be reunited with my daughter just in time to watch her die. Below Songbird's describes the reunion:

> "It was good to see you again. I felt comforted when you got to the E.R. I was surprised how worried you were. Not that I ever thought you didn't love me or cared about me. I wasn't sure how you would react. I never expected the kindness and compassion that I got because I didn't deserve it. How could you be so kind and forgiving after all that I had done? You loved me though, and I felt that and still feel it. All I needed was love and that's what got me through."

The prognosis was not promising. Specialists advised transporting Songbird to the university hospital in case a liver or kidney transplant was necessary, and so an airlift was scheduled:

"I was scared because everything was happening so fast and, at the time, I was just doing what they said. I didn't want to be transported. I didn't realize how close to dying I was. Not until later, after I was out of ICU, did I really understand everything.

ICU

Songbird was moved to ICU for observation while arrangements were made. I can't remember if it was because of fog or a storm or availability, but the airlift was delayed until the next morning. In the meantime, Songbird continued to take the antidote and nutrition intravenously. Her heart rate was monitored, and blood samples were taken every three hours throughout the night. Her skin tone was an awful shade of yellow, and she had monitors, tubes, and various medical devices coming from everywhere.

Mary and I took shifts pacing, praying, and napping when we could - just being there. A few hours before dawn and the scheduled airlift, blood tests indicated that she was stabilizing. The medical team informed us that, when that type of toxicity rescinds, there was a good chance that it would not get worse. Songbird had signed a form to allow us to make medical decisions for her, and so we were given the option of postponing the airlift and waiting to see how things went. By then, the airlift could mobilize at any time, and we decided that there was little to lose, and much to gain, by waiting—we didn't think Songbird would survive a transplant anyway. She weighed about 80 pounds, and she would not get our full emotional support 500 miles away. Songbird agreed. We postponed the airlift, waited, and prayed. Songbird remained in ICU for four days and then was moved to a room on the medical floor for another two days:

"The staff were all great, and I didn't feel judged or looked down at by any one of them. The visits from family helped me a lot. Ruthie bought me coloring books and crayons, and Lizzy brought me pajamas and nail polish. They were so nice, taking the time to visit me and bring me things. It helped keep my spirits up. I am grateful for their kindness, and I felt their love surrounding me. My brother and his wife brought me movies and were there for me. My friend's mom even came, and that surprised me.

After all these years, she was there to help me and encourage me. I also enjoyed Sarah's visits, and she talked and got my mind off of the pain that I was feeling. Her bubbly attitude was just what I needed. I thought they would be angry, but they weren't. I think they were feeling happy that I didn't die. After seeing my family, I wanted to live. My will wasn't that strong, but I didn't want to die anymore."

Going Home

Finally, Songbird was released to our care. "I think I wore sweatpants and a hoodie. The weather was sunny, and the snow was melting. I remember it was slushy on the ground. It was warm for March. The air smelled so wonderful outside the hospital! It smelled fresh and clean. Not like antiperspirant and latex. I was thinking that I shouldn't drink again. My family loved and cared about me deeply. I felt like I still didn't deserve everyone's love and kindness. I felt guilty and ashamed. I still didn't really like myself.

"I loved being back in my old room. It was very cozy with the chair in the corner and, the way Mary set it up for me, I could tell she really worked hard at cleaning it up and had done it with love and thoughtfulness. The rest of the family received me with love and kindness. They all were very caring and understanding. My immediate goals were to find a job and stay sober. My long-term plans were to go to school again and drive and work. I thought I was adjusting pretty well.

"I was a little depressed, but my family was always there to support me. I felt useless because I wasn't doing anything with my life but trying to end it. I also felt guilty because Ruthie and Liz were in school and sacrificed their time to come over and do things with me. I had anxiety that went up and down- mostly about my mom because she didn't know what had happened and also about the rest of my family who didn't live in Crossbridge. It was difficult for me to tell them what I had done. At first, I slept a lot because my body needed it. The doctor told me I could never drink again and, although I did later, at that time I was scared to drink."

Scene at the Ballpark

Songbird tried to deal with her addictions through out-patient services and participation in Alcoholics Anonymous, but it did not last long. She began drinking again, and the chaos that resulted reached a climax when she caused a scene at her younger brother's Little League baseball game. She was talking stupidly and being obnoxious. Mary was with her and called for my assistance. I met them in the parking lot, snatched Songbird's vodka laced Gatorade, dumped it, put her bicycle in the back of the truck, and curtly told her to get in. I was not pleased, patient, or pleasant. Nevertheless, her recent attempt to die by suicide softened my demeanor. I was gravely aware of the likelihood of future attempts, and I did not want to trigger another. From working with chemically dependent youth, I knew I should detach from the situation and focus on the behavior but, as a father, it was not easy.

I took Songbird home and we talked in her room. First, I scolded her and that brought tears. She was utterly drunk, and I don't know what else. She may have taken too many of her medications or not taken them at all. I didn't know what else to do, so I suggested that we ask for divine guidance and help. When she nodded, we knelt by her bed and prayed. She was high, but the prayer was voluntary, and I felt it was sincere:

"When we prayed together, I was drunk, but I knew God heard me anyway. I don't know that my whole heart was in it because of my state of mind, but it was the right thing to do." Afterward, we embraced and talked about in-treatment care:

"I knew I needed to be an in-patient again because I just couldn't stop on my own. My family was mad at me. I was hurting everyone around me and, most of all, myself. I couldn't go on destroying my family, and I could die if I didn't get help. I was definitely ready."

I told her I would arrange things in the morning. She had just recovered from acute liver and kidney failure, still weighed about 80 pounds, and had binged on vodka, possibly mixed with medication. During the night, I looked in her room several times and listened to make sure she was breathing.

Relapse Four: Back to Rehab

A room was available at the residential facility, arrangements were made, and Songbird was admitted the next day. She graduated from the program, got a job at the Salvation Army and began taking online classes. We thought that might suit her learning style, and it did. She obtained some equilibrium and seemed to be gaining momentum:

"My life was wonderful after getting out of rehab. My family relationships were being restored; I had a car, I found a great sponsor and I was ready to start living life sober, happy and free. Of course, it wasn't all rainbows and butterflies. I went through a lot of cravings, but I worked on my program and took it one day at a time."

In a Ditch

Songbird was clean for eight months, the longest time in seven years. "I had a good relationship with God. Better than it had ever been. I actually looked forward to going to church. I loved reading my Bible and talked to God throughout my day. I felt close to Him. I planned on finishing online classes for paralegal studies and getting a degree. I also planned on living independently at some point and maybe even sponsoring a member of AA if the opportunity came up. I read a lot also and work helped me feel good about myself. Looking back, my religious life could definitely have been improved, but I knew God and had a relationship with Him, so I felt pretty good about where I was."

She mentioned how going to college made her feel accomplished. And elaborated elaborates on the content of her coursework and how she began to internalize it. "Liberty University was where I learned mostly about the Bible and the Christian lifestyle. I wasn't fully living the Christian lifestyle, but I was learning about it."

When she asked to move in with her brother's family across town, we helped her, but a month later, I got a call from a lady across town who found her passed out in a drainage ditch next to their driveway. Before I got there, she had gotten up and walked away, so I thought she may have wandered to a friend's house—or a bar. In either case, it was not likely that I would find her, and so I went home and listened for the telephone. Before long, I got a call from the same lady. She and her husband had looked around nearby hiking trails and found Songbird passed out in the woods behind a school. They led me to her, lying under a tree and reeking of vomit. She had been drinking heavily and was not dressed adequately for the weather. She was markedly underweight, and alcohol lowers body temperature exacerbating hypothermic effect. The temperature fell to 35° that night, and the hospital report indicated that she would have been at-risk for exposure.

When I spotted her, she was conscious, so I offered her my hand. I held it as I led her to the truck making sure she did not fall on the uneven ground or stumble into traffic. My first concern was her physical condition and, as always, her emotional state. We drove around town to sort out the options, and I suggested that she go to the psychiatric unit for a few days. She agreed, reluctantly, perhaps because at that point she was homeless.

While she was in the psychiatric unit, Mary and I scrambled to find some place for her to go afterward. Songbird agreed that a long-term program would be best; one that had an immediate opening. In addition, we wanted the treatment to be faith-based (Christian) and as near to home as possible. I searched the internet and made several phone calls.

Mission Bible Training Center

With the aid of a GPS we drove north, winding our way through narrow, rough, unlit roads to the mission. We came to a 100-year-old farmhouse that was the women's dorm. Adjacent to that was the men's dorm, chapel, and two barns. There was a garden surrounded by a twelve-foot fence to protect the produce from foraging deer, and a chicken coop, pig pen, and cattle yard—all occupied. The air carried a cool, fresh fragrance unique to northern climates. The facility looked more like a mid-century homestead than a treatment center for desperate, lost souls.

Songbird looked relieved as we pulled in the long driveway and parked the van. We were greeted by a young, perky woman who escorted us into the admissions area. She assured us that Songbird had come to the right place to deal with her problems, whatever they may be, and promised that she would be well cared for.

While there, Songbird described her experience at the mission, reflecting on her blossoming spirituality and how it helped her.

"Now that I am Living a Christian lifestyle as best I can, I see myself as a better person. I feel God's love and God's blessing. The Bible really taught me discernment and what God wants me to do. When I don't do or act what the Bible says I should, I see myself as not who God wants me to be. I feel guilty, and I don't feel good about myself. The Bible has taught me that God loves me unconditionally just the way I am, and that makes me see myself a lot differently than before. Because God loves me, I love me and have faith in me because God does.

"I talk to God and thank Him throughout my day. When I feel like doing something that's not good for me, I now know that that is a sin and it's not what God wants me to do. It's Satan's temptation. This has really helped me. I try to help others and show God's love. I give my problems to God the best I can and pray daily to not be in my flesh. I have a great spiritual life, but I feel that it could still improve. I know God is with me always. I pray and write down scripture verses and want to be one with God.

"Over the years, I'd felt like more of a failure each passing year. I feel God has a path for me though, and he hasn't given up on me. I see myself as a stronger person getting through my failures and setbacks. Life is not all rainbows and butterflies, and the Christian lifestyle is definitely a process. Before, I was in my mess and felt criticized and useless. I couldn't stop drinking and I didn't have a relationship with God. I felt so alone and helpless. Since being saved again, I knew God has hope for me and loves me. I know that if I'm honest, loving towards others, and don't hold grudges, I'm living for God. He created me and wants me to live for Him. I know that. Plus, it's a sin to kill yourself.

"Having a relationship with God has made me look at myself in a different light. He loves me unconditionally just the way I am, and so I am praying to love myself just as He does. He has a future and a hope for me and that is why I wake up every morning wanting to change into a better person."

Fast Forward

It is Valentine's Day, 2015 and storming—snow, ice, wind and frigid temperatures. When we headed out, the wind chill factor was -27° with snow and 31 mph winds. I said a prayer for safety, warmed up the F150, put it in four-wheel drive, and hoped for the best. It was going to be a long 66.4 miles.

There had been a young man milling around when we had checked Songbird in at the mission. That night, he told his good friend that he was going to marry her. And this was the day. Gregg was driving from Green Bay and she from the upper peninsula of MI, to a little church in between. She and Gregg had waited a long time and the weather was not going to get in the way. I was to give Songbird away, and Lizzy was going to be the maid of honor, but the roads were treacherous. I advised the rest of the family not to try it, but I had to get through no matter what. For one thing, my wife was catering, and she had the food! As it was, I had to double as the maid of honor, and my wife had to double as the photographer. It was the same road, three years prior, that I traveled to reunite with my daughter after her suicide attempt. It was the same road Songbird had travelled two hours earlier when the road had been passable, but a lot of snow can fall very quickly in the county that sometimes has the highest snowfall in the country.

The road was closed, and we hesitated but skirted the barricade. My wife was driving because I am night-blind but, as an accomplished back-seat driver, I was more than willing to tell her what to do. The headlights reflected off the driving, swirling snow and she lost sight of the road, and so I told her to stop the car. When the flurry let up, we realized that she had stopped on the wrong side facing on-coming traffic. Fortunately, we were the only kooks out there. We pressed on and we made it! Marriage vows were exchanged, the wedding dinner enjoyed, and that evening I danced with that adorable, fanciful, beloved new bride to *He Knows My Name*, recorded by Francesca Battistelli:

> Spent today in conversation
> In the mirror face to face with
> Somebody less than perfect
> I wouldn't choose me first if
> I was looking for a champion
> In fact I'd understand if
> You picked everyone before me
> But that's just not my story
> True to who you [God] are
> You saw my heart
> And made
> Something out of nothing
> I don't need my name in lights
> I'm famous in my Father's eyes
> Make no mistake
> He knows my name
> I'm not living for applause
> I'm already so adored
> It's all His stage
> He knows my name. (Fields, Battistelli, & Mosley, 2014)

CONCLUSION

"Although we cannot draw conclusions about suicides in general from the examination of one individual case of suicide, we can learn a good deal by analyzing such a case" (Lester, 1997, p. 157). This chapter featured two cases. The participants described how suicidal ideation started, progressed and dissipated. I didn't know Mad Dog before he attempted suicide. I met him many years later when we both worked at a residential facility for chemically dependent youth. He strolled into my classroom wearing a goofy hat and a smile, introduced himself as Mad Dog, and we became fast friends. Mad Dog was an icon there. I don't even know how he got that goofy name, and he doesn't seem to remember! Residents looked up to him, supposing that if he could recover, even thrive, they could. He had found his purpose. We lived a few blocks from each other. Sometimes we sat on his porch, and I saw how he struggled with the consequences of consuming drain cleaner. He would spit incessantly, and sometimes get up and launch intestinal acid off the side of the porch. Once, we traveled from the Midwest to the east coast together (he is a terrible driver!), and I witnessed other struggles first-hand. Up much of the night because of severe acid reflux, he just sat, tried to read his Bible or watched television. At home, a hospital bed that lifts his upper body gives some relief, but the acid projects, and he must always be ready. It seems like he is always traveling to the hospital (over 300 miles away) or coming back. Because of his difficulty talking, his social life is affected too. For instance, once we were at a wedding reception, and he went out of his way to ask me if we could sit together. Understand that Mad Dog is an extrovert. He has more friends than I do, but there are times when it is especially difficult to hear and understand him. A loud wedding reception is one of them. He indicated that he noticed others avoiding eye contact and assumed it was because they did not want to try and understand what he was saying. Another time, after he had his voice box removed, he was over for dinner and he confided, "My world is getting smaller, Frank."

He is limited physically, and his disability cannot be hidden which can compound psychosocial issues (Park, Faulkner, & Schaller (2003). Yet despite circumstances that have become worse, he adjusts and no longer entertains thoughts of suicide. His explanation is simple. "I carry-on because of Jesus." The overall process was congruent with the self-regulatory principles of non-classical psychology (Leontiev, 2007) and belief theory (Nespor, 1987), and is allied with the literature indicating that spirituality and religiosity inversely impacts suicidal ideation (Dew, et al., 2008), and leads to happiness (Sharma & Sharma, 2016).

Mad Dog's remarkable transformation progressed from: "I had become a freak. My entire life had been a matter of survival, not thriving," to "I am special. God knit together in my mother's womb. I was made in the image of God. I have a purpose, God has plans for me, and it gives me hope. I began seeing things differently. My spirit began to lift."

How Songbird felt about herself, her sense of purpose, and how she viewed circumstances, seems to correspond with the level of engagement with her faith (which is consistent with the literature). As a child she was involved in church activities, interested in God, and happy. As a young teen her enthusiasm waned, but she remained active, and it seemed to help her maintain her equilibrium in ways similar to how it helped the adolescents studied by Laird, Marks and Marrero (2010). As a middle teen, Songbird's religious activities ceased, and her substance abuse increased. Miller, Davies and Greenwald (2000) confirmed earlier studies showing the inverse effect of religiosity on substance abuse. At the height of her distress, Songbird reported no religious activity and ambiguous spirituality. Reclaiming the faith of her youth fostered stability and improved self-esteem similar to a trend discovered by Hayman, et al. (2009).

Songbird's circumstances did not immediately change for the better. Nevertheless, spirituality and religiosity prompted a dramatic change in her thinking. As Walsh (2009) found for coed college students who were engaged spiritually, Songbird began to deal with life's challenges more productively, view her situation without self-pity, and regard her disability more academically. Written interviews, conversations, and observations revealed a transformation.

She moved from, "I just wanted out of the Hellhole I was living in. I saw myself as hopeless, a failure, friendless, worthless, and ugly person. I saw myself as self-centered with no talents, and nothing to live for. I thought others saw me as selfish, irresponsible, and untrustworthy. I didn't want to be alive anymore. I was thinking that my life was hopeless and there was no way out. I just wanted to die and not be on the earth anymore," to "Now that I am Living a Christian Lifestyle as *best I can,* I see myself as a better person. I feel God's love and God's blessings. Having a relationship with God has made me look at myself in a different light. He loves me unconditionally just the way I am, so I am praying to love myself just as He does. He has a future and a hope for me, and that is why I wake up every morning wanting to change into a better person. I talk to God and thank Him throughout my day. I try to help others and show God's love. I know that God is with me always."

Songbird attributes her growing ability to reframe circumstances to her new spirituality and religiosity or "living a Christian lifestyle." Since her spiritual epiphany, she has experienced setbacks, unemployment, and even homelessness, yet she no longer considers suicide an option. She reported having found purpose, if nothing more than the act of looking for it. She no longer believes that her learning disability is a character defect. "I thank God every day for rescuing me from dying and my own negative thoughts. That is so far behind me. That was a different me."

I also thank God. She got her nickname because of her delightful, melodic laugh. It has been years since I have bolted awake in the middle of the night worrying about her.

Practical Implications and Application

Spirituality and religiosity can bolster mental health, relieve emotional suffering, and promote coping mechanisms across ethnic backgrounds, age and demographics (Koenig, 2009). Spirituality and religiosity can also "influence…the meaning of symptoms" (Walsh, 2009). The implication is that spirituality and religiosity can provide a way to frame symptoms positively. The results of a mixed methods study by Yocum (2010) indicated that spirituality and religiosity can give rise to tremendous hope, and those who practice it can frame (or reframe) their circumstances in ways that give them a sense of purpose. Using mixed-methodology, Yocum studied how college students viewed spirituality and the effect spirituality had on their senses of self, purpose, and optimism. Quantitative analyses were augmented with qualitative, face-to-face interviews and focus group methodology. He found a significant connection in all three areas. Yocum concluded, “An increased sense of spiritual self-actualization gives people a more positive outlook on life, and generally makes them feel happier and more successful” (p. 114).

Despite substantial empirical evidence that religiosity and spirituality assuage suicidal ideation and behavior, they are not typically introduced to children and adolescents who experience them by secular counselors or in public schools. Political correctness, anti-religious sentiment, and interpretation of the separation of church and state are a few of the reasons. School counselors may fear retribution, non-theist or irreligious counselors may ignore the data due to personal bias, and political correctness hinders any religious content in a world that seems to have become more antagonistic to expressions of faith. The cost of this is great. “Spirituality and religiosity foster a propitious sense of self, purpose, optimism, and hope ad infinitum” (Bailey & Yocum, 2005).[2]

Limitations and Recommendations for Further Research

Participants can be guarded in what they reveal which is a major reason for the shortage of qualitative research on delicate issues in general (Dickenson-Swift, James, & Liamputtong, 2008), and suicidal ideation in particular (Lakeman & FitzGerald, 2008). This was an exceptional opportunity to study two very different individuals and their experiences regarding an intensely personal and delicate topic. However, the same intimacy that gave me access to their inner world may have affected my ability to interpret data objectively. Creswell (2017) recommends biographical methodology if the goal is to “let the voices of participants speak” (p. 43), but Mad Dog’s difficulty communicating required

[2] The unbridged version of this chapter, obtainable from the author, presents a case study of counseling an adolescent.

interpretation, and Songbird's deposition may have been affected by her writing skills.

Comparable research explicating the G factor and suicidal ideation is limited. Follow-up studies in a similar format or other style affording rich description could support and elucidate the issue more. Given the strength of evidence regarding the protective factors associated with religiosity and spirituality, further research to understand the reluctance of practitioners to put aside personal biases to best serve the client or to refer clients to other counselors would be helpful. Further research regarding how counselors might safely and effectively assess a client's potential benefit from religious and spiritual care would also be helpful. An applied research format would give clinicians additional resources.

REFERENCES

Bailey, F. & Yocum, R. (2015). Auditory processing learning disability, suicidal ideation, and transformational faith. *Journal of Research on Christian Education, 24*(1), 3-24.

Bailey, F. (2014). *Songbird's journey: A personal experience, narrative exploration of auditory processing disabilities, suicidal ideation and the reframing essence of the Christian faith.* Unpublished doctoral dissertation, Lynchburg, VA: Liberty University.

Beck, A. T, Brown, G., & Steer, R. (1989). Prediction of eventual suicide in psychiatric inpatients by clinical ratings of hopelessness. *Journal of Counseling & Clinical psychology, 57,* 309-310.

Creemers, D. H. M., Scholte, R. H. J., Engels, R. C. M. R., Prinstein, M. J., & Weirs, R. W. (2012). Implicit and explicit self-esteem as concurrent predictors of suicidal ideation, depressive symptoms, and loneliness. *Journal of Behavior Therapy & Experimental Psychiatry, 43*, 638-646.

Creswell, J. W. (2017). *Qualitative inquiry and research design: Choosing among five approaches* (4th ed.). Thousand Oaks, CA: Sage Publications, Inc.

Dew, R. E., Daniel, S. S., Armstrong, T. D., Goldston, D. B., Triplett, M. F., & Koenig, H. G. (2008). Religion/spirituality and adolescent psychiatric symptoms: A review. *Child Psychiatry & Human Development*, *39*, 381-398.

Ellis, T. E. (2014). Psychotherapy with suicidal patients. In D. Lester (Ed.) *Suicide prevention: Resources for the millennium,* (pp. 129-152). New York: Routledge.

Fenstermacher, G. (1979). A philosophical consideration of recent research on teacher effectiveness. In Shulman, L. S. (Ed.), *Review of Research in Education,* (Vol. 6) (pp. 157- 18). Itasca, IL: F. E. Peacock.

Fields, M., Battistelli, F., & Mosley, S. (2014). He knows my name [Recorded by Francesca Battistelli]. *On If we're honest* [CD]. Seattle: Amazon Music.

Frankl, V. E. (1963). *Man's search for meaning: An introduction to logotherapy.* New York: Simon & Schuster.

Gerber, P. J., Reiff, H. B., & Ginsberg, R. (1996). Reframing the learning-disabled experience. *Journal of Learning Disabilities, 29*(1), 98-101.

Heisel, M. J. & Flett, G. L. (2004). Purpose in life, satisfaction with life, and suicide ideation in a clinical sample. *Journal of Psychopathology & Behavioral Assessment, 26*,127-135.

Klonsky, E., Saffer B., & Byron C., (2018). Ideation-to-action theories of suicide: A conceptual and empirical update. *Current Opinion in Psychology*, 22, 38-43.

Koenig, H. G. (2009). Research on religion, spirituality, and mental health: A review. *Canadian Journal of Psychiatry, 54*, 283-291.

Laird, R. D., Marks, L. D., & Marrero, M. D. (2010). Religiosity, self-control, and antisocial behavior: Religiosity as a promotive and protective factor. *Journal of Applied Developmental Psychology, 32*, 78-85.

Lakeman, R., & FitzGerald, M. (2008). How people live with or get over being suicidal: a review of qualitative studies. *Journal of Advanced Nursing, 62*(4), 114-126.

Leontiev, A. (2007). "Units" and levels of activity. In *Journal of Russian & Eastern Europe Psychology, 44*(3), 3-7.

Lester, D. (1997). *Making sense of suicide.* Philadelphia, PA: Charles Press.

Linehan, M. M., Goodstein, J. L., Nielsen, S. L., & Chiles, J. A. (1983). Reasons of staying alive when you are thinking of killing yourself. *Journal of Consulting & Clinical Psychology, 51.* 267-286.

Manani, P., & Sharma, S. (2013). Self-esteem and suicidal ideation: a correlational study. *MIER Journal of Educational Studies, Trends & Practices*, *3*(1), 75-83.

Miller, L., Davies, M., & Greenwald, S. (2000). Religiosity and substance use and abuse among adolescents in the National Comorbidity Survey. *Journal of the American Academy of Child & Adolescent Psychiatry, 39*, 1190-1197.

Minkoff, K., Bergman, E., Beck, A. T., & Beck, R. W. (1973). Hopelessness, depression, and attempted suicide. *American Journal of Psychiatry, 130,* 455-459.

Nespor, J. (1987). The role of beliefs in the practice of teaching. *Journal of Curriculum Studies*, 19, 317–328.

Park, J. H., Faulkner, J., & Schaller M. (2003). Evolved disease-avoidance processes and contemporary anti-social behavior: Prejudicial attitudes and avoidance of people with physical disabilities. *Journal of Nonverbal Behavior 27*(2), 65-87.

Peterson, C. (2009). Positive psychology. *Reclaiming Children and Youth, 18*(2), 3-7.

Rasmussen, M. L., Dyregrov, K., Haavind, H., Leenaars, A. A., & Dieserud, G. (2018). The role of self-esteem in suicides among young men. *Omega*, *77*, 217–239.

Robbins, D. (2010). Guest editor's introduction. *Journal of Russian & East European Psychology, 48*(4), 5-16.

Schwandt, A. (2015). *The Sage dictionary of qualitative research* (4th ed.). Thousand Oaks, CA: Sage.

Seligman, M. E. P., & Csikszentmihalyi, M. (2000). Positive psychology: An introduction. *American Psychologist, 55*, 5-14.

Sharma, S., & Sharma, O. (2016). Spirituality leads to happiness: A correlative study. *International Journal of Indian Psychology, 3*(2), 50-54. Retrieved from http://oaji.net/articles/2016/1170-1459010814.pdf

Shneidman, E. S. (1996). *The suicide mind.* Oxford, UK: Oxford University Press.

Soto-Sanz, V., Piqueras, J. A., Rodríguez-Marín, J., Pérez-Vázquez, M. T., Rodríguez-Jiménez, T., Castellví, P. & Cebria, A. (2019). Self-esteem and suicidal behaviour in youth: A meta-analysis of longitudinal studies. *Psicothema*, *31*, 246-254.

Walsh, F. (Ed.). (2009). *Spiritual resources in family therapy* (2nd ed.). New York: Guilford.

Wilburn, V. R., & Smith, D. E. (2005). Stress, self-esteem, and suicidal ideation in late adolescents. *Adolescence, 40*, 33-45.

Yocum, R. (2010). *Spiritual hunger and recipes for spiritual satiety (a spiritual needs/motivation/volition framework for educators).* (Unpublished doctoral dissertation, Pensacola, FL: University of West Florida).

Yocum, R., James, S., Staal, L., & Pinkie, E. (2012). *Education and spiritual development: A mixed-methods study.* Unpublished paper presented at the 2012 Hawaii University Conferences: Education, Math & Engineering Technology, Honolulu, HI. Retrieved from http://huichawaii.org/assets/e---yocum,-russ.pdf

EDITOR'S CONTACT INFORMATION

David Lester, PhD

Psychology Program, Stockton University, New Jersey, USA

Email: david.lester@stockton.edu

LIST OF CONTRIBUTORS

Frank S. Bailey, EdD

Liberty University, Lynchburg, VA School of Education
Contributor Email: fsbailey@liberty.edu

Eleanor Beale, BA

Department of Psychological Sciences
Case Western Reserve University, Cleveland Ohio
Contributor Email: eeb72@case.edu

Mahboubeh Dadfar, PhD, MPH

School of Behavioral Sciences and Mental Health-Tehran Institute of Psychiatry, International Campus,
School of Public Health, Student Committee of Education and Development Center (EDC), Spiritual Health Research Center, Iran University of Medical Sciences, Tehran, Iran
Contributor Emails: dadfar.m@tak.iums.ac.ir; mahboubehdadfar@yahoo.com

Stephanie Gomez, BA

Department of Psychological Sciences
Case Western Reserve University, Cleveland Ohio
Contributor Email: stephaniegomez961@gmail.com

John F. Gunn III, PhD

Rutgers, The State University of New Jersey,
Center on Gun Violence Research
Contributor Email: jgunn3@scarletmail.rutgers.edu

Jenny Huen, MPhil

Department of Psychology,
The Chinese University of Hong Kong, Hong Kong, China
Contributor Email: Huen_Mei_Yiu_Jenny@alumni.cuhk.net

Karolina Krysinska, PhD

Centre for Mental Health, School of Population and Global Health
The University of Melbourne, Australia
Contributor Email: karolina.krysinska@unimelb.edu.au

Jennifer L. Laffier, PhD

Faculty of Education
Ontario Tech University, Ontario, Canada
Contributor Email: Jennifer.laffier@uot.ca

Bob Lew, MSc (Forensic Psychology), MBA, BEc

Department of Social Psychology, Faculty of Human Ecology, Putra
University of Malaysia, Malaysia
Contributor Email: boblew@asiacrux.com

James C. Overholser, PhD, ABPP

Department of Psychological Sciences
Case Western Reserve University, Cleveland Ohio
Contributor Email: overholser@case.edu

Cathy Pederson, PhD

Department of Biology, Wittenberg University, Ohio USA
Contributor Email: cpederson@wittenberg.edu

Steven Stack, PhD

Director, Center for Suicide Research
Troy, MI 48098
Contrubutor Email: steven_stack@hotmail.com

Liliana Varman, BA

Department of Psychological Sciences
Case Western Reserve University, Cleveland Ohio
liliana.varman@case.edu

INDEX

C

D

E

F

G

H

I

J

K

L

M

Q

R

S

T

U

V

W

Y

Related Nova Publications

UNDERSTANDING THE RISK FACTORS FOR SUICIDAL BEHAVIOR

EDITOR: Horace N. Ballou

SERIES: Psychology of Emotions, Motivations and Actions

BOOK DESCRIPTION: In this compilation, the authors provide a literature review of the relationship between hormones including testosterone, prolactin, leptin, hypothalamus-pituitary-adrenal axis hormones, hypothalamus-pituitary-thyroid axis hormones, oxytocin, ghrelin, estradiol and progesterone, insulin, melatonin and suicidal behavior, which has potential public health and clinical significance.

SOFTCOVER ISBN: 978-1-53616-468-8
RETAIL PRICE: $82

THE PSYCHOLOGY OF SELF-CONTROL

EDITOR: August van Looij

SERIES: Psychology of Emotions, Motivations and Actions

BOOK DESCRIPTION: *The Psychology of Self-Control* reviews evidence that indicates low self-control is among the most important individual risk factors for criminal offending. A developmental pathway that begins with this risk factor and leads to criminal offending is presented, and treatment recommendations for reducing the risk that low self-control poses for criminal offending are discussed.

SOFTCOVER ISBN: 978-1-53616-576-0
RETAIL PRICE: $82